Sybex's Quick Tour of Wind[ows]

THE DESKTOP

The Desktop is where your applications, folders, and shortcuts are located. You can choose between the classic Windows Desktop, which is familiar from previous versions of Windows, or you can use the new Active Desktop, which brings the Web directly to you.

My Computer lets you browse the contents of your computer, open folders, open documents, and run your favorite applications.

My Documents is a desktop folder you can use to store documents, graphics, and other files that you want to access quickly.

Internet Explorer starts up the Internet Explorer Web browser.

Network Neighborhood opens a viewer that presents system information about your computer's place in a network.

Recycle Bin makes it easy to delete and undelete files and folders.

The Microsoft Network opens a connection to Microsoft's online service.

My Briefcase lets yo[u] chronize files betw[een] computers.

Online Services allows you to access one of the popular commercial service providers, such as AOL.

Outlook Express opens the Outlook Express e-mail program.

The **Start button** pops up the Start menu, from which you can run almost all of your applications.

The **Quick Launch toolbar** provides an easy way to start frequently used applications.

The **Taskbar** displays a button for every program running on your computer.

site without first opening your Web browser.

Every **Window** has a **Minimize**, **Maximize** (alternating with **Restore**), and **Close** button.

The **Standard toolbar** provides fast access to common functions.

The **Address toolbar** shows the location of the page currently displayed in the main window; this may be an Internet address or a file or folder stored on your hard disk.

The **Links toolbar** lets you access different parts of Microsoft's Web site.

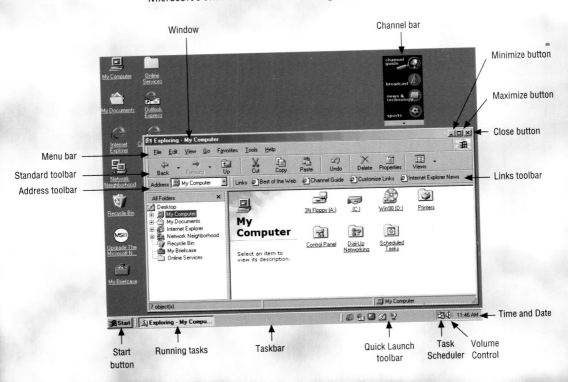

Windows 98 and Internet Explorer bring the Internet right onto your Desktop. There are Internet access points available in every folder, and you can add Web content to your Desktop and folders to customize the way your system looks and feels.

CONFIGURING WITH THE CONNECTION WIZARD

Use the Connection Wizard to find an Internet Service Provider (ISP) and open a new account, or to configure an existing account. Plug your modem into the phone jack and choose Start ➤ Programs ➤ Internet Explorer ➤ Connection Wizard, then follow the instructions on the screen.

USING INTERNET EXPLORER

Once you have established an Internet account, click the Internet Explorer icon on the Desktop and start your explorations; you can also start Internet Explorer from the Quick Launch toolbar.

TUNING IN TO CHANNELS

The Channel bar on the Desktop lets you access the Channel Guide quickly and easily. You can use it to subscribe to the Web channels that you want to view or place on your Desktop. The channel content is updated by the content provider on a regular basis; all you have to do is sit back and watch.

BROWSING FROM EVERYWHERE

You will find Go and Favorites menus in all the windows, including Explorer, My Computer, My Briefcase, the Control Panel, the Printers folder; even the Recycle Bin has them.

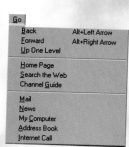

You can also use the Address toolbar or the Links toolbar, available in all these windows and on the Taskbar, to access Web sites on the Internet. The Auto Complete

feature automatically completes a Web address that you have previously visited as you start to type the address into the Address toolbar.

You can even access certain technical support Web sites from within the Windows 98 Help system.

WEB-RELATED APPLICATIONS

But it doesn't stop there; in addition to the Internet Explorer browser, Windows 98 also contains several other important Web-related applications, including:

Address Book Identifies the computers and individuals to which you may send and receive files and e-mail.

FrontPage Express A quick-and-easy Web-page editor you can use to create or customize your own Web pages.

NetMeeting A conferencing application which allows people working in different locations to collaborate simultaneously on the same project.

NetShow Player A viewer that displays streamed audio, video, and illustrated audio files downloaded from a Web site without waiting for long downloads.

Outlook Express An application used to send and receive e-mail and read and post messages to Internet news groups.

Personal Web Server Provides a Windows 98-based Web server you can use to set up a Web site on your local network or intranet, or to develop and test your Internet content before uploading it to your Internet Service Provider (ISP).

Web Publishing Wizard Manages the process of posting new Web content to a Web site.

Sybex, Inc.
1151 Marina Village Parkway
Alameda, CA 94501
SYBEX® Tel: 510.523.8233

Sybex's Quick Tour of Windows 98

Every application running on your computer and every open folder gets its own button on the Taskbar. The Taskbar may also show other icons from time to time, indicating that an e-mail message is waiting or that you are printing a document.

You can switch from one task to another by clicking its button on the Taskbar, but when you have a lot of applications running, the Taskbar can get pretty crowded. You can make it bigger by simply dragging the top edge of the Taskbar upward.

MOVING THE TASKBAR

You don't have to have the Taskbar at the bottom of the screen. If you'd prefer, you can have it at the top of the screen, on the left side, or on the right side. Just click a blank part of the Taskbar (not on one of the buttons), and drag the Taskbar to the new location.

TASK SWITCHING WITH ALT+TAB

Another quick way to switch from one running task to another is to hold down the Alt key on the keyboard and then press the Tab key once. A dialog box that contains an icon for each application running on your system will open. Each time you press the Tab key, a different icon is highlighted. This indicates the application that will run when you finally release the Alt key.

The name of each application or folder is displayed at the bottom of this dialog box.

ADDING A TOOLBAR

Windows 98 includes a default set of toolbars that you can add to your Taskbar.

Address Allows you to open an Internet address without first opening Internet Explorer.

Links Contains a set of Internet addresses, which users can add, remove, or re-arrange.

Desktop Adds a toolbar containing all your Desktop icons to the Taskbar. Because this toolbar is longer than the screen is wide, you can use the small arrows to see the other icons.

Quick Launch Adds buttons for commonly used applications.

To add one of these toolbars, right-click a blank part of the Taskbar, choose Toolbars from the pop-up menu, and then select a toolbar by name.

CREATING YOUR OWN TOOLBAR

To create a new toolbar, right-click an empty area on the Taskbar, and select Toolbars ➤ New Toolbar. Type the path to the folder (or the Internet address) that you want to appear as the toolbar and click OK.

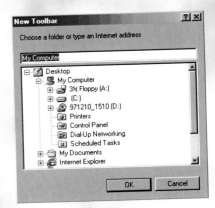

Drag the new toolbar to the Desktop, and then position and size it accordingly.

USING THE QUICK LAUNCH TOOLBAR

The Quick Launch toolbar, located on the Taskbar, provides shortcuts to several often-used Windows features.

 Opens Internet Explorer.

 Opens Outlook Express.

 Opens the TV Viewer.

 Brings the Desktop back to the front.

 Views selected Web channels.

START MENU

Click the Start button to do almost anything on your computer, from running an application to configuring your printer.

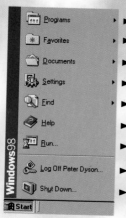

► Gives you access to the program groups and files on your computer.

► Gives you access to Channels, Links, and Software Updates.

► Gives you access to the last 15 documents you opened.

► Provides access to the Control Panel, Printers, Taskbar & Start Menu, Folder Options, and Active Desktop controls.

► Searches for a file, folder, device, or computer. You can also search the Internet and look for personal contact information.

► Opens the extensive Windows 98 Help system and gives you access to the Troubleshooters.

► Opens the Run dialog box so that you can run a program or open a folder by typing its path and name.

► Logs off the system quickly so that you can log back on with a different user profile or so that another user can log on.

► Prepares the computer to shut down or to be restarted.

RUNNING A PROGRAM

To start an application, click Start ➢ Programs, choose a program folder to open the next menu (if required), and then click the name of the program you want to run.

ADDING AN APPLICATION TO THE START MENU

The quickest way to add a program to the top of the Start menu is to open the folder that contains the program, and then drag the program's icon onto the Start button.

FINDING THINGS QUICKLY

Windows 98 adds several powerful items to the Find menu, which in addition to finding files and folders, now includes options for finding a computer, information on the Internet, or information about people.

To locate a file, click Start ➢ Find ➢ Files or Folders. Type the name (or part of the name) into the Named field, enter any text you think the

file might contain into the Containing text field, and click Find Now. A window opens displaying the files that match as Windows finds them.

To locate a computer, click Start ➢ Find ➢ Computer, enter the name of the computer into the Named field, and click Find Now. To track down information on the Internet, use Start ➢ Find ➢ On the Internet. This option connects you to a single Web site giving you access to some of the most powerful and popular search engines on the Internet, including Infoseek, AOL NetFind, Lycos, Excite, and Yahoo. To find information such as a person's e-mail address, click

Start ➢ Find ➢ People. In the Look In list, select the name of the directory service you want to use, type in the information on the person you are looking for (usually just the first name followed by the last name), and click Find Now.

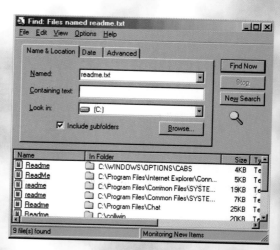

ABCs of
Windows 98

ABCs of
Windows® 98

Sharon Crawford
and Neil J. Salkind

SYBEX®

San Francisco - Paris - Düsseldorf - Soest

Associate Publisher: Gary Masters
Contracts and Licensing Manager: Kristine Plachy
Acquisitions & Developmental Editor: Sherry Bonelli
Editor: Shelby Zimmerman
Technical Editor: Kim Wimpsett
Book Designer: Catalin Dulfu
Electronic Publishing Specialist: Kate Kaminski
Production Coordinators: Theresa Gonzalez, Beth Moynihan, and Rebecca Rider
Indexer: Ted Laux
Cover Designer: Design Site
Cover Illustrator: Design Site

Library of Congress Card Number: 98-84013
ISBN: 0-7821-1953-0

Manufactured in the United States of America

10 9 8 7 6 5 4 3 2 1

Acknowledgments

Even though our names are on the cover, the book you're reading was the effort of many different people, all of whom deserve thanks. We'd like to acknowledge our editor, Shelby Zimmerman, for her sunny disposition and skill in pulling everything together; our technical editor and wizard, Kim Wimpsett, for making sure every last detail was accurate; our production coordinators, Beth Moynihan, Theresa Gonzalez, and Rebecca Rider; and our electronic publishing specialist, Kate Kaminski. Thanks to all of you for your help.

Contents at a Glance

Table of Contents

Chapter 16: A World of Windows 98 Applets 261

Introduction

The phenomenon known as Windows 98 has arrived. And the publicity and hype, while not at the level that it was for the introduction of Windows 95, still runs high.

If you're now confronted (voluntarily or involuntarily) with learning to use Windows 98, this book is all you need to get started. Windows 98 is designed to be explored—that is, given enough time, you can learn all there is to learn all by yourself. But how many of us have unlimited time to learn a new system? Not many.

This book will guide you quickly through the elements of Windows 98 and point you to where all the time-saving and cool stuff can be found.

Who Is This Book For?

This book is written for the person coming to Windows 98 for the first time. There are occasional references to earlier versions of Windows, but previous knowledge of Windows is definitely *not* required.

We assume that you are a reasonably intelligent person, so we don't talk to you as if you're a dummy. On the other hand, lots of smart people don't know much about computers, so everything is explained with the absolute minimum of techie talk or jargon. And if a bit of jargon is necessary, it will be defined in clear terms.

Also assumed is that you want to get going with Windows 98 as soon as possible. You can read just the chapters about subjects that interest you and come back to the others when you're ready, though we recommend not skipping Chapters 1 and 2 because they give you some basic facts about Windows 98 that will help make you Windows 98-competent that much more quickly.

What's in This Book?

Inside you'll see 17 chapters plus some appendixes. We have arranged the chapters so the first seven or eight are the basic stuff that you'll need to move around in Windows 98. The rest of the chapters are also basic, but some will interest you more than others, so feel free to dip into them as questions come up. Here's how the chapters break down:

Chapter 1: Introducing Windows 98

This is a short chapter on the things that make Windows 98 different from what has come before. It includes simple definitions of the terms you've heard tossed around at the local computer store, plus a summation of the new features that make Windows 98 useful and efficient.

Chapter 2: Visiting the Windows 98 Desktop

In this chapter you will learn how to deal with the Desktop you see when you first enter Windows 98. We'll explain what the elements are and how to make them work for you, how to use the Start menu, and how to choose a style for your desktop that suits you best.

Chapter 3: Making and Taking Shortcuts

Here we'll give you more on those wonderful tools: shortcuts. In fact, you'll learn everything you'll probably ever need to know about making and using them, including what to call them and where to put them.

Chapter 4: Mousing Around

In this chapter we reveal details about what the mouse can do now and how you can configure it to do even more. It includes settings for your mouse and using mouse pointers of many types, including animated ones!

Chapter 5: The Windows 98 Explorer

The abilities of the Explorer are described here. Plus you'll learn how to change window views and navigate through your hard drive's contents.

Chapter 6: Working with Files and Folders

Here's where you'll find out about moving, copying, renaming, and deleting files and folders. There's also a section on the great search tool called Find and how to use long file names.

Chapter 7: Running Programs

This is an introduction to all the ways you can run programs so you can set up all your Desktop operations in a way that makes sense to you.

Chapter 8: Using The Recycle Bin

Chapter 8 introduces another great tool in Windows 98: The Recycle Bin lets you decide the exact margin of safety you want for deleted files. And we tell you the easy way to approach setting up the Recycle Bin.

Chapter 9: Connecting to the Outside World

Time to connect…to the Internet, that is. Learn what you need to connect, how to establish a connection, and how to add and delete service providers.

Chapter 10: Using Outlook Express

The Internet is great, but you may like e-mail even better. Send e-mail to individuals and groups, use your address book, add attachments to your messages, and subscribe to newsgroups.

Chapter 11: Browsing the Web

The Internet is a wonderfully rich set of connections between thousands of computers. Learn to navigate it with confidence, tune in to channels, and use FrontPage to create your own Web page.

Chapter 12: DOS and Windows 98

DOS is still here and sometimes handy. Windows 98 will run your DOS programs better and faster than ever before. Tame even the most aggressive game with this chapter.

Chapter 13: Hardware Changes with Windows 98

Adding new hardware to Windows 98 is easier than ever. Even when you run into trouble, you'll find plenty of help to get you back on track.

Chapter 14: Seeing and Hearing Multimedia

This chapter describes all the really cool multimedia features that come with Windows 98, including new sound and video capabilities. You'll see how easy it is to record and play back your own sound files and use the CD player to listen to your favorite music.

Chapter 15: Controlling the Control Panel

Here's where you'll find explanations for all the icons in the Control Panel. Find out what they mean and how to make them work.

Chapter 16: A World of Windows 98 Applets

This chapter has simple instructions on how to extract the maximum benefit from the many included programs such as the calculator, HyperTerminal, Paint, and more.

Chapter 17: Keeping Your System Healthy

Fortunately, Windows 98 comes with a number of system utilities that are handy and, in some cases, essential for keeping your computer happy. This chapter tells you which ones are essential and how to use them.

Appendixes

Appendixes A and B will help you install Windows 98 whether you're currently using Windows 3.1 or Windows 95. Appendix A covers the Windows 95 installation while Appendix B assists the Windows 3.1 user.

Glossary

This is a glossary of useful computer terms. Some of these words are not discussed in the book but they do float around any environment where you find computers. Knowing what they mean can be helpful.

TIP   You'll see a lot of these—quicker and smarter ways to accomplish a task, based on many, many months spent testing and using Windows 98.

NOTE   You'll see these Notes too. They usually represent alternate ways to accomplish a task or some additional information that needs to be highlighted.

WARNING   In a very few places you'll see a Warning like this one. There are few because it's hard to do irrevocable things in Windows 98. So when you see a Warning, do pay attention to it.

Getting Going

Now it's time to flip the page and get started. We'd be delighted to hear from you if you find the book useful or even if you find it missing something you'd like to see included in a future edition. Our e-mail address is `ABCWindows@scribes.com`. And don't hesitate—we love getting e-mail.

Hope you enjoy the book—We're *sure* you'll enjoy Windows 98.

Chapter 1

INTRODUCING WINDOWS 98

- **Web integration**
- **Single-click launching**
- **Multimedia advances**
- **All the new features**

As an operating system, Windows 98 is designed to be "discoverable." This means that as you putter about, you can find many of the features and shortcuts all by yourself. However, most of us have work to do and lives to live, so we don't have endless hours in which to discover the best, shortest, and easiest way to do things. This book will give you a quick start on how to use the features of Windows 98 to your best advantage.

In this chapter, we'll talk a little about how Windows 98 came to be and what's new about it. It's not at all necessary to learn a bunch of technical stuff to use Windows 98, but a little information about the basics goes a long way toward making the whole system more understandable and accessible.

A Little History

Every computer requires an operating system. This, at a minimum, is a set of instructions for setting up a file system and for launching programs. DOS (for Disk Operating System) has been the dominant system for PCs since the first PC in 1981. At first, DOS was perfectly adequate for the hardware that existed. It could only use a limited amount of memory but that didn't matter because computers didn't *have* much memory.

With DOS, you could only run one program or process at a time. So once you'd finished writing your document, you had to cool your heels waiting for it to print. If your letter needed numbers from your spreadsheet program, you had to close the word processor, open the spreadsheet, get the numbers, close the spreadsheet, open the word processor—you get the picture. In addition, DOS commands were cryptic, consisting of statements such as "format a: /s." With Windows, you just point and click, making this graphical interface greatly preferable to DOS.

Over time, with Windows 3.1 and Windows 95 and now Windows 98, the interface has become more discoverable and easier to use. And features have been added that make the most recent Windows operating system much more comprehensive. For example, rather than having to go out and buy software to back up your files, Windows 98 includes a nice, easy-to-use package.

So What's New?

Aside from the continuing technical wizardry and the ability of Windows 98 to handle complex memory issues, Windows 98 offers many new features. Some are merely cosmetic, while others truly add a new and improved degree of functionality and ease of use. Which ones are considered cosmetic and which ones are major improvements depends, in part, on the individual. As with many things in life, one person's indispensable item is another's frippery. But don't worry: There are enough of these new features that everyone will be able to find some that are very handy or even essential.

Simple User Interface

The Desktop that greets you when Windows 98 starts is free of clutter and has an obvious entry point: the Start button. And you can customize this working area to your heart's content so that it meets all of your access and software needs.

With this new version of Windows, the interface includes single-click launching and an easy-to-customize Start menu. This is the Active Desktop, and it allows you to create a work environment that is fully integrated with Microsoft's Internet Explorer, integrating the World Wide Web with your everyday Windows activities. When we say integrated, we mean that your Desktop and other Windows applications can look and act like a Web document, complete with single-click links, back and forward buttons, and HTML-based documents. Chapter 3 provides a quick start on the Desktop elements and how to use them.

You can switch between the Active Desktop and the non-Web–like desktop (where you need to double-click things to open them) by right-clicking anywhere on the desktop, clicking Active Desktop, and then turning the View as Web Page option on and off.

> **NOTE**   **Throughout the book, we will be presenting steps using the Active Desktop style. If you are not using this view, you may need to double-click in instances where the text says to click.**

The Update Wizard

Tired of having to update your system every few months? That's no longer the case with Windows 98. The Update Wizard uses the Microsoft Web site to automate driver and system updates. The Wizard determines what sort of software and hardware your system uses. And (if you want it to) it will automatically update your system to maximize performance.

Better Help

There is a local version of Help as there was in previous versions of Windows. But Windows 98 brings Help one step further with a connection to Microsoft's online Help through the Internet. From this online Help site you can page through extensive collections of Help documents or send a message to a Microsoft technician. While most beginner problems can be solved using the Help that comes with Windows 98, the opportunity to connect directly to Microsoft puts a whole new level of assistance right at your fingertips.

Better Operation

The Tune-Up Wizard will automatically scan your disk to fix errors, make more room, and even eliminate old or unneeded files. And all this can take place automatically on a schedule that you specify. If you're not interested in a complete tune up, you're welcome to use one of several system tools that can enhance the operation of Windows 98 and your computer. One of these is an improved version of the FAT (File Allocate Table), allowing for the more efficient use of space.

Enhanced Internet Capabilities

Well folks, let's face it: The age of the Internet is upon us. So some of the biggest and best new features of Windows 98 are aimed at making the Internet easier and more enjoyable to use. Windows 98 enhances some of the biggest pluses. And it also tackles some of the worst pitfalls of using the Internet, from finding an ISP and connecting to making the Internet and the rest of your system work together seamlessly. With Windows 98, the Internet is more accessible, more user-friendly, and easier to publish to.

Total Web Integration

Windows 98 Explorer and Internet Explorer integrate both local and Web-based resources in one Active Desktop view. In this view you can customize your desktop, easily and quickly launch programs, and switch between files. For example, part of the clean and efficient look of the Active Desktop is the Taskbar, where the Start button rests. The Taskbar is the home for icons representing all your open programs. Windows 95 was the beginning of the Taskbar, but with Windows 98, its capabilities have been expanded. It can now be configured to meet many of your work needs more effectively. For example, it can include standard toolbars as well as customized toolbars.

The Internet Connection Wizard

And it's easier than ever to connect to the Internet using the Internet Connection Wizard. You can choose to establish an Internet connection via phone or cable using an established Internet local area network. You can even have the Wizard help you find an Internet Service Provider! And on the Desktop you'll find a folder full of everything you need to sign up with commercial services such as CompuServe, Prodigy, America Online, and AT&T WorldNet. You'll also find Microsoft's commercial service, the Microsoft Network, right on your Desktop when Windows 98 finishes its installation. (Or, if Windows 98 came already installed on your machine, the Microsoft Network will be on your Desktop ready to go.)

Favorites and Channels

Some of the really cool features of this Web integration are improved listings of favorites and previously visited Web sites and support for all Internet standards such as Java and Channels. Channels one of the hot new features of Windows 98; they deliver content from your favorite Web site(s) right to your computer. You can have the information delivered only when you want, or select to have it automatically downloaded so you can read it offline. E-mail, which is just as easy to use as Channels and Outlook Express, allows you to do everything from send and receive mail to fax and filter your mail for particular messages or from selected people.

FrontPage Express

Finally, consistent with the Web-based theme of the Desktop, FrontPage Express is included with Windows 98. FrontPage is a WYSIWYG (What You See Is What You Get) HTML editor that allows you to create your own home pages as simply as you create a letter using a word processing program.

Faster Operation and Improved Reliability

A lot of what determines how fast Windows 98 operates has to do with your particular computer's configuration. But no matter what you have as the basics (see the installation appendixes for what you must have to run Windows 98), Windows 98's new design will ensure that your computer runs smoother.

For example, the Tune-Up Wizard will make your programs run faster and check your hard drives for errors that could create significant problems. You can even schedule a daily or weekly tune-up when you are not working (for example, overnight) on your computer to ensure that things stay in tip-top shape and you don't have any unwelcome surprises.

One of the major components of the Tune-Up utility is the Windows 98 Disk Defragmenter. This utility cleans up all the broken file pieces that can litter your machine and optimizes the speed with which your applications load into the computer and run. When your disk is not fragmented, everything runs faster and smoother.

Windows 98 comes with a FAT32 utility that allows even those very large hard dives that come with today's powerful computers to be easily and quickly accessible—another element in making all your Windows 98 operations run more smoothly.

As for increased reliability, the Windows 98 Update Wizard feature ensures that you have the latest files and drivers to make your system continue operating smoothly. And the System File Checker keeps track of the important files that make Windows 98 run in the first place. If you accidentally move one of these files, the checker knows and makes sure the file is replaced in the correct location. And Windows 98 keeps running while all these corrections take place in the background, so you're not slowed down and you are rarely even aware that these utilities are silently keeping your system in top order.

New Innovations

All along, Microsoft has tried to integrate new and unique features into all their Windows releases. Windows 98 brings some nice new surprises. You already read about how the Explorer is integrated with the Web, making file management, information retrieval, and dealing with documents much easier and more intuitive.

But there are some other very cool new functions and features. For example, multiple display support allows you to use several different monitors simultaneously to increase the size of your work area, run different programs on separate monitors, or even play some of the hottest new games with multiple views.

Better Accessibility

People with disabilities will find Windows 98 easier to use than any other version of Windows. Features such as StickyKeys, ShowSounds and MouseKeys all enhance the usability of the product and open Windows 98 to people who previously found the operating system too cumbersome to use.

Improved Multimedia Features

New multimedia capabilities are in demand because there are new hardware and software products that require such capabilities; and Windows 98 delivers. Now you can not only play music CDs, view video clips, and record your own sound files, but also watch movies on your DVD player, play high quality movies and other video files with DirectShow, or watch television right through Windows 98. All are possible with the right equipment and Windows 98.

NOTE You can watch television with Windows 98 as long as you have a TV tuner board installed in your computer. You'll also need a constantly updated program guide, which should soon be available.

What's Next?

In this chapter, we have presented only a few of the features that make Windows 98 special and that you'll find easy to master with the help of this book. In the next chapter, we cut straight to the chase and tell you a couple of important skills and concepts that will give you a head start using Windows 98. In fact, after Chapter 2 you'll be equipped to start your own explorations if you're the adventurous type. However, if you continue on with the rest of the book, you can save yourself some time discovering the capabilities you will find most inviting and useful.

Chapter 2

VISITING THE WINDOWS 98 DESKTOP

- **Using the Start button**
- **Using the Taskbar and Toolbars**
- **Understanding the main features of the Desktop**
- **Setting the Desktop's look**
- **Getting help when you need it**

In this chapter, we'll do a quick tour of the screen you see when Windows 98 starts up. There'll be a description of each item you see on the Desktop as well as how to get more information on each item. Of course, everything can't be covered in detail here, so there are frequent references to later chapters—but we'll try not to bounce around any more than necessary.

The Start Button

The opening screen in Windows 98 (see Figure 2.1) is a mostly blank Desktop with a Taskbar running along the bottom of the screen and two or more icons located along the left-hand side of the screen. Fortunately, there's a clear signal where to begin in the form of a start button in the lower-left corner.

FIGURE 2.1:   The Windows 98 Desktop displays the Taskbar and various icons.

NOTE	Your Desktop can contain many icons depending upon how Windows 98 was originally configured when it was installed. If you purchased a computer with Windows 98 already installed on it, there are probably items on the Start menu and the Programs sub-menu as well as on the Desktop, in addition to the items that appear on your Desktop by default.

Start   Click the Start button once to open a menu of choices. (To close the Start menu, click somewhere else on the Desktop.) Initially there will be only a few items, but they're enough to get you going. Starting from the top, here's what you'll see:

Programs   Slide the mouse pointer to Programs and you'll get a cascading menu that includes all the programs currently installed plus access to a DOS prompt used to launch programs from a command line (more about this in Chapter 12), the Internet Explorer used to browse the Internet (covered in Chapter 11), and the Windows Explorer used to work with files and folders (addressed in Chapter 5).

You can add programs to the Start menu and change what's on the Programs menu quite easily. Take a look at Chapter 7 for the steps to do just that.

Favorites   Want to find out the score of the Yankees game? Where to have dinner in Cleveland? How about the latest reviews of a Disney movie? These are just some of the options that are available on the Favorites portion of the Start menu. Here you can use the Channels feature (uncovered in Chapter 11) to arrange for information to be updated and to connect with various Internet sites.

Documents   Windows 98 remembers the files you recently worked on and puts them on this menu. To clear all the entries on the Documents menu:
1. Click the Start button.
2. Point to Settings and select Taskbar & Start Menu.
3. Select the Start menu Programs tab.
4. Under the Documents menu, click the Clear button.
5. Click OK or Close.

There's no way to clear this menu selectively. It's all or nothing.

Settings   Branching off this item, you'll find the Control Panel folder, the Printers folder, the Taskbar & Start Menu settings, Folder Options, and an Active Desktop sub-menu. The Control Panel (explored in detail in Chapter 15) allows you to customize the way that Windows 98 looks and works. The Printers folder (refer to Chapter 13) is the place to go to add or modify the way a printer operates. You already know that the Taskbar & Start Menu option helps you customize what appears on both the Programs menu and the Start menu. Folders Options allows you to determine what items you want to appear on your Desktop and how you want them to look; and Active Desktop allows you to switch the Desktop view, including whether you want to view the Desktop as a Web page, (see Chapter 6) and to customize the Desktop appearance.

Find This is a neat little program that will let you search for files (and folders) or even a particular piece of text within a file. Chapter 6 has more information on using Find to search for almost anything. You can search your whole computer, just a particular drive, or just selected drives. If you're on a network, you can search for a particular computer by name. You can even search for something on the Microsoft Network or the Internet (see Chapter 11 for more details), or e-mail a long lost friend.

Select Find and then Files or Folders to begin a search for one of these items. Figure 2.2 shows the dialog box that appears if you select to find files.

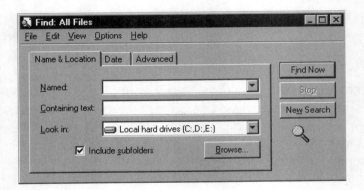

FIGURE 2.2:
The Find: All Files dialog box

As you can see from the tabs, you can search by name and location and by the date a file was created or modified. The Advanced tab has an option for searching for a particular word or phrase. The menus include options to make your search case sensitive or to save the results of a search.

The really nice thing about Find is that once you locate the file or folder you want, you can just click to open it or you can drag it to another location. In other words, the file or list of files displayed at the end of a search is "live" and you can act on it accordingly.

TIP To launch a search when the Desktop is visible, press the F3 key.

You can also use the Browse button on the Name & Location tab to look around for the file you want. And if you click the downward arrow on the Named box, you get a drop-down list of all the recent programs you've run from this box.

Help The Help option on the Start menu is where you want to go to get help with anything and everything about Windows 98. When you click Help, you have the option of going to the Help files that were installed along with Windows 98 or using the Internet to access help. Help is so important that we'll spend extra time on it later in this chapter in the section called "Getting All the Help You'll Ever Need."

Run   Those who loved the command line option popular in earlier versions of Windows will be equally happy here. Select Run from the Start menu and you can type in the name of any program you want to launch. Or use the Browse button to go to the specific location. You can even enter an Internet site and Windows 98 will see to it that Internet Explorer takes you there.

Log Off   Log Off closes all programs, disconnects your computer from the network (if you're connected), and prepares your computer to be used by someone else. It does not shut the computer down.

Shut Down   This Start menu option is only used when you want to shut down your computer, restart it, or restart it in MS-DOS mode.

Taskbars Galore

The Taskbar appears at the bottom of your screen and contains the Start menu button and other helpful tools. Every open program has a button on the Taskbar associated with it. This is extremely handy because it means you don't have to close windows or move them aside to find other ones. Just click the button and the corresponding open item will become active.

You can modify the Taskbar's appearance and location to make its use even more convenient.

NOTE   While you can have many different buttons visible on the Taskbar, only one can be active. The active button is always the one that appears in a lighter shade of gray, as if it is depressed.

Changing the Taskbar's Location and Size

To change the location of the Taskbar, drag it to the top of the screen or to either side. (Make sure your cursor isn't over a button when you drag it.) To increase its size (so you can fit more buttons), position the mouse pointer at the edge of the Taskbar and when you see a double-headed arrow, drag the border to where you want it.

Making the Taskbar Disappear

If you have a smallish monitor, you may want the Taskbar to disappear except when you need it. This gives you more room on the Desktop. To try this look, follow these steps:

1. Click the Start button and select Settings ➤ Taskbar & Start Menu.
2. On the Taskbar Option page, click the Auto Hide box.
3. If you want to access the Taskbar even when you're running a full-screen program, select Always on Top as well.
4. Click Apply to preview the changes or OK to accept them and close the box.

Now the Taskbar will only appear as you move the mouse pointer towards the bottom of the screen. Once you move the mouse pointer away from the bottom, the Taskbar will no longer be visible. You can reverse this by deselecting the Auto Hide box in Taskbar Options.

TIP   **You can also quickly get to the Taskbar Properties window by right-clicking between Taskbar buttons and selecting Properties.**

Also on the Taskbar

The Taskbar contains the all-important Start menu and buttons for each open item, but it also contains other items to make your Windows 98 activities that much easier.

To the right of the Start button is the Quick Launch toolbar with buttons that can be used to access Internet Explorer (the Windows 98 Internet browser), launch the Windows 98 mail program, Outlook Express, (discussed in Chapter 10), change the view of the Desktop, and use Windows 98 Channels to access information.

The right corner of the Taskbar is interesting as well. That's where you'll find active bits of hardware. If you have a sound card and it's working, there'll be a little speaker icon on the Taskbar. Also, when you're printing or faxing, a miniature printer appears in the same area. Position the mouse pointer over the clock display and a box showing the day and date will pop open. To change this, either double-click, or right-click and select Adjust Date/Time. If you install software that opens when you start

Windows 98 and remains available at all times, a corresponding icon will appear as well in this area of the Taskbar.

Selecting the Taskbar's Toolbars

The Taskbar can contain a series of different toolbars. To display a toolbar, point to a blank place on the Taskbar and click the right mouse button. Select toolbars and then select the toolbar you want to use. The menu includes ready-made toolbars plus the opportunity to make your own.

Quick Launch Toolbar

The Quick Launch toolbar is on the Taskbar by default. It consists of icons representing Internet Explorer, Outlook Express, the Desktop, and Channels.

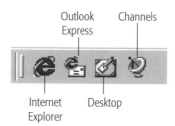

A single click will open Internet Explorer or any of the other programs represented. When you have a bunch of windows open and you want to get at something on your Desktop, just click the Show Desktop icon to minimize the current windows. Click the icon again to return the open windows to their original positions.

Desktop Toolbar

Select the Desktop Toolbar and every icon on your Desktop will be represented in the Taskbar. Click any of the icons to open the file or program it represents.

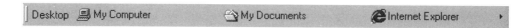

Address Toolbar

Select Address to open a toolbar that allows you to enter a Web address without having to open an Internet browser first. The address can be on your own computer, on your intranet, or on the Internet.

TIP **The Address and Links Toolbars may not be available on your computer depending on whether or not you have established an Internet connection.**

Type in an address or click the drop-down arrow to select a recently visited site.

NOTE **For more on using Web addresses, see Chapter 11.**

Links Toolbar

The Links Toolbar is another Web-based toolbar. It contains all the shortcuts to Web sites that are listed in the folder WINDOWS\FAVORITES\LINKS (or in Start ➤ Favorites ➤ Links). You can add shortcuts and delete the ones you don't want (see Chapter 3).

Right-clicking on the Taskbar allows you to select the Toolbars option and choose which toolbars are displayed on the Desktop.

Creating a Toolbar

After right-clicking on the Taskbar, select Toolbars ➤ New Toolbar to create a toolbar of your own design. In the New Toolbar window (see Figure 2.3), select a folder and then click the OK button. The items in the folder you selected will appear as a toolbar.

FIGURE 2.3:
Selecting a folder
that will become
a toolbar

Making Room for All the Toolbars

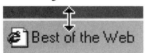

Opening even two toolbars at the same time will surely overcrowd the Taskbar. To make more room for an individual toolbar, point to the top of the Taskbar so your cursor looks like this vertical bar. When your pointer grows two heads, click once and drag the vertical sizing bar to the position you want.

If you want even more room, point to the right or left edge of a toolbar and when the pointer turns to a double-headed arrow, click and drag to make it wider. Now you can have all the toolbars you want!

Configuring Toolbars

Are the icons on the toolbar too small? Right-click a blank part of the toolbar and select View ➢ Large. You can make one toolbar large and leave the others at their default setting.

To change the contents of a toolbar, right-click it and select Open. In the window that opens, delete items you don't need and add shortcuts to files or programs you want. Below is the Quick Launch Toolbar with the addition of a shortcut to Quicken. Either of these programs can now be opened by single-clicking on the Taskbar.

WARNING   It's a big help that each of the toolbars can be adjusted. It can be a challenge to find a truly blank spot to right-click once you have several toolbars on the Taskbar.

What My Computer Can Do For You

The My Computer icon is on every Windows 98 Desktop. Single-click the icon to see icons for all your drives, plus a folder for the Control Panel and a Printers folder, as well as folders used in creating dial-up connections. My Computer is one of several ways to access information about the drives on your computer and your printer. It's the perfect place to go to highlight a hard drive and then right-click to find out about some of the drive's properties, such as how much space is available through its Properties option.

Right-click the My Computer icon and select Properties for a look at your hardware. (Chapter 13 has more on using this feature to get reluctant hardware to work properly.)

Click the My Computer icon and select Folder Options from the View menu. On the General tab, you can select whether you want Web Style, Classic Style, or a combination of the two. Web Style is where only one window is displayed at a time, which is probably preferable unless you have a very large monitor. On the average monitor, having every click open a new window (with all the old ones remaining) can turn your Desktop into a crowded mess very quickly.

NOTE   If the name My Computer is just too cute for your tastes (and it is for ours), right-click the icon and select Rename from the menu. Then edit the existing name or type an entirely new one.

Recycling Unwanted Files and Folders

The Recycle Bin, as you might imagine, is where old, deleted files hang out until you may need them again, or until you send them to a quick and painless death (meaning they are no longer recoverable).

Despite the name, the deleted files aren't actually recycled unless you rescue them from the bin before they're deleted permanently. Nevertheless, the Recycle Bin gives you a nice margin of safety. When you delete a file, you have days or even weeks (depending on how you set things up) to change your mind and retrieve it.

Chapter 8 is all about the Recycle Bin, how to configure it and use it to your best advantage. In the meantime, here are two important facts about the Recycle Bin:

- The Recycle Bin icon cannot be renamed or deleted.
- Files that are deleted using DOS programs or any program that is not part of Windows 98 are not sent to the Recycle Bin. They're just deleted, so be careful.

The Windows 98 Properties Sheet

Sometimes, it's important to have information about files, folders, and programs. For example, you might be having trouble running a certain program and need the size and location of a particular file. In Windows 98, it's a snap to use Property Sheets and find out about objects that appear on your Desktop. You can try it by right-clicking the object you want to learn more about and selecting Properties.

When you select Properties, you open what's called a *Properties sheet* (shown in Figure 2.4). Properties sheets vary, of course. Some types of files will have multiple pages in the Properties sheet; others will have only one page and very few options. The one you see in Figure 2.4 is a simple Property sheet for a file created using Microsoft Word.

Properties sheets contain valuable information about files, programs, devices, and virtually anything else that can be represented by an icon). So when you find yourself with a program or a piece of hardware that isn't working the way you want it to, right-click it, select Properties, and then examine the contents of the Properties sheet.

You'll learn more about Properties sheets in later chapters. For example, the Properties sheets for DOS programs are covered in Chapter 12, and the Properties sheets for printers are covered in Chapter 13.

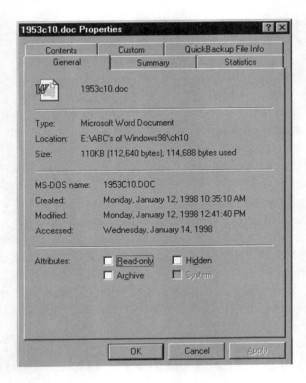

FIGURE 2.4:
A Property sheet for a simple Microsoft Word file

Setting Up Your Desktop

The default Windows 98 Desktop screen you saw in Figure 2.1 probably does not elicit cries of joy on first glance. But this can be easily changed. One of the most convenient and friendly features that Windows 98 offers is that you can change the appearance of the Desktop and almost any of the elements it contains such as the color of the display or the resolution of the objects on the Desktop.

WARNING **When you begin changing default Windows 98 settings, it's a good idea to write down the old settings just in case you end up with something you like less than the original. This will make it fairly easy to switch back to the original settings should you need to.**

Remember that you can use the entire area of your monitor's screen in Windows 98. You can have many folders, a few, or none at all. You can have all your programs on menus that fold out of the Start button's menus or you can have program icons on the Desktop where you can open them with a mouse click. You can also have colors, fonts, and Desktop wallpaper of many types. You can do just about anything you can imagine, so experiment until you find a setup that works like you do. Here's how to get at all the settings that affect the Desktop.

To get to the Property sheets that control the Desktop, move the pointer to a blank spot on the Desktop and right-click the mouse. Select Properties from the pop-up menu and you'll see the Display Properties dialog box (see Figure 2.5) with seven pages of labeled tabs.

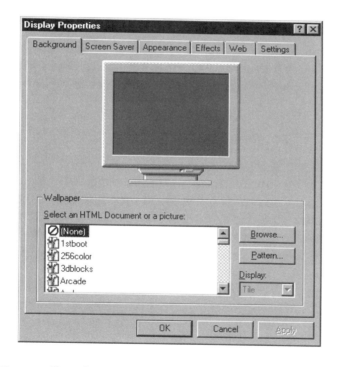

FIGURE 2.5:
The Display Properties dialog box allows you to change the appearance of your Desktop.

Next, we'll explore the contents of each individual page that is part of the Display Properties sheet.

Background

The wallpaper and background pattern is what appears as your Desktop. On the Background page, you can set both of these elements. If you have a special type of pattern, you can use the Browse button to locate that file and use it as your wallpaper.

Any file that is in a bitmap format (.BMP) or device-independent bitmap file format (.DIB) can be used as wallpaper.

WARNING When Windows 98 is installed, it uses the minimal amount of memory necessary to maintain the Desktop display. Changes, such as adding complex patterns to the Desktop, use valuable memory. If you don't want to use memory resources, minimize the number of Desktop settings you change.

TIP The Apply button lets you see how a setting will work without having to close the Display Properties box. It also allows you to try several different settings before you make a decision as to which one you want to use.

Screen Saver

When personal computers were relatively new, monitors could be damaged if the same image was left on the screen for an extended period of time. Screen savers, a constantly moving and repetitive display, came to the rescue.

If you installed a screen saver—the one that comes with Windows 98 or some other one—you can adjust the settings on this page. All the installed screen savers are in the Screen Saver drop-down list.

Click the Preview button to get a full-screen view of the selected screen saver. Move your mouse or press any key on the keyboard to return to the Display Properties screen.

Appearance

This page allows you to change the color scheme of the different Desktop elements, such as the title bar and how text will appear on the Desktop.

Click any of the elements in the window at the top of the Appearance page and the name of the element appears in the Item box as well as the colors and any other settings. Change the size or color, or both. If there's a font that can be changed, the current one will appear in the Font box.

And if you're just not in a very creative mood, select one of the many different color schemes ranging from Desert to Lilac. How pretty.

Effects

This page, a new addition to Windows 98, allows you to work with the various icons used to represent files and folders on the Windows 98 Desktop, and it even allows you to hide all the icons on the Desktop if you are viewing it as a Web page. You can also adjust visual effects such as the size of the icons on the Desktop, and even smooth the edges of those pesky fonts that refuse to cooperate.

Web

The Web tab gives you the opportunity to create different configurations of items on the Windows 98 Active Desktop, and to open a series of Channels or links, which you can go to using Internet Explorer (see Chapter 11), with a click. You can also place other active resources (links to other Internet sites) on your Desktop and change the way you click the Desktop icons using the Folder Options button.

Settings

Of all the pages in the Display Properties dialog box, this page offers the changes that have the most direct impact on your working environment. Here's where you can change how your screen actually looks (as well as what Windows 98 knows about your display hardware).

You can change the number of colors that are used (which is limited by the type of monitor you have and the capability of the video driver), the size of the fonts used on the Desktop (by clicking the Advanced button), and most important, the area of the Desktop that is used by Windows 98 (also limited by your hardware and software capabilities).

Changing Resolutions

Displays are described in terms of their resolution—that's the number of dots (or pixels) on the screen and the number of colors that can be displayed at the same time. The resolutions you can choose using the slider under the Screen Area are limited by the hardware and software you have. You can't make your monitor and video card display more than is built into them. As the resolution increases, objects become more defined, but they become smaller as well. Also, as the relocation increases, more of your computer's memory is devoted to appearance rather than performance.

Most computers and most people are happy with the 800x600 setting. Resolution choices are based on what you like to look at—constrained by the capabilities of your monitor and video card. At the lowest resolution, you may not be able to see all the elements of some programs, so try the next higher resolution. At the highest resolutions, screen elements are very small, so you may want to try Large Fonts from the Font Size box (by clicking the Advance button). That will make the icon captions on the Desktop easier to see.

Here are the most likely display settings:

- 640x480   A standard VGA display that's 640 pixels wide by 480 pixels high.
- 800x600   A typical SVGA display (super VGA).
- 1024x768   This is the upper limit of SVGA and the beginning of more advanced systems such as 8514/A and XGA. This is a very fine (that is, non-grainy) resolution, but if your monitor is 15 inches or smaller, you'd better have very good eyes.
- 1280x1024   A very fine resolution but one that requires a large monitor. Even with a 17-inch screen, you'll need good eyes.

You'll notice as you move the slider toward higher resolutions that the number of colors displayed in the Colors box changes. As resolution numbers go up, color numbers have to go down because they're both competing for the same video memory. That's why, if you want the most realistic color represented on your screen, you'll need a video card (also called a display adapter) with 2, 4, or more megabytes of its own memory.

As with many display changes, you'll have to restart your computer to see the effect of these changes.

NOTE **If you change your screen resolution, you may end up with some very peculiar arrangements of your icons. They may be way too far apart or so close together that they're difficult to use. The Appearance page has controls for the spacing of icons. Pull down the Item drop-down list and select one of the Icon Spacing choices, and then adjust the spacing using the Size box.**

Getting All the Help You'll Ever Need

Who needs Help with Windows 98? Sooner or later, almost everyone. Windows 98 provides extensive help that is easily accessible and easily understood.

The most direct way to get Windows 98 Help is from the Start menu. Click the Start button and then click Help. The initial Windows 98 Help screen shown in Figure 2.6 opens.

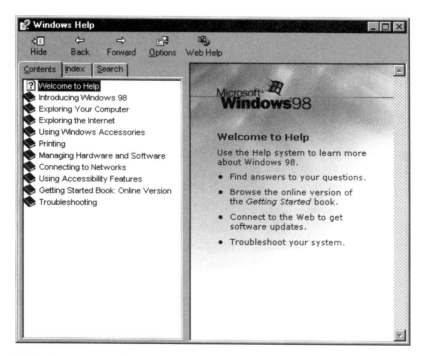

FIGURE 2.6:   From the Help menu, you can select local Help or the Web Help button from the Internet browser.

You can elect to access offline Help or access Web Help through your Internet connection. Offline, Windows 98 will use the files stored on your computer to provide you with assistance on the topic of your choice. If you click the Web Help button, Windows 98 will use your Internet connection to make a direct connection to Microsoft and you can access help there.

Which help should you use? The offline option is great for most common problems, and you can probably find the help you need. But, if you have a fast Internet connection and want to access all the help and services at your disposal, try the Web Help option. In a nutshell, offline is faster, but the Web Help option is more comprehensive.

TIP   Earlier versions of Windows allowed the user to press the F1 key and get help on the selected dialog box option. This easiest of help approaches is still alive and well. At any time in any Windows 98 dialog box, you can press the F1 button and get help on the Desktop or the current action you are undertaking. It's quick, it's handy, and it works.

Using Offline Help

Offline Help allows you to select from three different ways of getting help (see Figure 2.7). One is through a search of the Contents of Windows 98, which includes general Help categories. Here you click the category in which you are interested (such as Printing) and then work your way through the selection of options until you find the topic on which you need help. Just follow the instructions provided to get the assistance you need.

A second way to get Help is through clicking the Index tab. This action produces a list of all the topics contained in Windows 98 Help and allows you to scroll through the list or type in a keyword or two to find the topic on which you need assistance.

The third way of using offline Help is to use the Search tab to look for a particular term or operation you want to perform. Windows 98 will find terms that relate to whatever you enter and provide you with Help on that topic.

One of the nicer features of Windows 98 Help is that you can continue performing those Help steps without worrying about the Help screen retreating to the background as you click a new Window or select a menu option. The Help screen only disappears when you close out if it.

NOTE   Clicking in the right frame of Help allows you to perform many different operations, including printing the contents of the Help topic. You can then make up your own little book of special Help tips. You can also save Help screens as wallpaper, copy them as graphic files, or create a shortcut for a particular topic.

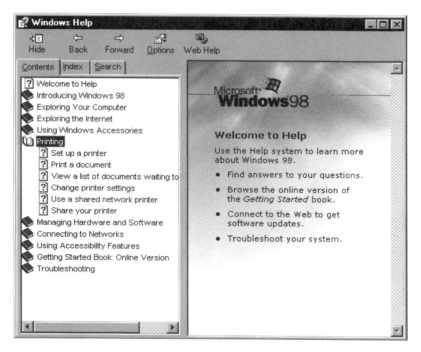

FIGURE 2.7: Use Local Help to find out about printing documents.

Using Web Help

Using Web Help allows you to use your browser and connect to Microsoft's Windows 98 Support Home Page. Here, you can get extensive help on almost any aspect of Windows 98.

There are just too many topics for which you can receive support to go through them all here, but when you use online help, you access an entire knowledge base of help topics. You can also submit a question to a Microsoft technician, find out phone numbers if you'd rather talk with someone, and get information about other support options.

What's Next?

Now that you've been at least casually introduced to Windows 98, we'll move to specifics. In the next chapter you'll learn about *shortcuts*—indispensable little tools that will make you a more efficient Windows 98 user. And they're also great fun! So, good work so far and let's move on.

Chapter **3**

MAKING AND TAKING SHORTCUTS

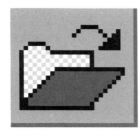

FEATURING

- Creating, naming, and moving shortcuts
- Setting shortcuts to work for you
- Placing shortcuts where you want them
- Starting programs when Windows 95 starts
- Using other shortcuts
- Using the keyboard

There are many different ways to accomplish the same task in Windows 98. For example, you can open the Windows Explorer and click the program application you want to start. Or, you can create a shortcut for that program, place it on the Desktop, and click it when you're ready to use it. Shortcuts introduce a new level of convenience and customization to Windows. They're meant to be convenient ways to get at all the things on your computer or network: documents, applications, folders, printers, and so on. In this chapter, we'll cover all the ways to make and modify a shortcut and how to place the shortcuts you want in the places you want them to be.

NOTE At the end of the chapter you'll find a different type of shortcut—a set of keyboard combinations you can use to perform many of Windows 98's most important functions.

A shortcut is identified by the small arrow in its lower-left corner (see Figure 3.1).

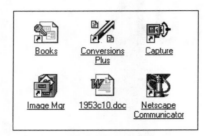

FIGURE 3.1:
This is a sample of shortcuts representing various Windows 98 files and applications.

The arrow isn't there just to be cute. It's important to know (particularly before a deletion) whether something is a shortcut or a real object. You can delete shortcuts at will. You're not deleting anything that you can't re-create in a second or two. But if you delete an actual file or folder, you'll have to reinstall it or rummage around in the Recycle Bin to retrieve it. And if it's a while before you notice it's missing, the Recycle Bin may have been emptied in the meantime, and the object may be gone.

Here's an example. Let's say that on your hard drive you have a folder called FrontPad (and you do, unless you've deleted it). On the Desktop, you can put a shortcut to that folder just like the shortcuts in Figure 3.1. You can get to the contents of the folder by clicking the shortcut. If you delete the shortcut folder on the Desktop, the folder on the hard drive remains untouched.

If you delete the folder on the hard drive but not the shortcut on the Desktop, the shortcut will still be there, but it will be pointing to nothing. When you click the shortcut, you will get a dialog box telling you that Windows 98 is looking for the file to which the shortcut refers. Most of the time, if what the shortcut is pointing to is still on your computer somewhere, Windows 98 can find the target. And if it can't, you can click the Browse button in the dialog box that appears to search for it manually. But if you've deleted the file or folder it's looking for, Windows won't be able to locate it and neither will you. The best thing to do in this situation is delete the shortcut from the Desktop.

Shortcuts are an excellent tool for configuring your Desktop to suit you. You can create shortcuts to folders, to programs, and to individual files. In fact, you can create a shortcut to any Windows 98 object. Arrange them any way you want on the Desktop, inside other folders, or on menus.

Creating Shortcuts

The Create Shortcut option can be found in many different places including:
- On an object's pop-up menu (see Figure 3.2)
- From various drop-down menus
- On the Desktop pop-up menu as New ➤ Shortcut

FIGURE 3.2:
Create Shortcut is an option almost every time you use the right mouse button to click an object.

Shortcuts are pointers to objects. So you need to either find the object you want to create a shortcut to or be able to tell Windows 98 where the object is located.

The easiest way to create a shortcut is to use My Computer or the Windows 98 Explorer to locate the object for which you want to create the shortcut. Then, right-click the object and click Create Shortcut. A new icon named Shortcut to… will appear.

NOTE   **There are some special circumstances you need to keep in mind depending upon where the original object is located. The next few sections will address these.**

Creating a Shortcut When You Can See the Object

To create a shortcut when you have the original object in view inside the Explorer or My Computer window, follow these steps:

1. Right-click the object for which you want to create a shortcut.
2. Click the Create Shortcut option on the pop-up menu.

The new shortcut is created with the name Shortcut to *Name* (where *Name* is the name of the program or file). You can now drag the short-cut to any location you choose, including another folder, the Start menu, or even the Desktop.

Here's a shortcut to the Word for Windows program. This shortcut, when clicked, will open the Word for Windows program.

Creating a Shortcut When You Can't See the Object

If the original object isn't handy or you don't want to go hunting for it (which means you probably can't remember where it is or never knew in the first place), you can still create a shortcut by following these steps:

1. Right-click the Desktop and select New ➢ Shortcut.
2. In the dialog box that opens, type in the location and name of the original object. If you don't know the path (and who ever does?), click the Browse button.
3. Using the Browse window, mouse around until you find the file or object you want to link to. You may have to change the Files of Type item in the Browse window to the All Files option.
4. Highlight the file with the mouse (the name will appear in the File Name box) and click Open. The Command Line box will now contain the name and location of the object.
5. Click Next and either accept or change the name for the shortcut.
6. Click Finish and the shortcut appears on your Desktop.

Renaming a Shortcut

To rename a shortcut, right-click the icon and select Rename from the menu that opens. Type in the name you want. Click a blank spot on the Desktop when you're through.

What to Name Shortcuts

When you name or rename a shortcut, take full advantage of the long file name feature (up to 255 characters) that Windows 98 makes available. No need to get carried away, but you might as well call a folder "March Budget Reports" rather than "MAR BUD."

As with naming any file, certain characters aren't allowed in shortcut names, including:

Backslash	\
Forward slash	/
Greater-than sign	<
Less-than sign	>
Pipe symbol	|
Colon	:
Double quotation mark	"
Question mark	?
Asterisk	*

Just be a bit creative, and learn to live without these characters in your shortcut names.

Shortcut Settings

As is the case with other Windows 98 objects, each shortcut has a Properties sheet associated with it that you can see by right-clicking the shortcut icon and selecting Properties from the pop-up menu. For shortcuts to Windows objects (as opposed to DOS programs), the most interesting page is the one labeled Shortcut (shown in Figure 3.3).

Finding the Target

Forget what object is represented by the shortcut and where it's located? The path or address for the target, or the object from which the shortcut was created, can be found in the Target text box on the Shortcut page of the Properties sheet.

If you want to find out what the shortcut is pointing to and be delivered to that location, click the Find Target button. When you click this button, a window opens into the folder containing the application or file the shortcut is for. You can then click the file or application to open it.

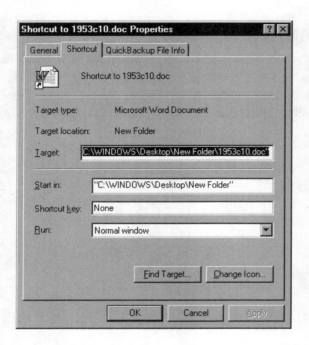

FIGURE 3.3:
The Shortcut page
of the Properties
sheet

Changing a Shortcut's Icon

Shortcuts to programs will usually display the icon associated with that program. You can, however, change the icon for a shortcut by following these steps:

1. Right-click the shortcut icon and select Properties from the pop-up menu.
2. Select the Shortcut tab and click the Change Icon button.
3. Use the Browse button to look in other files (WINDOWS\MORICONS.DLL has a bunch). Click the icon you want to use.
4. Click OK twice and the new shortcut icon will be displayed, taking the place of the old shortcut icon.

TIP **Many icons are available from icon libraries that are distributed as shareware, and an especially great place to find them is on the Internet. Just use the Search tools found in Internet Explorer or any other browser. More about this in Chapter 11.**

Putting Shortcuts Where You Want Them

The point of shortcuts is to save time and effort. Indiscriminately placing a bunch of shortcuts on the Desktop may help you, but it also may just clutter up the Desktop. There are a number of other ways and places shortcuts can be made useful, including placing them at locations other than the Desktop.

Putting a Start Menu Item on the Desktop

When you click the Start menu and follow the Programs arrow, you'll see a hierarchical display of programs installed on your system. All those menu items are just representations of shortcuts. To create the shortcuts you want on your Desktop, you'll need to (if you'll pardon the expression) go Exploring.

1.   Right-click the Start button and select Open or Explore.
2.   Click the Programs icon.
3.   Find the programs you want here. (You may have to go down another level by clicking one of the folders.)
4.   Right-click the shortcut you want and drag it to the Desktop, selecting Create Shortcut(s) Here from the menu that opens when you release the mouse button (shown in Figure 3.4).

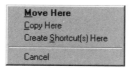

FIGURE 3.4: Select Create Shortcut(s) Here from the pop-up menu to create a shortcut.

Adding a Program to the Start Menu

You undoubtedly have some objects that you'd like to get at without having to go through the menus or without searching around the Desktop.

To add a program to the top of the Start menu, just click a shortcut and drag-and-drop it on the Start button. Then when you click the Start button, the program will be instantly available.

You can remove programs from the Start menu by selecting Start ➤ Settings ➤ Taskbar & Start Menu. Click the Start Menu programs and then the Remove button. Then select Close and OK. Highlight the program you want to remove and then click the Remove button. Once again, the shortcut (which appeared on the Start menu) is removed, but the actual program to which the shortcut refers remains.

Adding a Shortcut to *Send To*

When you right-click most things in Windows 98, one of the choices on the pop-up menu is Send To. By default, the Send To menu includes shortcuts to your floppy drive (or drives) and also may include (depending on your installation) shortcuts to mail and fax recipients.

A great example of using shortcuts effectively is to add one that represents a printer to the Send To folder. That way, all you need to do is right-click a file icon, then select the printer. The application associated with the icon will open and the document will print. Pretty nifty.

To add a shortcut to Send To, follow these steps:

1. Click the Start button and select Programs ➤ Windows Explorer.
2. Locate the Windows folder in the left pane of the Explorer and open it.
3. Locate the Send To folder and click it.
4. Now drag any item you want to appear on the Send To menu into the Send To folder.

You may have to open a second instance of the Explorer to get at other folders if the shortcuts you want are not on the Desktop.

TIP When you use Send To, you're actually doing the equivalent of drag-and-drop. The item you highlighted will be dropped on the selection you make in Send To.

Starting a Program When Windows Starts

You may have programs you want to have started and ready to run when you start Windows—for example, your calendar or another application you want immediate access to. Windows 98 includes a StartUp folder for just such purposes.

To start a program when Windows 98 starts, you must first create a shortcut for that program and then place it in the Windows 98 StartUp folder. Here's how:

1. Right-click the Start button and select Open or Explore from the pop-up menu.
2. Click the Programs icon and then click the StartUp folder icon.
3. Drag whatever shortcuts you want to start to the StartUp folder.

NOTE   **If you want to leave the original shortcut where it is, drag with the right mouse button and choose Copy Here from the menu that pops up when you release the button.**

Now that you've got the shortcut in the StartUp folder, how do you want the window to appear when it starts? It can appear as minimized (on the Taskbar), normal (as it would if normally opened), or maximized (using the entire Desktop area).

To specify how you want programs to look when Windows 98 starts:

1. Right-click the shortcut and select Properties.
2. Click the Shortcut tab.
3. In the Run window, select Minimized (or Normal Window or Maximized).
4. Click OK when you're done.

Starting a Program with a Keyboard Shortcut

You can click a shortcut placed anywhere on the Desktop to work with a file, a folder, or an application. And you can also use a keystroke combination as a shortcut.

What's great about this Windows 98 feature? Imagine having a maximized window on your Desktop where all you can see is the document. You need to open another application. Even if you have a shortcut to what you need, you can't use it because you can't see it! A keystroke shortcut is just what you need. If you have a keyboard shortcut, you can use that to open the application without any other fuss.

To create a keyboard shortcut, follow these steps:

1. Right-click the shortcut and select Properties.
2. On the Shortcut page, click in the Shortcut Key field.
3. Type in a letter and Windows will add Ctrl+Alt. (So if you enter a W, the keyboard combination will be Ctrl+Alt+W.)
4. Click OK when you're finished.

Now whenever you want to use the shortcut to access the application, just use that key combination.

TIP To remove a keyboard shortcut, you need to go to Properties again and click in the Shortcut Key field and press the Backspace key.

NOTE It's best to limit keyboard shortcuts to just a few programs or folders because these shortcuts have precedence in Windows. This means that if you use a keyboard combination that's also used in a Windows 98 program for a shortcut, that program loses the ability to use the key combination.

Shortcuts to Other Places

Shortcuts quickly become a normal way of accessing files and programs on your own computer, but they're a much more powerful tool than you'd first suspect.

DOS Programs

Shortcuts to DOS programs are made in the same way as other shortcuts. Find the program file in the Explorer and do a right-mouse drag to the Desktop. However, the Properties pages for a DOS program are more complex to allow for individual configuration of older programs. Chapter 12 covers these settings in some detail.

WARNING Windows 98 will always try to find the target for a shortcut, even if you move the target to another location. But, you might not be that lucky with DOS programs. So if you move your game to another drive or rename a batch file, plan on making a new shortcut.

Disk Drives

Right-click a disk drive in the Explorer or My Computer and drag it to the Desktop to create a shortcut to the contents of a drive. When you click the shortcut, you'll see its contents almost instantly—it's much quicker than opening the entire Explorer.

Keyboard Shortcuts

The mouse is the mouse, but some people prefer to keep their hands on the keyboard and perform as many Windows 98 operations as possible from there. In fact, you can perform practically every Windows 98 function using either the mouse or the keyboard.

Of course, you probably can't be bothered memorizing all these keyboard combinations, but you may want to consider a few for your memory bank (the one in your head), particularly if there are actions you do repeatedly that you find the mouse too clumsy for. The more you use keyboard shortcuts that best fit your needs (such as Ctrl+S for Save or Ctrl+X for Cut), the easier they will be to remember, and the more proficient you'll be as a Windows 98 user.

The following table includes the most useful (and in many cases, undocumented) keyboard shortcuts:

Key	Action
Alt+Esc	Activate open applications
Alt+F4	Close the current application. If no application is open, it will activate the Shut Down window
Alt+PrintScreen	Copy the active window to the Clipboard
Alt+Tab	Open files and folders (see Figure 3.5 at the end of this table). Hold down the Alt key and press Tab to move the cursor from item to item
Alt+Shift+Tab	Move the cursor through the open items in the opposite direction from Alt+Tab
Alt+Spacebar	Open the Control Menu (same as clicking the icon at the far upper-left corner of the application or folder window)
Alt+Enter	View item properties
Alt+hyphen	Show system menus for those same programs
Alt+underlined letter on menu items	Carry out the same command as if you selected the menu option with the mouse
Backspace	Move up one level in the folder hierarchy
Ctrl+A	Select all

Key	Action
Ctrl+X	Cut
Ctrl+C	Copy
Ctrl+V	Paste
Ctrl+Z	Undo
Ctrl+F4	Close the current window in programs that allow several windows to be open (like Word or Excel)
Ctrl+Esc	Open the Start menu
F1	Get Help from the Desktop and Help for a selected dialog box item
F10 or Alt	Put the focus on the menu bar. To move between menus, use the left ← and right → arrow keys. The ↓ or ↑ key will open the menu
F2	Rename the file or folder that's highlighted
F3	Open Find
F4	Open the drop-down list in the Address toolbar. Press F4 a second time and the drop-down list will close
F5	Refresh the view in the active window
Left arrow (arrow graphic)	Collapse the highlighted folder. If it's already collapsed, move up one level in the folder hierarchy
Print Screen	Copy the current screen to the Clipboard, from which it can be pasted into Paint or another graphics application
Right arrow (arrow graphic)	Expand the highlighted folder. If the folder is already expanded, go to the subfolder
Shift+Del	Delete immediately and do not place in the Recycle Bin
Shift+F10	View the shortcut menu for the selected item
Shift+Tab	Move the selection cursor in the opposite direction from Tab
Tab or F6	In Explorer view, each time you press this key, the focus will move from the drop-down window on the toolbar in the left pane to the right pane and back again

The Clipboard mentioned above is not an actual application; it's a special place in memory. However, there is a Clipboard Viewer (available under Programs ➤ Accessories ➤ System Tools) that can see whatever you copy. If it's not installed, go to Add/Remove Programs in the Control Panel. Select Windows Setup and then Accessories.

FIGURE 3.5:
Use the Alt+Tab key to scroll through active programs. Here the program that will become active is Microsoft Word.

What's Next?

Shortcuts can really speed things up and make you a better and more efficient Windows 98 worker. Whether you create shortcuts and place them on your Desktop or in a dedicated folder, they do their job very well. Next we'll move on to working with that all-important input device, the mouse.

Chapter 4

MOUSING AROUND

- **Understanding clicks**
- **Using the right mouse button**
- **Setting up your mouse**
- **DOS mouse**

One of the great advances made in personal computing was the introduction of the graphical user interface (GUI) and the use of a mouse to navigate within that interface. There are other pointing devices you can use with Windows 98 (such as a tablet or a stylus), but the mouse is king. The Windows user interface has always depended on a mouse or another pointing device, and with Windows 98, that reliance is even more pronounced. You can still do most things from the keyboard (Chapter 3 has a whole list of key combinations), but everything is much easier when you're using a mouse. Fewer steps are required, and there's no memorization necessary.

Everywhere you go in Windows 98, you can click with the mouse to produce an action—whether it's opening a file, getting helpful information, or sending your recently composed thank you note to a floppy drive for backup. In this chapter, we'll discuss how the mouse works and how you can customize most functions to fit the way you work.

One Click or Two

A single-click is one click of the left mouse button, while a double-click is two rapid clicks of the left mouse button in succession. If you've used any version of Windows before, you know all about single clicks and double clicks. However, the click options have changed in Windows 98. As Chapter 1 explained, you can have it your way when it comes to clicks—most of the time anyway.

Windows 98 attempts to reduce the number of clicks needed by offering right-click options (also offered in Windows 95) and the Active Desktop view, which eliminates some of the double-clicking that older versions of Windows required. Throughout this book, we assume that you're using the Active Desktop view. This new Desktop view works very well when you're operating in Windows 98 components, including Internet Explorer. But in applications that are not designed for Windows 98—and we all have plenty of those—you'll still need to double-click on occasion.

For example, if you're using Quicken 6, you'll still have to double-click to open an account. On the other hand, when you're selecting a file to open in some applications, a single-click will often work just fine.

Double-Click Speed

You can adjust the amount of time allowed between mouse clicks for two successive clicks to be considered a double-click. To do this, open the Mouse icon by selecting Start ➤ Settings ➤ Control Panel. On the Buttons page, move the slider under

Double-Click Timing toward Slow or Fast. Double-click in the Double-Click Test area to try out a different setting. Click OK when you've found a speed that you like.

If you click too slow, you end up highlighting the object once and then highlighting it again. If you click too fast, you'll only highlight the object. This takes a bit of practice, but soon your clicking speed will be in synch with the mouse setting. See the "Mouse Settings" section later in this chapter for more information.

The Right Mouse Button

You know the left mouse opens an object, but it's the right mouse button that really adds power to Windows 98. You can right-click everything on the Desktop, as well as the Desktop itself, to produce menus full of options. In addition, all the programs that come with Windows 98 and all programs written specifically for Windows 98 will use the right mouse button extensively.

For example, in Outlook Express (see Chapter 10), you can right-click the person you are sending an e-mail message to and use one of the options to enter that person's e-mail address in the Address Book.

Right-Clicking a File

Right-clicking a file icon presents you with a menu of multiple options, including opening the file with its associated program.

If there's a Quick Viewer associated with the file, you can get a look at the contents by choosing Quick View from the menu. This is a great "look-see" option, since you are not actually opening the file, but just "peeking" in.

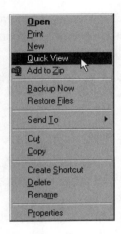

You can see every available command for a file or folder by selecting the file or folder and holding down the Shift key as you right-click.

If the file is of a registered file type, you can get still another option. Hold down the Shift key while right-clicking and you get Open With—an option that lets you open the file with a different application.

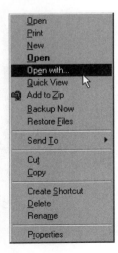

A number of programs will add other entries to the right mouse button menu. For example, the archiving program WinZip puts the item Add to Zip on the menu so you can select files to be added to an archive.

Right-Clicking a Folder

The menu that opens when you right-click a folder is similar to the one for a file. If you choose Open, you'll see the contents of the folder. Explore does much the same thing, except the folder will be shown in the Windows Explorer view—two panes, with the left pane showing the folder and its location on the hard drive, and the right pane detailing the contents of the folder.

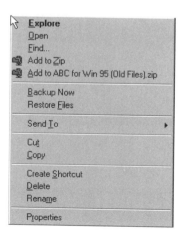

You can also select Find to search the folder for a particular file either by name or by contents. (There's more on using Find in Chapter 6.)

Right-Clicking the Start Button

Place your pointer on the Start button and right-click to bring up three choices:
- Open: Opens the Start Menu folder. This is the folder that contains the files and folders you've dropped on the Start Menu as well as another folder called Programs that contains all the shortcuts that make up the Programs menu that cascades off the Start Menu.
- Explore: Opens the Start Menu folder in the Explorer view
- Find: A shortcut to finding a file in the Start Menu folder

The first two choices on the menu are quick ways to get at the items on the Programs menu so you can move a program up a level or two, or remove one from the menu entirely. If you choose Explore, the window that opens will have two panes, the left one showing the folder and its location, the right pane showing the files inside whatever folder is chosen on the left. If you choose Open, the view is of a single window. When you click a folder, another window opens showing the folder's contents.

Right-Clicking the Taskbar

To perform additional tasks, there are tons of places on the Taskbar where you can right-click, including the Start button, icons on the Taskbar, the Taskbar itself, the Quick Launch or Desktop toolbar on the Taskbar, and even the buttons on these toolbars! Lots of options!

When you right-click a blank spot on the Taskbar, a menu pops up with the following options:
- Toolbars
- Cascade
- Tile Horizontally
- Tile Vertically
- Minimize All Windows
- Properties

NOTE

The Desktop toolbar on the Taskbar (right-click and select Toolbars) displays all the items on the Desktop (My Computer, etc.) as a series of icons. The Quick Launch option lists the standard Taskbar items, including Launch the Internet Explorer, Show Desktop, and View Channels. The New Toolbar option allows you to add a folder icon to the Taskbar.

WARNING

If you find that right-clicking on the Taskbar (or any element on the Taskbar) does not produce the results that we discussed, you probably have clicked in the wrong area (an easy thing to do). Remember that the Taskbar has a Start button, icons representing active documents, toolbars, and icons on the toolbars. You need to click on or between these Taskbar elements to view the options you want.

Right-Clicking Icons on the Taskbar

Active programs and folders will each have an icon on the Taskbar. Right-click the icon, and if the item isn't open on the Desktop, you'll get the option to Restore (in other words, expand a window on the Desktop), Maximize (restore it full screen), or Close the file.

For items that are active on the Desktop, clicking the icon will bring that window to the front. A right-click will bring the window to the front plus open the same pop-up menu.

Move and Size are keyboard options. Select one of them and you can move the window or change its size using the arrow keys. Press the return or Enter key to complete the operation.

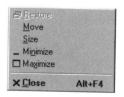

Right-click other icons in the far right corner of the Taskbar and you'll get a chance to adjust characteristics of what the icon represents. For example, you can adjust the date and time or adjust the volume on your sound card. Other Startup icons appear in this section of the Taskbar depending on the hardware and software installed.

Right-Clicking the Toolbar

The toolbar can contain the Desktop and the Quick Launch toolbars and right-clicking presents these additional options:

- View: Allows you to see toolbar icons in large or small format
- Show Text: Produces the text alongside of the toolbar icon
- Refresh: Brings the toolbar up to date after any changes are made
- Show Title: Shows the title of the toolbar

To see these options, you have to click between the buttons or anywhere on the toolbar where empty space is available.

Right-Clicking My Computer

Right-click the My Computer icon on the Desktop and you have the option of opening My Computer in a regular window or in the Windows Explorer view. You can also find files or computers, or open the Properties sheets for your system. There's considerably more about My Computer in Chapter 5.

Mouse Settings

Because the mouse (or any other pointing device) is used so much in Windows 98, it's important to have it set up comfortably. To change how your mouse operates, settings are available in the Mouse icon in the Control Panel.

If you have installed another device such as a trackball or a touchpad, there will be an icon in the Control Panel window that you need to open to make changes to the way that pointing device operates.

> **NOTE** **Dead mouse? It happens. If your mouse doesn't work, check that the cable is inserted tightly into the back of the computer. These cables have a way of slowly loosening over time. You'll probably have to restart your computer once you reseat the cable. How about a sick mouse? Dirt easily gets into the mechanism and the surface on which the mouse rolls, contributing grease and other dirt to the inside workings of the mouse. Open the mouse up, remove the mouse-ball, and clean the dirt with a cotton swab and alcohol.**

Right- or Left-Handed

Not everyone is a righty. If you want to use the mouse with your left hand, you can change your right-handed mouse to a left-handed one. To do this, follow these steps.
1. Open the Mouse Properties menu by clicking Mouse in the Control Panel.
2. Click the Buttons tab (if it isn't already displayed).
3. Click Left-Handed to reverse the normal button functions. The graphic will show you what each button does.
4. Click Apply, then OK.

Pointer Speed

As you move the pointer around the Desktop, perhaps you find you have to move the device too much to get a small result on the screen. Or vice versa, you move the mouse just a little and the pointer moves way too far. To adjust this, click the Mouse icon in the Control Panel.

1. Select the Motion tab.
2. Move the slider under Pointer Speed one notch to the left or the right.
3. Click the Apply button and try the new setting.
4. Repeat until you have a speed you like and then click OK.

Making the Pointer More Visible

If you're working with a smaller screen—particularly the kind on a laptop, you may find the pointer "disappearing" sometimes. To make the pointer more visible, open the Mouse icon in the Control Panel and select the Motion tab (see Figure 4.1).

Click the box next to Show Pointer Trails (despairingly, but with humor, also called "mouse droppings"). Use the slider to adjust for long or short trails. You can see the results as you move the slider, without having to use the Apply button. Click OK when you find something you like.

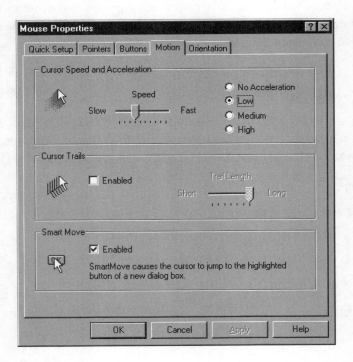

FIGURE 4.1:
The Mouse Properties screen is where you can adjust the cursor and trails.

Mouse Pointers

Windows 98 comes with an assortment of new mouse pointers, so you can choose ones you like. You'll probably find them a big improvement on the default pointers. A few of the pointers included with Windows 98 are animated, and many more animated cursors come with the Plus! Package (available for Windows 95 but compatible with Windows 98).

Animated cursors are becoming the kind of cottage industry that icons were with earlier versions of Windows. Animated cursors can be downloaded from many online services and are also distributed as shareware.

NOTE **Your display must be set to at least 256 colors for the animated cursors to work. To check your settings, open the Display icon in the Control Panel and click the Settings button. The color palette must be set for 256 Colors, High Color, or True Color.**

Figure 4.2 shows the Pointers page under Mouse Properties. These default pointers are described in the table that follows. Once you understand what each pointer represents, you're better able to select appropriate substitutes. For example, you wouldn't want an animated pointer for Text Select because the animation would make it very difficult to make a precise selection.

Pointer	What It Does
Normal Select	The normal pointer for selecting items
Help Select	Click on the ? button and move the pointer to the area you want information about and click again
Working in Background	Something is going on in the background, but you can often move to another area and do something else
Busy	Just hang in there. Windows 98 or an application is doing something and can't be disturbed
Precision Select	Cross-hairs for very careful selection
Text Select	The I-beam that's seen in word processors and used to select text

Pointer	What It Does
Handwriting	When you're using a handwriting input device
Unavailable	Sorry, you can't drag a file to this location either because the area is unacceptable or the application won't accept drag-and-drop
Vertical Resize	Cursors that appear when you're moving a window border
Horizontal Resize	
Diagonal Resize 1	
Diagonal Resize 2	
Move	Select Move from the System menu or a right-click menu and you'll get this cursor, allowing you to move the window using the arrow keys
Alternate Select	Used in the FreeCell card game. Probably other uses to come

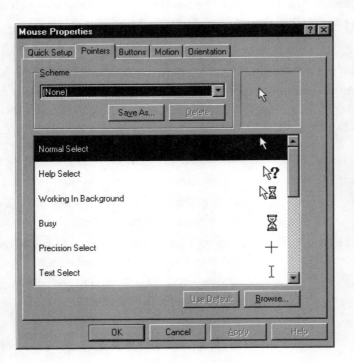

FIGURE 4.2:
Working with other mouse pointers

Changing Pointers

You can change one or more pointers and even have more than one set of pointers that you can switch among. To change one or more pointers on your system, follow these steps.

1. Click the Mouse icon in the Control Panel and select the Pointers tab.
2. In the middle of the screen, you'll see a display of the pointers with their function. Highlight a pointer you want to change and click the Browse button.
3. The window shown in Figure 4.3 will open. When you click a selection (files with the .ANI extension are animated), it will be displayed in the Preview.
4. Click the Open button when you have selected the one you want.

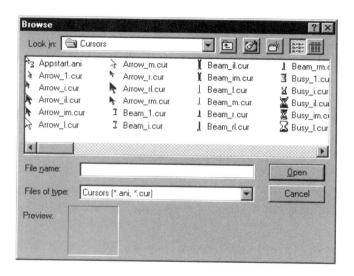

FIGURE 4.3:
Selecting a new cursor

If you accumulate a large number of animated cursors, you may want to gather them together in a folder inside the Cursors folder.

TIP

The animated cursors that come with Plus! are located in the PRO-GRAM FILES\PLUS!\THEMES folder. Copy them over rather than moving them. If you do move them, the Plus! themes may not work correctly (since they use the animated cursors).

To save a selection of pointers as a set, click the Save As button and enter a name for the scheme. After you save it, the set will be listed in the Scheme drop-down list and you can select it any time.

The DOS Mouse

DOS programs that use mouse movements and button presses should work fine in Windows 98. Windows 98 passes the mouse information along without the need to install special DOS mouse drivers.

However, if you have occasion to run a program in the special MS-DOS mode (described in Chapter 12), you'll have to load a mouse driver for that program. The mouse driver is a program that came with the mouse when you bought it or is available on the Internet at the manufacturer's Web site. Or if you upgraded by installing Windows 98 over Windows 95 or Windows 3.1, it's probably still on your machine. Consult the mouse documentation to find the name of the driver file.

What's Next?

Now that you're acquainted with all the mouse functions, in the next chapter we will move on to the all important Windows Explorer, the most often used tool for working with files and folders. You'll also see how the a new Windows 98 feature allows you to view Explorer information as if you were connected to the Internet.

Chapter 5

THE WINDOWS 98 EXPLORER

- **What the Windows 98 Explorer can do**
- **Navigating Windows 98 using the Explorer**
- **Working with file extensions**
- **Using My Computer**

Windows 98 is flexible and can easily meet the needs of people who work in different ways. One of the most powerful tools that Windows 98 offers is the Windows Explorer, which provides the tools you need to work with files and folders, and associate files with applications. Another Windows 98 tool, My Computer, also offers many of the same features. In this chapter, we'll examine both and show you how to use them.

What Is the Explorer?

The Explorer is the main tool for viewing the files and folders on your hard drive, floppy drives, or any other storage medium. It's "Windows 98 central" because it's from here that you can do everything from copying a file to another folder to launching an application to examining how much space is available on your hard drive. To open the Explorer, click the Start button and select Programs ➤ Windows Explorer.

Explorer

Many of the programs you'll use will be started using shortcuts that are located either on the Start menu or on the Desktop. But you'll still need to use the Explorer to find the objects you want to create shortcuts to and to locate the executable files for applications that are not automatically installed on the Desktop or the Start menu.

When you install a program on your computer, the program's folders are placed on the hard drive—usually in the form of a main folder and subfolders (folders inside the main folder). Sometimes there are even sub-subfolders. In Windows 98, many new applications are installed in the folder named PROGRAM FILES.

Figure 5.1 shows an open Explorer window with the hierarchy of folders shown on the left. If you look closely, you can see that one of the folders in the left column is shown as "open." The contents of that folder are displayed in the right-hand pane. You use the scroll bars on either side to move up and down through the listing.

In the left pane, folders may have either a plus or minus sign next to them. A plus sign means there are subfolders—click directly on the plus sign to expand the view. When expanded, the plus sign turns into a minus sign.

TIP　　Perhaps the best shortcut you can create is one for the Windows Explorer. The Explorer is such a handy tool, you'll find yourself using it all the time. It's located in the WINDOWS directory on your hard drive. See the section "Creating a Shortcut to Explorer" later in this chapter fro more details.

Understanding What the Explorer Does

While in the Explorer, slide the scroll bar for the left pane (if there are enough files expanded for it to be displayed) all the way to the top. Note that the hard drive C and the floppy drive A are connected to the My Computer icon by dotted lines. This indicates their connection to My Computer. But even further up is the top folder called Desktop.

FIGURE 5.1: The Explorer view showing an open folder

In the Explorer's terms, the Desktop is the top of the hierarchy (see Figure 5.2) with My Computer and all its pieces connected to it.

The dotted lines show the connections, like in a flow chart. Lines that come from the bottom of an icon and connect horizontally to other icons indicate that the destination items are contained inside the object represented by the top icon. For example, you can see that floppy drive A and hard drive C are part of My Computer. Inside drive C are numerous folders (notice the minus to the left of the C drive icon). Folders with plus signs next to them have subfolders (click the plus sign to see them). Folders without plus signs have no other folders contained within them.

Special folders such as the Control Panel and Printers folders are displayed on the same level as the disk drives so they're easier to find. You'll also see icons for the CD-ROM drive, other hard and floppy disk drives, and any other hardware Windows 98 recognizes.

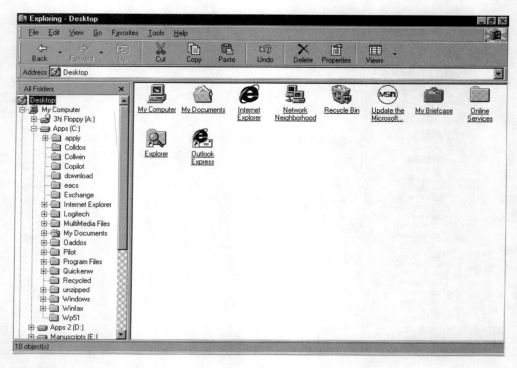

FIGURE 5.2:   The Desktop is organized as a hierarchy of files and folders.

Folders you have placed directly on the Desktop will also show up in the left pane. Shortcuts to folders won't show up in the left pane because shortcuts are only pointers to the actual folders or files. The original folders are found along with other folders on your hard drive. To see the shortcuts that are on your Desktop, click the Desktop icon in the left pane. The shortcuts will then be displayed—along with the rest of the stuff on the Desktop—in the right pane.

NOTE	Other items that don't show up in the left pane are the Inbox for Outlook Express, the icon for the Microsoft Network, and any individual files that are on the Desktop. All these are visible in Explorer's right pane when you click the Desktop icon in the left pane.

Exploring a Folder

Right-click any folder in the Explorer's left pane (except Desktop)—including My Computer or Network Neighborhood—and select Explore. The folder will open in Explorer view, with the hierarchy of folders shown in the left pane and the content of the open folder shown in the right pane.

Creating a Shortcut to the Explorer

To put Explorer at the top of your Start menu, open the Explorer and find the file called EXPLORER.EXE in your Windows folder on drive C. Drag-and-drop it on the Start button. Similarly, you can put Explorer on your Desktop. Right-click EXPLORER.EXE and drag it to the Desktop. You may have to adjust the size of your Explorer window so you can see both it and the Desktop. When you release the mouse button, select Create Shortcut(s) Here.

You will now be able to start the Windows 98 Explorer from the Start menu or from the Desktop.

TIP Since the Explorer is used so often, why not create a keyboard shortcut (addressed in Chapter 3)? Use the Ctrl+Alt+E key combination and you can access the Explorer from any screen, any time.

Creating a Shortcut to the Desktop

Try as you may, you can't drag the Desktop icon from the Explorer's left pane and create a shortcut that way. But you can create a shortcut to the Desktop by following these steps:

1. Click the Windows folder in the Explorer.
2. In the right pane, right-click the Desktop folder and drag it to the Desktop. Again, you may have to adjust the window size. Also, you may have to select Show All Files under View ➤ Folder Options.
3. Release the right mouse button and select Create Shortcut(s) Here.

When opened, this shortcut will contain all the folders and files and other icons on the Desktop—except the system-type folders like My Computer and Recycle Bin.

Using Two Explorers at Once

If you're working with and moving around a number of files or folders, it's easier if you can have two Explorer windows open at once. Just select Explore from the Start menu or the Programs menu for each copy you want.

To arrange the Explorer windows so you can access them easily, right-click the Taskbar and select Tile Horizontally or Tile Vertically. Figure 5.3 shows two instances of Explorer tiled horizontally.

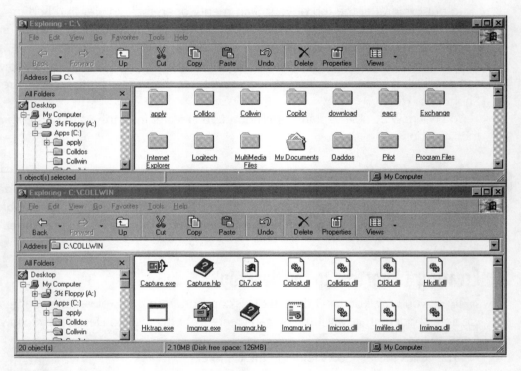

FIGURE 5.3: Using multiple copies of the Explorer

The Two Faces of the Explorer

You can view the contents of the right pane of the Explorer as a conventional listing of files as you are used to in Windows 95, or as a Web page.

To view the right pane as a Web page, follow these steps:

1. Open the Explorer.
2. Right-click in the right pane of the Explorer.
3. Select View ➤ As Web Page.

The right pane of the Explorer will appear as a Web page as shown in Figure 5.4.

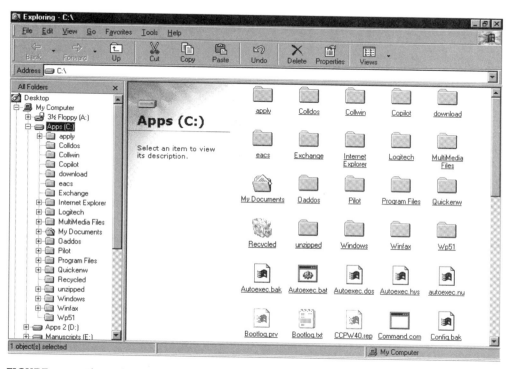

FIGURE 5.4:   The Web Page view of the Explorer

WARNING   Be careful not to confuse the Web Page view on the Explorer Toolbar with the Web Style view in the Folder Options dialog box (see Chapter 2). The Web Page view provides a view of the files and folders in the Explorer as a Web page. The Web Style option changes the way icons behave when they are pointed to and clicked.

As you can see in Figure 5.4, the Web Page view provides you with all the important information about whatever file or folder is pointed to (in Web Style) or single-clicked (in Classic Style). One of the big advantages of viewing the right pane of the Explorer as a Web page is that the right pane is more visual in nature and the relevant information is more easily available.

Navigating the Desktop with the Explorer

As mentioned before, when you see a plus sign next to an icon in the Explorer, it means that at least one subfolder is inside that folder. Click the plus sign to expand the view. Click the minus sign and the subfolders will be collapsed inside the main folder. You can slide the scroll boxes to view items that are outside the pane view.

TIP

Scroll boxes are proportionate in Windows 98. That is, the scroll box shows how much of the window's contents is being displayed. A scroll box that fills half the bar tells you that you're looking at half of what there is to see (in that particular window).

There are several ways to get at the contents of a folder using your mouse:

- Click a folder in the left pane of the Explorer and the contents are displayed in the right pane.
- Right-click a folder in the left pane and select Open. A new folder will open on the Desktop displaying the contents of the folder you clicked.

Working with the Explorer Toolbar

The Explorer Toolbar is a visual device that's been used in most Windows applications. It's a collection of icons that provide quick access to the functions on the menus. Position the mouse pointer over any button on the Explorer Toolbar and a small window or ToolTip opens telling you what the button does.

From left to right, the functions on the toolbar are:
- Move back to a previously visited folder in the left Explorer pane.
- Move forward to a previously visited folder in the left Explorer pane.
- Move up one folder in the folder hierarchy.
- Cut the highlighted item(s).
- Copy the highlighted item(s).
- Paste what you've just cut or copied.
- Undo the last operation.
- Delete the highlighted item(s).
- View the Properties sheet for the highlighted item.
- Change the view or how the Explorer's contents appear.

TIP You can cycle through the different views of the Explorer (Large Icons, Small Icons, List, Details) by clicking the Views button on the Explorer Toolbar. If you want to select a particular view, click the down triangle to the right of the View button and select the view you want.

The View Menu

The View Menu takes on particular importance when using the Explorer Toolbar because of the options that are available for the appearance of the left pane when you select View ➤ Explorer Bar. No matter what Explorer Bar view you use, the right pane of the Explorer window will always show the folders and files for the current folder which you have selected.

The Explorer bar options are as follows:
- Search allows you to search the World Wide Web using Internet Explorer (see Chapter 11) from within the Explorer.
- Favorites provides a list of those locations that are specified as favorites on the Start menu.
- History provides a list of the Internet sites you have visited, organized by the week.
- Channels lists the available channels (Chapter 11 contains information about channels).
- All Folders returns you to the traditional view of files and folders.
- None removes the left pane from the Explorer window.

Which view of the Explorer is best for you depends on how you work. For example, if you're comfortable with the appearance of Windows 95, the All Folders option might be best for you. If, on the other hand, you want to work with the files and folders you listed on the Favorites menu, Favorites is the best choice.

TIP You can negotiate the Explorer and locate any file or folder by clicking the Back, Forward, and Up buttons. That way, you can have whatever Explorer Bar view you want in the left pane and still work with files in the right.

Other Tools and Buttons

The Explorer, like other folder windows, has a number of additional tools and buttons all useful in making your file and folder management activities easier.

Minimize, Maximize, and Close

In Explorer, click the rightmost button (the one marked with an X) and the window will close. The button on the left minimizes the window to the Taskbar. The middle button maximizes the window. If the window is already at its maximum size, the middle button will restore the window to its normal size.

Sizing a Window

The odd little graphic effect in the bottom right corner of some windows is called the sizing handle. Click and drag the sizing handle to change the size of a window. A Windows 98 window without a sizing handle can't be resized. Application windows can be resized as they always have been—by dragging a corner or border.

Sorting Buttons

The sorting buttons are only visible and accessible in Details view. In that view, click a button to get the following results:

Name Clicking this button will sort contents in alphabetical order. A second click will sort the files in reverse alphabetical order.

Size When you click the Size button, files will be sorted in ascending size order. A second click will reverse the size order.

Type Files   Clicking this button will sort alphabetically by type, with folders first, then files. A second click will reverse the order.

Modified Files   Clicking this button will sort files by the date they were last changed from most recent to oldest. A second click will reverse the order.

All of the above sort methods are also available on the View menu under Arrange Icons.

> **TIP**   You can adjust the width of the Name, Size, Type, or Modified columns in any folder by dragging on the line that separates the names of the columns in the title bar.

Changing the View of a Folder's Contents

Through the Explorer, the contents of a folder can be viewed as large icons, small icons, a list, or a detailed list. Pull down the View menu in any folder window to try out different looks.

> **NOTE**   You can also right-click in the right pane of the Explorer to get a pop-up menu of the same options available on the View menu. It also can be found on the Views button's drop-down list.

If you use large or small icons, you can select View ➤ Arrange Icons and toggle Auto Arrange on or off. Remove the check mark from in front of Auto Arrange and you can drag the icons around inside the folder. With Auto Arrange selected, the icons snap to an invisible grid.

If you turn off Auto Arrange and have moved your folder icons every which way until you've made a mess, you can select Line Up Icons from the View menu and the file icons all snap to an invisible grid. You can only use the Line Up Icons option when the view is either large or small icons.

Customizing the Look of a Folder

New to the Windows 98 Explorer is the Customize this Folder option on the View menu. When you select this option (see Figure 5.5), a wizard walks you through the steps to create one of two types of customization: an HTML document (the language used to create home pages on the World Wide Web (more about this in Chapter 11) or a background picture (discussed in Chapter 16).

FIGURE 5.5:
The Customize this Folder Wizard

If you really want to get fancy, you can start fooling with HTML and create a folder look that includes just about any element you might like, including links to Web sites, newsgroups, fancy graphics, and even animated icons.

The background picture option is less ambitious, but can provide some attractive effects.

To remove any customization, click the Remove Customization button in the Customize this Folder Wizard dialog box. Click Next and continue following the prompts. Select Finish to save changes or Cancel to exit the Wizard without saving the changes.

Files and Extensions

If you've ever used any version of DOS or Windows, you're probably familiar with the file-naming conventions that are used. A DOS file name can have a maximum of eight characters plus a three-character extension (such as TERM3.DOC). The short file name requirement has historically been one of the more irritating facts about using a

PC—not because naming a file is especially hard, but because six months later you're probably going to have a hard time remembering what CZMLHTL.DOC is all about.

With Windows 98, long file names are permitted, so you can give that file a name like LETTER TO HOTEL IN COZUMEL. But because the underlying file structure is unchanged, the actual name of that file will be LETTER TO HOTEL IN COZUMEL.DOC.

NOTE   **Remember, a file name can be up to 255 characters, including spaces. It cannot contain the characters / \ : * ? " < > |.**

By default, Windows 98 hides most file extensions. If Windows 98 knows what program was used to create the file, the extension doesn't need to be seen. All you have to do is click the file and Windows 98 will open the associated application.

Seeing Extensions

If you want the file extensions displayed, follow these steps:

1. Select Folder Options from the View menu.
2. On the View page, be sure that no check mark appears in front of Hide File Extensions for Known File Types.
3. Click OK.

Seeing All Files

Windows 98 also hides a whole assortment of files from normal view, including system files and various kinds of device drivers. These are hidden for two reasons. First, most users don't need to see these files and they just clutter up the Desktop. Second, if you were to accidentally change or delete one of these files, it could cause a particular program—or even your whole system—not to work.

If you really want to see all the files on your system, you can do so easily. Just select Folder Options from the View menu and on the View page (see Figure 5.6), select Show All Files.

Unfortunately, there's no way to pick and choose among the files that are designated as hidden. Either they're all displayed or none are.

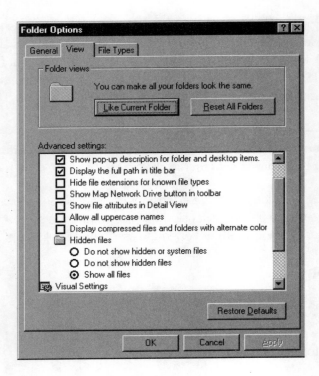

FIGURE 5.6:
Select Show All Files in the View tab of the Folder Options dialog box to see hidden files.

Associating Files with Programs

One thing that Windows 98 does very well is determine which files go with which programs. For example, you can click in the Explorer on an Excel file icon, and Windows 98 knows to open that file in Excel.

But what about files that don't necessarily have associations? You may have to establish that relationship. But, once Windows 98 knows that a certain type of file is associated with a particular program, you can click *any* file with that extension and cause the program to open.

NOTE   **Associating a file type with a program is the same as registering it. So when Windows 98 talks about registered file types, the reference is also to associated files.**

Creating New Associations

Most of the time, merely installing a program is enough to teach Windows 98 which files go with what program, but this is not always the case. If a file is of a registered type, when you right-click it the first option on the menu is Open. If it's not registered, the first option will be Open With. Select Open With and you can select from the list of applications, as shown in Figure 5.7.

FIGURE 5.7:
Creating an association

NOTE　**You can tell what application a file is associated with by highlighting it in the Explorer window, clicking View ➤ Folder Options, and clicking the File Types page. In the Folder Options box, you'll see the name and the icon that represents the application.**

If the file is not registered and the Open With window is displayed, click the name of the application you think can be used to open the file.

If you want all your files of a particular type to always open with a particular application, you need to tell Windows 98.

To register a file type, follow these steps:

1.　Open Explorer and from the View menu, select Folder Options.

2. Select File Types and click New Type.

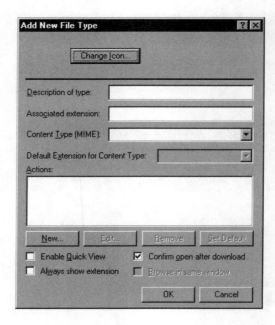

3. In the Description of Type box, enter how you want this type of file to be shown in Windows in Details view. This is for your information, so you can describe it in any way you choose.

4. In the Associated Extension box, enter the three letters that make up this file type's extension. These three letters *are* important because all files with the same extension will display a particular icon and be treated the same way as far as the operating system is concerned.

5. Click the New button. In the Action text box, type in the action you want performed when you double-click files of this type and the application used to perform the action.

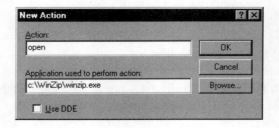

NOTE   Almost all the time you'll want the associated program to open the file. That is, the program will start and then load a file with the specified extension. To do this, type **open** in the Action text box.

6. In the Application Used to Perform Action box, type where the program that you want to use is located. If necessary, use the Browse button to find the exact location of the application you want used. Click OK.

7. Back in the Add New File Type box, you can click the Change Icon button to select a different icon for the associated files. Click OK after you've highlighted one you like. Click Close twice when you're done.

NOTE   Windows 98 knows more about other programs than any previous version of Windows. So you can be fairly confident that Windows will know most, if not all, of the associations necessary for you to open almost any file.

Using My Computer

When you first set up Windows 98, there'll be several icons on the left side of your screen. The number will vary, depending on the options you chose when installing. One of them—in fact, the first one in the top left corner—is named My Computer. Click it and you'll see a window similar to the one shown in Figure 5.8. It may not be exactly the same as yours because the contents of computers vary from user to user.

NOTE   The My Computer name is what the Windows 98 designers have assigned this icon. You can rename it as you can any icon, but just be sure that you remember what you renamed it to and that other users (of this particular computer) know that the change has occurred.

The items displayed in the window are symbols for the physical contents of your computer, including the floppy drives, hard drives, and CD-ROM drives. There'll also be a folder labeled Printers (even if you have only one or none), one for the Control Panel, folders for creating connections to the Internet and other remote locations

(Dial-Up Networking), and a folder named Scheduled Tasks, used to schedule disk maintenance, backup, and other computer housekeeping tasks (discussed in Chapter 17).

FIGURE 5.8: The contents of My Computer

NOTE Because so many settings are accessed through the Control Panel, it makes sense for it to be available in a variety of locations: off the Start menu, in My Computer, and in the Explorer. Plus you can make shortcuts to the Control Panel and put them wherever you like.

TIP If you don't see the My Computer icon on your Desktop, it may have inadvertently been renamed. Open the Explorer and click the icon representing the C drive. Then look for an icon that looks like a small computer. That's probably My Computer, regardless of what it's named. Now you can rename it My Computer if you like.

Highlight an icon that represents a drive and the disk's capacity and free space will appear in the status bar at the bottom of the window. Click one of the icons and a window will open displaying the contents. For example, click the hard drive labeled C: and you'll see all the folders contained on the C drive.

This feature provides the same information as what you saw in the Explorer window. The big difference is that the My Computer window offers limited file and folder management options.

My Computer's Properties

Right-click the My Computer icon and select Properties. There's a great deal of information to be found in these Properties sheets. Of particular interest is the Device Manager page (see Figure 5.9). Click any of the hardware items in the list to see exactly what's installed on your system.

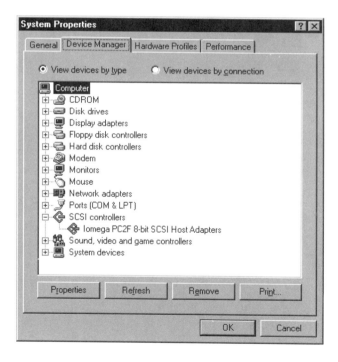

FIGURE 5.9:
The contents of the Device Manager page on the My Computer Property sheet

Highlight a specific piece of hardware and click the Properties button to see some of what Windows 98 knows about it. There are a number of other settings—particularly under the Performance tab—that you may want to take a look at. Most of these settings *never* need to be changed, but you should know where they are.

TIP To create a shortcut to the Device Manager, right-click the Desktop and select New ➤ Shortcut. In the Command Line box, type this *exactly*: **c:\windows\control.exe sysdm.cpl,system,1**. If you're working with hardware conflicts or want to fine tune hardware installations, this shortcut can be very handy.

Disk Properties

Right-click one of the disk drives and select Properties in My Computer. You'll get a Properties sheet (see Figure 5.10) that reports the used space and free space in detail and in living color. You can also rename the icon for the drive. The dialog box calls the icon's name its Label.) There are several tabs on this page, including some that might result from other software that you may have installed (such as Norton Utilities).

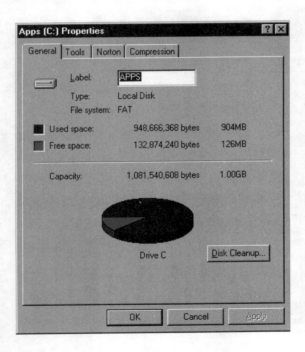

FIGURE 5.10:
Look at the General tab of the Properties sheet to see how much space is available on a drive.

The Disk Cleanup button will help you free up space used by temporary files as well as files that are currently in the Recycle Bin. Disk Cleanup deletes these files on your command.

The Tools tab will let you check the disk for errors, back it up, or defragment it. There's more on these tools in Chapter 17.

The Compression tab allows you to compress the data on your hard drive to create free space.

One Window or Many

Click the View menu and select Folder Options in a window (like My Computer), click the General tab, and you can choose from three ways that folders are displayed on the Desktop (as shown in Figure 5.11).

Web Style   The folders on the Desktop will act like the World Wide Web (more about this in Chapter 11). In this view, a click on a folder will open that folder in the same window. This will fill up your screen pretty quickly, but it will give you a clear indication of where you are and how you got there.

Classic Style   The folders behave according to Windows default settings. In this style, each folder opens in its own window, which means that as you double-click through multiple layers of folders, the contents of the current folder fill the window.

Custom   The folders operate the way you design them.

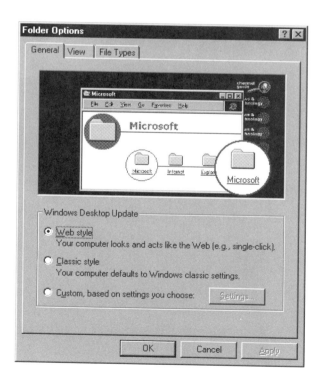

FIGURE 5.11: In the General page you can design how your folders operate.

Which one you select depends on how you like to work as well as how many windows you need open at any one time to complete the task at hand.

Some Special View Folder Tricks

If you like using the Classic style folder option most of the time, you can switch to a single window on occasion. Instead of a simple double-click on a folder to open a new window, hold down the Ctrl key as you double-click. This will open the contents of the clicked folder in the current window.

Hold down the Shift key as you double-click a folder and the folder will open in the Explorer view. Make sure the focus is on the folder you want to open this way, otherwise Windows 98 will open all the folders between where you clicked and the folder you intended to focus on.

What's Next?

These days, connecting is a major part of personal computing. In the next chapter we'll really start to have fun introducing you to Windows 98's connection tools, including the different online services that are available.

Chapter 6

WORKING WITH FILES AND FOLDERS

- **Selecting and working with files and folders**
- **Creating new files and folders**
- **Working with file and folder properties**
- **Moving, copying, and deleting files and folders**
- **Undoing mistakes**
- **Working with floppy disks**
- **Finding files and folders**

In this chapter, we'll continue some of the discussion from Chapter 5 with an emphasis on the basics of making and manipulating files and folders, and getting them organized in ways you find comfortable.

This chapter will teach you just about everything you need to know concerning working with files and folders, including how to create them, move and copy them, name them, and find them.

Selecting Files and Folders

Before any action can be taken on an object such as a file or a folder, it must first be selected. A single file or folder is selected by clicking it once with the left mouse button. You know a file or folder is selected when it appears in reverse color. Once an object is selected, you can then move or rename or copy the object as described later in this chapter.

Selecting Everything

To select a group of files or folders so you can perform the same operation on all of them at once (such as Print), open the window where the objects in question are and then click the Edit menu and click Select All. Everything in the window will be highlighted (see Figure 6.1). Right-click on any one of the highlighted icons and choose the action you want to take from the pop-up menu.

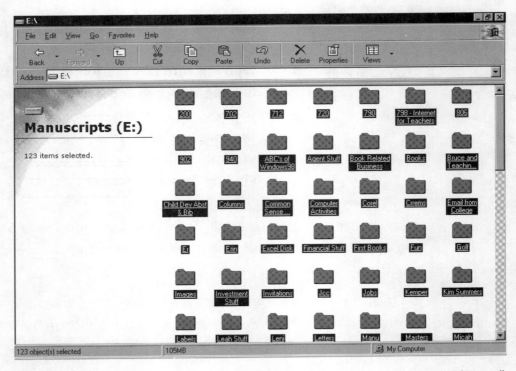

FIGURE 6.1: When you select all the folders or files in the window, you can perform one action on all of them.

TIP The Ctrl+A key combination will select all the files or folders in an open window.

Selecting Some Objects but Not All

You may not need to select all of the objects in a window. There are lots of ways to select some of the objects in a window, and the easiest way often depends on how you have the files and folders displayed.

If you have large icons displayed (as in Figure 6.1), you might want to simply lasso the items in question. Right-click an area near the first item and, holding the mouse button down, create a rectangle around the icons you want to select. When you're finished creating the box, the icons will be highlighted and the pop-up menu will appear, giving you a choice of actions. Figure 6.2 shows some icons selected in just this way. Notice that they are all next to one another.

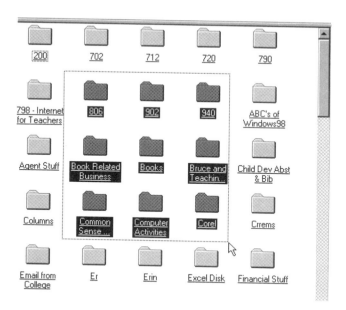

FIGURE 6.2:
A group of selected icons

If you have the icons displayed as a list or in the Details view, you can also lasso them. But since they are greatly reduced in size (from the large icon view), you're better off taking another approach. To select some but not all of the files and folders, hold down the Ctrl key and pass the pointer over each file or folder you want to select long enough for it to be selected. You can use this technique with any number of icons, be they contiguous or not.

To select more than one file or folder where they are located next to one another in a series, place the mouse on the first icon in the series, then hold down the Shift key and move the mouse pointer to the last item in the series. All of the files or folders you moved the mouse over will be selected.

Creating a New Folder

Folders are the equivalent of directories first used with DOS and then with Windows. Folders created in Windows 98 can contain shortcuts. These shortcuts can be to *real* folders in other locations, and can be placed right on the Desktop—a great improvement over earlier versions of Windows.

Creating a New Folder On the Desktop

To create a new folder on the Desktop, right-click the Desktop in some unoccupied space and select New ➤ Folder. A folder like the one shown in Figure 6.3 will appear with the cursor placed inside it, so all you have to do to name it is type the name you want.

FIGURE 6.3:
A newly created folder on the Desktop

This folder is also located on your hard drive in the Desktop folder inside the Windows folder, which you can examine using Windows Explorer. Figure 6.4 shows this new folder as it appears in the Explorer.

TIP   If you can't see the Desktop folder, it's because Hide Files of These Types is checked under View ➤ Folder Options in the Explorer. Check Show All Files instead and the Desktop folder appears.

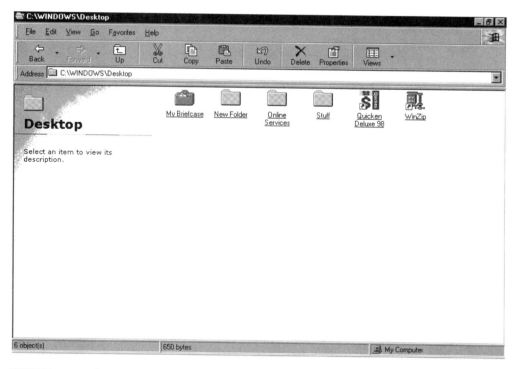

FIGURE 6.4:   The new folder on the Desktop can also be seen on the Windows Explorer.

Creating a New Folder Inside Another Folder

You can also create a folder inside another folder, allowing you to create a hierarchy of folders. To do this, follow these steps:

1. Open the Explorer. Use the scroll bars to locate the folder in which you want to place the new folder.
2. Expand the existing folder by clicking it.
3. Move your pointer to a blank spot in the right pane and click once with the right mouse button.
4. Select New ➤ Folder from the menu.
5. Type in the name for the new folder.

You can do this with any folder anywhere (on the Desktop or elsewhere). Just right-click once in a blank spot inside the open window.

TIP Most Windows applications such as Word or Excel also allow you to create a new folder inside the Save As dialog box. Click the folder icon with a star burst in the upper-right corner in the Save As dialog box, and the application will ask you to name the new folder. Click OK and you're set.

TIP Create a folder in the wrong place? Just right-click the folder and select Delete. You'll be asked to confirm that you want to send the folder to the Recycle Bin. Then you can create the folder where you intended for it to be.

Naming Folders

When you create a folder, Windows 98 automatically gives it the name "New Folder." If you create a second folder without renaming the first one, the second folder will be named "New Folder (2)." A third folder would be called "New Folder (3)." Pretty efficient, but not very descriptive. That's why you will probably want to rename the folder.

The easiest way to rename a folder is to right-click once on the folder, select Rename from the pop-up menu, and then type a new name. Windows 98 will not let you use an already existing name and will ask you to provide a new one should you try.

TIP You can also rename a folder in the Explorer window by highlighting it and selecting File ➤ Rename or by pressing the F2 function key.

Understanding Folder Properties

Since everything else has Properties sheets, it should come as no surprise that folders do too. Right-click a folder and select Properties from the menu. You'll see a window like the one shown in Figure 6.5.

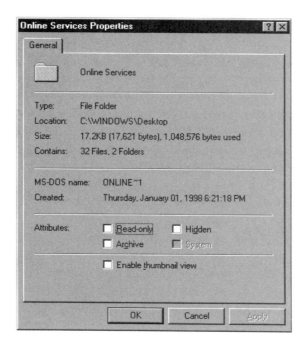

FIGURE 6.5:
The Properties
sheet for a folder

TIP   It's sometimes hard to find out how big a folder is. When you look at it in the Explorer, there's no accompanying size number next to it as there is for a file. To find out how big a folder is, examine the folder's Properties sheet and look at the value entered for Size.

The General Page

The General page provides information about the folder, including its title, type, location, size (just about the only place this is available), and the number of files and other folders to be found inside. As with properties sheets for individual files, there are also checkboxes for setting attributes:

Read-Only   This attribute prevents a folder from being written to. This makes it impossible to accidentally change something.

Archive   A check in this box shows the folder will be archived or backed up.

Hidden   This attribute shows whether the folder is hidden. If the box is checked, you cannot see the folder or use it unless you know its name.

System System files are required by Windows 98. You don't want to delete them. In any case, a whole folder cannot be designated as System, so this box is always grayed out when you're looking at a folder.

TIP To change a file or folder from hidden to visible, go to View ➢ Folder Options on a window's toolbar and select Show All Files. Find the file you want to change and open its Properties page. Then remove the check from the Hidden attribute.

Creating a New File

If you're using older software that was not designed for Windows 98, you'll probably create new files by opening the application and selecting New from the File menu. However, a number of applications create an option on the right-click menu, so you can easily create a new file for that application.

Creating a New File on the Desktop

To create a new file on the Desktop, right-click on the Desktop in some unoccupied space and select New from the menu. Select the type of file you want to create. A file like the one in Figure 6.6 will appear with the cursor already placed for you to type in a name.

FIGURE 6.6:
Creating a new file on the Desktop

This file is located on your hard drive in the Desktop folder inside the Windows folder.

Creating a New File inside Another Folder

To create a file inside another folder, such as in the Explorer, open the folder that will be the outside or the next folder up in the Windows hierarchy. Right-click a blank spot and select New from the pop-up menu. Then select the type of file from the list and type in the name for the new file.

TIP   **Create a file in the wrong place? Just right-click the errant file and select Delete. You'll be asked to confirm that you want to send the file to the Recycle Bin. Or, move it to the location where you want it.**

Naming Files

Files are named using the same procedures for naming folders. You first highlight the file by placing the mouse pointer on it, then right-click and select Rename. The file can then be named.

WARNING   **If you rename a file, be sure that you include the original extension name (such as .DOC or .XLS) in the new name. Otherwise, Windows 98 may not know what type of file it is and may not be able to create any type of association. For example, you can rename the Word file BUDGET FOR FALL.DOC to BUDGET FOR FALL, 1997.DOC, but not BUDGET FOR FALL, 1997 (without the extension).**

Long File Names

Back in the old days, when DOS-based personal computers first became popular, users were limited to file names that were no longer than eight characters. That was fine for a while, but then when lots of files were created using many different types of applications, things could, and did, get very confusing. Names were just too cryptic and hard to understand.

One of the most attractive features in Windows 98 is the ability to assign long names to files and folders. In fact, a name can be as long as 255 characters (including spaces). While you can use this many characters, it's still best to use as few as possible while being as descriptive as possible. Long file names take up valuable memory resources, and few files or folders need even 100 characters.

File names can include spaces as well as characters such as the comma, semi-colon, equals sign (=), and square brackets ([]). However, the following characters are not allowed to appear in either file or folder names:

\ / * < > : ? " |

File and folder names can also have both upper- and lowercase letters and spaces, and the system will preserve the casing and spacing you use. And Windows 98 does not care whether you capitalize part of a file or folder name, so you don't need to remember that information. Windows 98 will find it as long as the spelling is correct.

NOTE **Don't worry about case (upper or lower) when you work with file names. But do worry about it when you work with passwords. Passwords in Windows 98 are case-sensitive—so Windows 98 sees the password Zoomer differently than zoomer.**

Long File Names in DOS

While you probably won't be dealing with DOS in much of your Windows 98 work, the DOS commands that come with Windows 98 know how to handle long file names. Figure 6.7 shows some files and folders as they appear in an open window in Windows 98.

FIGURE 6.7: A Collection of long names for files and folders in Windows 98

Figure 6.8 shows the same files in an MS-DOS window.

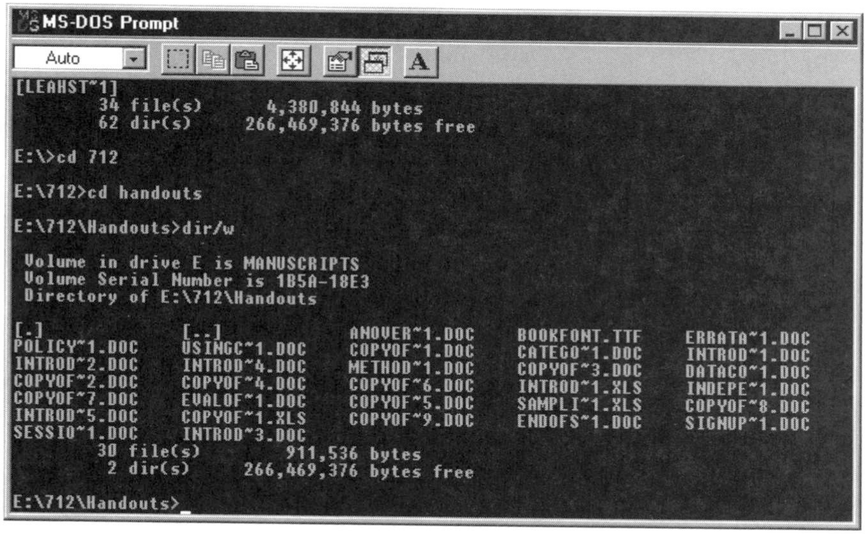

FIGURE 6.8: A collection of long names for files and folders in an MS-DOS window

DOS preserves the long file names on the right side of the DOS window while shortened versions appear on the left. As a rule, DOS will make the short file name by taking the first six letters of the long file name and appending a tilde (~) and a number. So if you have files named CHAPTER 1 and CHAPTER 2, they'll show up in a DOS window as CHAPTE~1 and CHAPTE~2.

Understanding File Properties

All files have properties or characteristics. Knowing about them can make our file management tasks much easier and keep us informed as to the size of files, where they reside, and other important information. Properties sheets for files consist of several different pages, as you see in Figure 6.9. The number of pages depends on whether the file is a document file (created using an application such as Word or Excel) or the actual application file (such as Word or Excel).

The various tabs on the Properties page include:

General   This page describes the type, location, and size of the file. It also includes information about the file's creation.

Summary   This page includes information about the title of the document, the author, comments, and other information that you might want to share with another person who may work with the same file.

Statistics   This page provides information about when the file was last modified and how much time was spent editing it.

Contents   This page provides a thumbnail sketch of the contents of the files.

Custom   This page allows you to examine the properties of the file and make alterations.

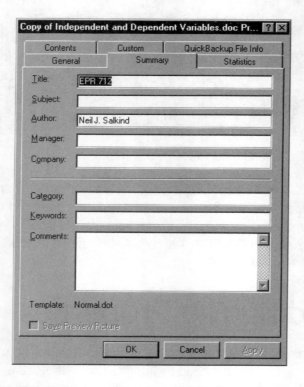

FIGURE 6.9:
The Properties sheets associated with a file created using Word

Depending on how your computer is configured, other Windows 98 programs may add something additional to the properties sheet of the file. As Figure 6.9 shows, the program QuickBackup added a QuickBackup File Info tab to the Properties sheet. This page provides information about the backed-up file.

Moving and Copying Files and Folders

Good file management involves knowing how and when to move, copy, delete, and rename files and folders. We'll start with the most basic of operations: moving and copying files and folders.

There are at least three different methods for moving and copying files or folders. You can adopt one method and use it all the time, or you can pick and choose from the various methods. Whatever works for you is the best way. Remember that when you move a file or folder, it is no longer in the original place it was created; and when you copy a file or folder, a copy is created (and perhaps placed in a new location) but the original still remains.

Moving or Copying Using Right Drag-and-Drop

Here's where Windows 98 and the right-click feature really shine. This is my personal favorite because it requires a minimum of effort:

1. Locate the file or folder in the Explorer or My Computer window. You have to be able to see the file or folder to drag it.
2. Right-click the object and drag it to its new location.
3. Release the mouse button and choose Move Here or Copy Here from the pop-up menu.

You may also want to open a second instance of the Explorer so you can drag-and-drop directly from one Explorer window to another Explorer window. Or you can move or copy the object to the Desktop, and then open the destination folder or drive, and drag the object a second time.

Moving or Copying Using Left Drag-and-Drop

This method requires a bit more attention because when you use the left mouse button to drag-and-drop, the result is a move only if the source and destination are on the same hard drive. If they are on different drives, the result will be a copy.

If you see a black plus sign in the transparent icon as you drag, that means that a copy will be made when you release the left mouse button.

In both cases, you can force a move to happen by pressing and holding down the Shift key before you release the left mouse button.

TIP   **If you decide while dragging to cancel the move or copy, just hit the Escape key before you release the mouse button. This stops the drag but leaves the files or folders highlighted.**

Moving or Copying Using Cut/Copy and Paste

This is the original Windows method for moving or copying a file or a folder.

To move or copy a file using cut or copy and paste, follow these steps:

1. Locate the file or folder you want to move or copy, using My Computer or the Explorer.
2. Right-click the object and select Cut or Copy from the pop-up menu.
3. Find the destination folder and open it.
4. Right-click a blank spot inside the folder and select Paste from the pop-up menu or the Edit menu.

TIP   **You can create a copy of a file or folder and move it at the same time by pressing the Ctrl key as you drag the file to a new location.**

NOTE   **There are a few objects, such as disk icons, that you can't move or copy. If you try to, you'll get a message informing you of this fact and asking if you want a shortcut instead. And, sometimes the shortcut will be created on the Desktop rather than where the file or folder is located. Windows 98 will ask you if you want to do that before you complete the operation.**

Deleting Files and Folders

The easiest way to delete a file or folder is to click it once with the right mouse button and select Delete from the pop-up menu. You can also highlight the object with the left mouse button and then press the Delete key on your keyboard. You will be asked if you want to send the object to the Recycle Bin.

Another method is to drag-and-drop the object on the Recycle Bin icon. A plus of this method is that you won't be asked to confirm that you want to delete the file.

For both of these methods, the Recycle Bin protects the user from over-hasty deletions because the deleted folder or file is not instantly deleted but can be retrieved from the Recycle Bin if you later decide you want it back. There's much more on the Recycle Bin in Chapter 8.

TIP   **To delete a file or folder without first sending it to the Recycle Bin, press the Shift key while you select Delete from the pop-up menu or while pressing the Delete key. It's gone (for good!).**

The Undo Command

When you move, copy, or rename something, the command to undo that action is remembered by Windows 98. And Windows 98 remembers the last action you performed first, the next to last second, and so forth.

To undo an action, click the Undo button on the window's toolbar, or right-click on the Desktop or in a free area of a folder, and the Undo command will be on the pop-up menu. Or you can select Undo from the Edit menu.

The most important thing about Undo is to use it as soon as you realize you've made an error. You don't want to continue working and then use Undo because you will undo what you've just done and not what you want to undo. So if you do make a mistake, stop and use Undo right away to set things straight. You can also continue to use Undo until you eventually get to the action you want to undo.

TIP   **If you don't remember what you did last and therefore don't know what Undo will undo, rest your mouse pointer on the button and the pop-up menu will tell you whether it was a move, copy, rename, or delete.**

Using Floppy Disks

Floppy disks remain a critical part of the computing arsenal even for people who work only on networks. Sooner or later, you have to put something on a floppy to transport it to another location or to back up your work.

Formatting a Floppy

When a disk is formatted, it is "wiped clean" and ready to use anew. Think of an unformatted disk as a newly constructed parking lot. The formatting places the yellow stripes where the cars are supposed to park. When a disk is formatted, there are the same kinds of "holders" for data defined on the newly formatted disk.

WARNING   **Windows 98 will not let you format your C drive. This is to protect you against accidentally erasing the Windows operating system. But, it will let you format other hard drives such as D or E, so be very careful when you use the Format command that you are formatting the disk you want.**

To format a floppy disk, put the disk in the drive and follow these steps:
1.   Open the Explorer.
2.   Use the scroll bars to move up to the point where you can see your floppy drive icon in the left window.
3.   Right-click the floppy drive icon and select Format. The window shown in Figure 6.10 will open. Make sure the choices selected are the ones you want. If not, change them.
4.   Click the Start button. When the formatting is complete (you'll see a progress bar at the bottom of the window), click the Close button.

WARNING   **Remember that when you format a disk, all of the information that was contained on that disk will be erased and will not be recoverable.**

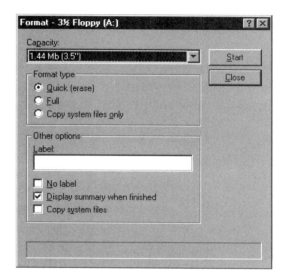

FIGURE 6.10:
Beginning the formatting process

TIP	If you try to format a floppy drive and are unsuccessful, it may be because you have the disk's contents displayed in the right pane of the Explorer and the disk is active. In order to format the floppy, click the C drive icon, right-click (only) the floppy drive icon, and then select Format.

TIP	The Quick format option allows you to speed up the formatting process, but only works when you are formatting (or reformatting) a disk that has already been formatted. The Full format option should be saved for those disks that have been used with another operating system (such as Macintosh or OS/2). Windows 98 will tell you if it cannot Quick format a disk and will default to the Full option.

Copying a Floppy

You may have the occasion when you need to make a copy of all the contents of a floppy disk on another disk. In this case, you might as well just make a copy of the whole floppy rather than each individual file one at a time.

To make an exact copy of a floppy disk, put the floppy in the drive and follow these steps:

1.   Open the Explorer.
2.   Use the scroll bars to move up to the point where you can see your floppy drive in the left window.
3.   Right-click the floppy drive and select Copy Disk.
4.   If you have more than one floppy drive, you'll have to specify the Copy From drive and click Start. With only one floppy drive, just click Start.

The system will read the entire disk and then prompt you to insert the disk you want to copy to. When you are done, you will have an exact copy of the original floppy. Also, if the disk you want to copy to is not formatted, Windows 98 will ask you if you want to format the disk before the copying process begins.

Copying Files to a Floppy

There are two approaches to copying folders or files to a floppy disk, depending on whether the material to be copied is smaller or larger than the capacity of a single floppy.

When the material you want to copy will fit on a single floppy, the process is easy. Put the floppy disk in the drive and use one of these approaches:

• Highlight the file or folder. Then right-click and select the Send To option on the pop-up menu. Then click the location where you want the file sent (which can be a floppy drive).
• Drag-and-drop the items to the floppy drive icon in the Explorer or My Computer. This is the fastest and easiest way to go.
• If you have a shortcut to a floppy drive on your Desktop or in a folder, drag-and-drop the items there.

TIP   **You can also copy more than one file to a floppy by holding down the Ctrl key when you click and then dragging to the destination.**

Finding Files and Folders

It's not at all unusual for even an experienced Windows 98 user to "lose" a file. What this means is that a file is created and saved, but it just can't be found when the time comes to work with it again. Fortunately, Windows 98 comes with a very sophisticated file-finding tool that makes it possible to find almost anything on your hard disk, even if you know very little about it. It's easy and it's fast.

When You Know the Name

To find a file or folder when you know the name (or part of it), follow these steps:

1. Click the Start button, point to Find, and then click Files or Folders.
2. Type in the file name, either whole or in part. You don't need to know how the file begins or ends. For example, a search for files with "new" in their names yielded the results shown in Figure 6.11.
3. The Look In box tells the program where to search. If you haven't a clue, use the drop-down list or the Browse button to select My Computer and the program will look everywhere on your system.
4. Click Find Now to start the search.

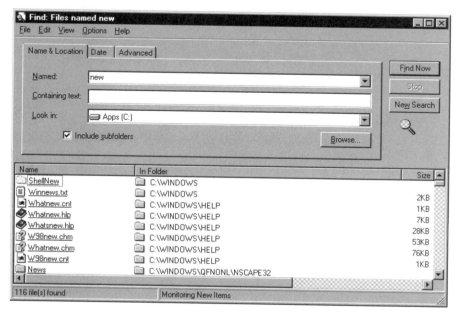

FIGURE 6.11: The Find File tool

NOTE **The results of file and folder searches can be saved by selecting Save Results from the Options menu. Then, select File ≻ Save Search. The search results will be saved in the form of an icon on your Desktop. Double-click the icon to open the Find window with the search criteria and results displayed.**

Once you find a file or a folder, you can right-click and perform many of the same operations you are already familiar with, including copying, opening, creating shortcuts, and sending the file to another location.

When You Know Something Else

Then there will be the time when you don't know *any* part of the file name, but you have an idea of when the file was last worked on. You can use the Date tab and specify a search between specific days or just look for files created or modified in some previous months or days.

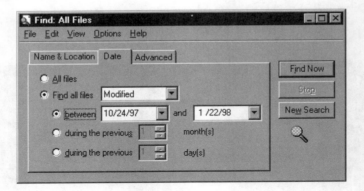

Maybe all you know is that the document you want is a letter written in WordPerfect and that it was addressed to a branch office in Poughkeepsie. Click the Advanced tab, select the file type from the Of Type drop-down window, and enter **Poughkeepsie** in the Containing text box.

Searches can be based on even skimpier information. You can have the program search all files and folders (look in the Of Type drop-down list) for files containing a certain word or phrase. Of course, the more information you can tell the program, the faster the search will be.

TIP Once you find the file you want, you can drag it to the Desktop or into another folder. You can click program files to open the program. If a file is associated with a program (as discussed in Chapter 5), click the file and the program will open with the file loaded.

What's Next?

No mater how well you understand the Windows 98 operating system, having Windows is not much fun or much use unless you can run other applications. In the next chapter, we'll show you how to work with Windows 98 applications.

Chapter 7

RUNNING PROGRAMS

FEATURING

- **Using the Start menu**
- **Using the right mouse button**
- **Starting programs using the Start menu**
- **Starting programs automatically**
- **Finding and using Program Manager**

In this chapter, we'll cover the essentials of launching programs. There are lots of ways to get programs started. Where you'll start them from often depends on how often you use them. The more frequently used programs can be placed in the most easily accessible spots, such as on the Desktop, and the infrequently used programs can be easily accessible but still not be in the way.

Starting a Program

As you might suspect, there are several different ways to start a program. You may prefer having shortcuts to your favorite programs on your Desktop or on the Start menu.

Creating a Shortcut to a Program

To create a shortcut to a program on your Desktop, you have to find the file that starts the program (which always has an .EXE extension) and drag it to the Desktop.

To create a shortcut:

1. Open the Windows 98 Explorer by selecting Start ➢ Programs ➢ Windows Explorer.
2. Locate the application file you want to create a shortcut for.
3. Right-click the file and drag it to your Desktop. When you release the mouse button, select Create Shortcut(s) Here from the pop-up menu.

TIP   **You can view the file type (to help you determine which file is an application) by viewing Explorer in Details view and clicking the Type button at the top of the right pane. To switch to Details view, select View ➢ Details (see Figure 7.1).**

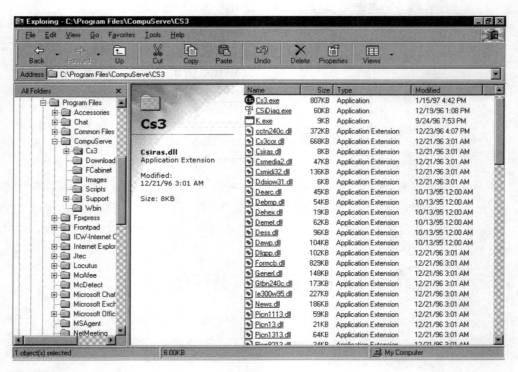

FIGURE 7.1:   Finding the application file to create a shortcut

TIP **If there's more than one file type labeled Application, you may have to guess which one is the actual main program file—either by the name or the icon. If worse comes to worse, click a file you think might be "it." If the program opens, you've hit the jackpot. If it doesn't, just close whatever did open and try again.**

A shortcut to a program can be put wherever you want; on the Desktop or inside a folder are only two of many locations.

Putting a Program on the Start Menu

If you want a program to appear on the Start menu (as shown in Figure 7.2), follow these steps:

1. Open the Windows 98 Explorer (Start ➤ Programs ➤ Windows Explorer).
2. Locate the application file you want to add to the Start menu.
3. Right-click on the application file you want and drag it to the Start button. When the pointer is on top of the Start button, release the mouse. The program will appear on the Start menu and will start when you point to it and release the mouse button.

TIP **To determine if a file is an application file switch to Details view, in Explorer, by selecting View ➤ Details. In the right pane of the Explorer, click the Type button at the top of the list. If the file in question is an application file, you can add it to the Start menu.**

FIGURE 7.2:
You can place programs, files, and folders on the Start menu.

> **TIP**
>
> **Like the idea of having a shortcut to the Desktop on your Start menu? Open the Explorer and find the Desktop subfolder inside your Windows folder. Right-click the Desktop folder, drag it to the Start button, and drop it. Don't forget that you can always return to the Desktop by clicking the Show Desktop icon on the Taskbar.**

Forcing the Order on the Start Menu

Programs on the Start menu are listed in alphabetical order, but suppose this isn't what you want? For example, you might want Access to be the last program on the list because it's the one you use least often. Since it starts with A, it's not likely to be last. To place it last, you'll have to change the order by following these steps:

1. Right-click the Start button and select Explore.
2. In the window that opens, you'll see a Programs folder (what you see when you select Start ➤ Programs) and shortcuts for the programs you've placed on the Start menu (see Figure 7.3).
3. Right-click the program you want to move to the top of the list and click the Rename option.
4. Rename it, making sure that the first character is an underscore (such as _Access).
5. Click the Start button and you'll see that the name that begins with an underscore has been moved to the bottom.

Using the Right Mouse Button

The right mouse button, not surprisingly, is useful for launching programs in addition to all its other talents. Right-click a program in the Explorer or on the Desktop and select Open from the menu.

If the top item is Open With… and you haven't a clue as to what program might be able to handle the file, make a shortcut to the file viewers by following these steps:

1. Click the Start button and select Find, then click Files or Folders.
2. Search for QUIKVIEW.EXE (note the spelling!). Or you can open Explorer and look in Windows ➤ System ➤ Viewers. You'll find QUIKVIEW.EXE in the last folder.

3. Right-click QUIKVIEW.EXE and drag it to the Desktop, selecting Create Shortcut(s) Here when you release the mouse button.
4. Open the Explorer, and open the folder Windows ➤ SendTo. Drag the shortcut to QUIKVIEW.EXE to the SendTo folder and drop it inside.

Now when you right-click an object, one of the options under SendTo will be Quikview. So when you see a file that you don't recognize, you can always send it to Quikview for a fast look.

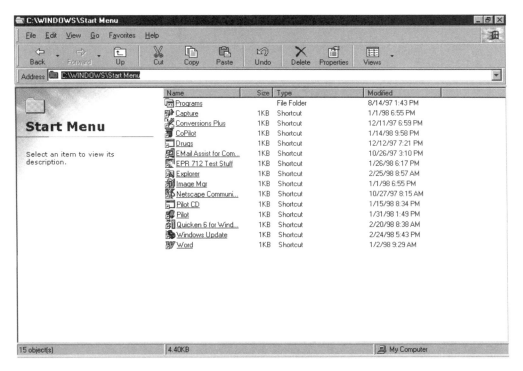

FIGURE 7.3: The Programs folder containing programs that appear on the Start menu

TIP If you cannot find the **QUIKVIEW.EXE** file, it probably was not installed when Windows 98 was initially installed on your computer. You can install Quikview by placing the Windows 98 CD-ROM in your computer, selecting a custom installation, and selecting only QuikView.

Starting with the Start Menu

The Start menu may be the way you choose to start programs in Windows 98 because many Windows 98 programs automatically create an item on the Programs menu.

Click once on the Start menu, slide the pointer up to Programs, and then select the program you want. This is an easy way to start any program on your system. However, you may dislike the multilevel menus—first there's a folder for each application and then another menu for all the stuff inside (see Figure 7.4). This is the default setup for Windows 98, but you can change almost all aspects of it.

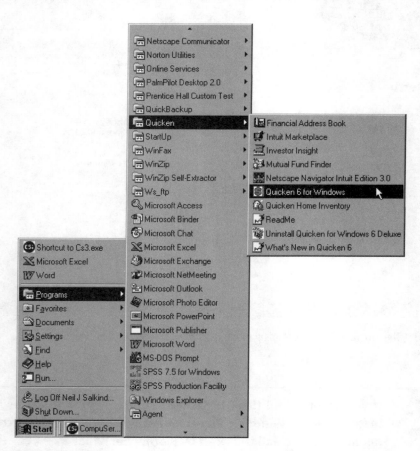

FIGURE 7.4: You can start a program from the Programs menu. But if you don't like this method, you can adjust the setup of your Start menu to avoid multi-level menus like this one.

Many of the menus in Windows 98 contain just a series of shortcuts easily accessible through the Explorer. If you can find the window that represents the menu, you can change it as you see fit. To change how programs appear on the Programs menu, follow these steps:

1. Right-click the Start button and select Explore.
2. Click Programs in the Start menu and you'll see a listing of folders and shortcuts that correspond to the Start ➤ Programs menu.
3. Click a folder to see the program inside. To move a program up a level, just drag-and-drop the program to the folder in which you want it placed.

You can drag shortcuts, or even the actual file, to any level of the file hierarchy using the Explorer. It's just a matter of how you want the different levels designed and what you want to see when you click the Programs menu on the Start button.

Adding a Program to the Start ➤ Programs Menu

You can add a program to the Start ➤Programs menu quite easily. Just follow these steps:

1. Click the Start button, then click Settings ➤ Taskbar & Start Menu.
2. Click the Start Menu Programs tab.
3. Click the Add button.
4. Enter the complete path of the file you want to add, or use the Browse button to locate the file. Highlight it and click OK.
5. Click Next and then choose the location where you want the shortcut placed. The default is the Programs menu, and since that's usually where you'll want it, you don't need to change the default.
6. Click Next and provide a name for the Program menu item and click Finish.
7. Select an icon and click Finish. The item will appear on the Programs menu.

WARNING All the items in the Programs folder and any subfolders *should* be shortcuts, though the icons are too small in many cases to verify this at a glance. If you have any doubts, right-click the object and select Properties. If there's not a Shortcut page with the Properties sheet, don't delete the file until you're sure it's not the *only* copy you have.

Removing a Program from the Start ➤ Programs Menu

To remove a program from the Start menu, click the Remove button on the Start Menu Programs tab, highlight the program you want to remove, and click Remove. Then, click Close and OK.

Another way to remove a program from the Programs menu is to open the Programs folder using the Windows 98 Explorer and delete it from the right pane. The program will no longer appear on the Programs menu, but since you deleted only a shortcut, the original file is left undisturbed.

TIP   **Icons can sometimes be difficult to decipher, and you certainly don't want to delete the wrong program. To help you discern which icon is which, select Large Icons from the View menu or right-click in the right pane and select Large Icons from the pop-up menu.**

Starting Programs When You Start Windows

Everyone has a program or two that they know they'll be using every single day. So you might as well have the program start when you start up your computer. For instance, those concerned about viruses can have a program such as Norton Utilities run automatically when they start Windows 98.

To add a program to the StartUp group, just right-click the Start button and select Explore. Click the Programs icon in the right pane. Then click the StartUp folder under Programs. In this folder are all the programs that will automatically launch when you turn on the computer.

Next, open a second instance of Explorer and find the programs you want in StartUp. Right-click your choice and drag it to StartUp. Release the mouse button and select Create Shortcut(s) Here from the menu. Or you can right-click any shortcut on your Desktop and drag it to the StartUp folder, also selecting Create Shortcut(s) Here when the menu appears.

WARNING Each time you add a program to the StartUp folder, it means that memory is taken up to keep that program active as you work. Too many open programs can ask too much of your machine and create memory problems. So you should only use automatic startup for programs you constantly use or programs that keep guard over your system (such as virus checkers) and leave the others for just when you need them.

Using the Program Manager

If you really miss Program Manager from way back in Windows 3.1, there's good news for you. It's included with Windows 98 just as it was with Windows 95. Look in your Windows folder for a file called PROGMAN.EXE. Right-click it and drag it to the Desktop to make a shortcut to it.

TIP When you know the name of the file, it's almost always fastest to use Find from the Start menu. Once Find locates the file, you can right-click the file and make a shortcut or a copy, or even move it from its folder or click it to start it.

Sometimes—even if you don't miss Program Manager—you'll still need to use it. Some older programs that work perfectly well in Windows 3.1 or Windows 95, just won't install in Windows 98. If you run into one of these uncooperative programs, try installing it from Program Manager by following these steps:

1. Use Find to locate PROGMAN.EXE in Windows 98.
2. Right-click and drag it to your Desktop to make a shortcut there.
3. Click the shortcut to PROGMAN.EXE.
4. Select Run from Program Manager's File menu.
5. If you've been prudent enough to check the program's floppy disk for the name of the install program (almost always INSTALL.EXE or SETUP.EXE), type in the path in the command line box. Otherwise, click Browse and check the floppy drive for the name of the install file.
6. Click OK twice and the program should install.

The program will be available in Windows 98, though if you want to put it in the Start ➤ Programs menu, you may have to do it by dragging a shortcut to the Programs folder (described in the section "Adding Programs to the Start ➤ Programs Menu" earlier in this chapter).

What's Next?

In the next chapter, we'll move on to one of the best tools in Windows 98: the Recycle Bin. We'll cover how to use it to its best advantage, as well as some of the Recycle Bin's limitations and how to overcome them.

Chapter 8

USING THE RECYCLE BIN

- **How the Recycle Bin works**
- **Deleting files and folders safely**
- **Recovering deleted files**
- **Setup and confirmation**

In the bad old days of computing, it was far too easy to accidentally delete a file from your system—and all you could do was wave bye-bye. You could buy a package of tools like the Norton Utilities that included a utility for retrieving deleted files (providing you acted quickly enough). Even DOS, starting with version 5, included a program you could use to undelete a file. The weakness of both approaches was that if you didn't undelete immediately, the file could easily be overwritten by another file and then there *really* was no way to recover.

Windows came to the rescue with the Recycle Bin. The Recycle Bin, always on your Desktop, will retain all your deleted files until you choose to empty the bin. And, as an added bonus, you can adjust the amount of space in the Recycle Bin, so you can go quite a long time without worrying about recovering files. Or, if you're more confident in your actions, you can set the Recycle Bin to delete recycled items often, deleting a file without any prospect of recovery!

What's the Recycle Bin?

The Recycle Bin is a reserved space on your hard drive where files and folders you no longer want can be disposed of. When you delete a file or folder, or drag it to the Recycle Bin icon to delete it, the file or folder itself is moved to that reserved space. If you have more than one hard drive, each drive has its own reserved space (and as you will shortly read, you can adjust the "comfort level" for each of those spaces). If you chose to manage your drives independently, there's an icon representing the Recycle Bin on each drive—though the contents displayed when you click any icon will be the same as the Recycle Bin on any other drive. If you want a deleted file or folder back, you can click the Recycle Bin icon to open it and retrieve any file by restoring it.

NOTE **See the section "Recycle Bin Settings" later in this chapter for information on how to determine the amount of disk space used by the Recycle Bin, as well as other adjustments you can make.**

The Recycle Bin functions as a first-in, first-out system. That is, when the bin is full, the first files or folders that were deleted will be removed from the bin to make room for the newest ones.

While there are many things about Windows 98 that can be set to reflect the way you work or your computing needs, such is not the case with the Recycle Bin. The Recycle Bin cannot be deleted, renamed, or removed from the Desktop.

Recycling a File, Folder, or Icon

By default, Windows 98 is set up to deposit all deleted files, folders, or icons in the Recycle Bin. When you right-click a file or folder and select Delete or highlight a file or folder and press the Delete key, you'll be asked to confirm if you want to send the file or folder to the Recycle Bin. After you click Yes, that's where the file or folder is moved to. (Deleted shortcuts are also sent to the Recycle Bin.)

Sending a Floppy Disk's Files to the Recycle Bin

Normally, files that you delete from a floppy drive are *not* sent to the Recycle Bin. They're just deleted. However, if that strikes you as just a little too impetuous (since they cannot be recovered from the Recycle Bin), there's an easy way to make sure that the files on your floppy do go to the Recycle Bin:

1. Open the Windows 98 Explorer.
2. Click the A drive icon so the contents of the drive appear in the right pane of the Explorer.
3. In the right pane, select the file(s) you want sent to the Recycle Bin.
4. Right-click the file(s) and select Cut. Right-click the Desktop and select Paste.
5. Highlight the file(s) on the Desktop. (If there's more than one, hold down the Shift key while you click each one in turn.) Right-click a highlighted file and select Delete. You'll be prompted to confirm that you want to send the file(s) to the Recycle Bin.

There's no more direct way to accomplish this because the Recycle Bin stubbornly refuses to see any files that are sent directly from a floppy.

WARNING Using the Recycle Bin with a floppy can be deceptive. You can drag a file from a floppy to the icon representing the Recycle Bin in the Explorer window, but the file will just be deleted and not placed in the Recycle Bin. You may think that this method deletes the file and places it in the Recycle Bin, but it only deletes the file.

Bypassing the Recycle Bin

If you've got a file that you know for sure you want to delete (forever) and that you don't want taking up space in the Recycle Bin, just hold down the Shift key when you select Delete. But be sure that's what you want to do because there's no way in Windows 98 to recover a deleted file that's bypassed the Recycle Bin.

NOTE If you have the Norton Utilities for Windows 98, you can use their Norton Unerase program to recover deleted files that are not in the Recycle Bin. When you install Norton Utilities, Norton Unerase is installed as well. You can tell when it's installed by the small N on a shield attached to the Recycle Bin.

Files That Won't Go Willingly

Some older programs (not written specifically for Windows 98) allow you to delete files from within the program. Files deleted this way will not be sent to the Recycle Bin. Similarly, files you delete at the DOS prompt (discussed in Chapter 12) will also disappear into never-never land rather than the Recycle Bin.

Therefore, you should make all your deletions through the Explorer or My Computer, or on the Desktop. If Windows 98 knows about the deletion, the file will automatically go to the Recycle Bin.

Recovering a Deleted File, Folder, or Icon

Retrieving a file, folder, or icon from the Recycle Bin is remarkably easy. Just click the Recycle Bin icon. The Recycle Bin window can be set up in any of the usual choices on the View menu. The most useful views are probably Large Icons (shown in Figure 8.1) and Details.

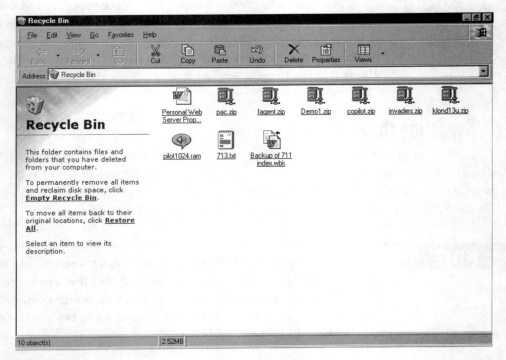

FIGURE 8.1: In the Large Icons view you can quickly identify files that were created in a particular program.

The Details view (shown in Figure 8.2) is the best view if you're looking for a file that was recently deleted. Just click the Date Deleted button on the bar at the top of the right window to arrange the files in order by the date they were deleted. Another click will reverse the order. Similarly, clicking the Name button will list the files in alphabetical order.

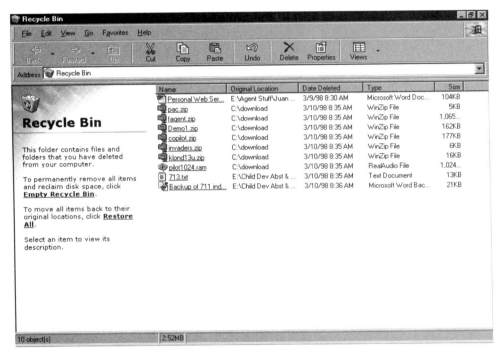

FIGURE 8.2:   You can arrange deleted files by different details in the Details view.

To retrieve a single file to its original location, right-click the file name and select Restore from the pop-up menu. You can also drag it from the Recycle Bin folder to any folder or to the Desktop.

Recovering More Than One File

To recover more than one file at a time, hold down the Ctrl key while selecting file and folder names from the Recycle Bin. Then right-click one of the highlighted names and select Restore. Or use Cut and Paste to send the whole bunch to a different location. Using either the right or left button, you can drag the files to your Desktop or another open folder.

To retrieve a number of files all in a series, point to the first file or folder icon to select it and then hold down the Shift key while you point to the last one in the series.

Let's say you deleted a whole folder and the only thing all the parts of the folder have in common is that all were deleted at the same time. Here's how to recover them:

1. Open the Recycle Bin.
2. Select Details from the View menu.
3. Click the Date Deleted button. Use the scroll bar to move through the list until you find the group of files you want to retrieve.
4. Point to the first file's name. Then, while holding down the Shift key, point to the name of the last file you want. All the files between the first and last click will be highlighted.
5. Right-click one of the highlighted files and select Restore from the pop-up menu.

All the files will be returned to their original location, and even though the original folder is not listed in the Recycle Bin, the files will be in the original folder.

TIP To open a file that is in the Recycle Bin, drag it to the Desktop and then click it. A single-click on a file or folder still in the Recycle Bin produces the Properties sheet for the file or folder.

Recycle Bin Settings

You can adjust the amount of space the Recycle Bin uses on any one hard drive and change other settings that affect how the Recycle Bin works. The setting you need to be most concerned with is how much space you want the Recycle Bin to use, since that directly affects how many deleted files of folders it can hold. Remember, eventually the Recycle Bin will fill up and then the last file or folder deleted will push out the first file or folder that was deleted.

TIP Empty the Recycle Bin on your own every week or so to be sure that it does not overflow and cause you to inadvertently lose files for good. Some programs such as the Norton Utilities Space Wizard look to the Recycle Bin for space that can be reclaimed and delete (with your permission) all the files and folders in the Recycle Bin. The Disk Cleanup button on the Disk Properties Sheet (accessed from My Computer) also gives you the option to delete all the files in the Recycle Bin as space is reclaimed.

How Much Space?

Right-click the Recycle Bin icon and select Properties. The Recycle Bin's Properties sheets will open as shown in Figure 8.3.

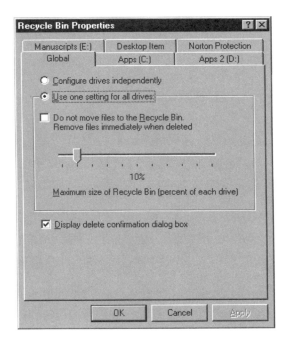

FIGURE 8.3:
The Recycle Bin's Properties sheet

As you can see, you can set the amount of space reserved for the Recycle Bin for each hard disk drive individually, or you can make a global setting. By default, 10 percent of each drive is set aside for the Recycle Bin. On a large drive, that's a lot of megabytes, so you may want to reduce the size a bit.

Click Configure Drives Independently and then click the tab representing each drive in turn. Set the amount of space you want free by clicking the sliding arrow to move it up or down until the Space Reserved is to your liking.

NOTE   **There's a numerical value (expressed as a percent) below the slide bar, showing the percentage of the drive that is currently reserved. If your drives are different sizes, you might want to make things easier for yourself by just reserving the same percentage on each drive.**

WARNING If you are confident that the files you delete should be deleted permanently and not first sent to the Recycle Bin, you can check the Do Not Move Files to the Recycle Bin checkbox. But remember, this means that any file you delete will not be recoverable.

Remember that the Recycle Bin is first-in, first-out, so if you make the reserved space very small, deleted files may pass into oblivion faster than you might wish.

Getting Rid of Confirmation Messages

On the Global page of the Recycle Bin Properties sheet, there's a box to clear if you don't want to be questioned every time you delete a file.

If there's no check in this box, you won't see any messages when you select Delete. If you like the comfort of being consulted about every deletion, check this box.

Emptying the Recycle Bin

To get rid of everything in the Recycle Bin, right-click the Recycle Bin icon and select Empty Recycle Bin. When the Recycle Bin is open, there's also an option to Empty Recycle Bin under the File menu.

To remove just *some* of the items in the Recycle Bin, highlight the file names, right-click one of them, and select Delete from the pop-up menu. You'll be asked to confirm the deletion (assuming you have the confirmation option turned on) and when you say Yes, the files will be deleted permanently.

What's Next?

Ever hear of such wonders as e-mail or the Internet? You're about to get your introduction to the basics of connecting electronically to your friend across the street or your business partner across the nation. Windows 98 allows you to connect to the world through a variety of tools, including Outlook Express and Internet Explorer. The next chapter will get you on your way.

Chapter 9

CONNECTING TO THE OUTSIDE WORLD

- **Adding or deleting services**
- **Connecting to an online service**
- **Making that Internet connection**

Ask any personal computer user, beginner to expert, what's hot these days and you'll get one answer—the Internet. Being connected to the Internet seems to be the focus of new hardware and software developments, and this is no place more apparent than in Windows 98.

Windows 98 incorporates more ways of connecting to the outside world than any other operating system. In addition to software for connecting to the major online services such as the Microsoft Network, it also includes Internet Explorer for browsing the Internet and Outlook Express for reading and sending mail, and participating in online discussions or newsgroups.

What Is the Internet and Why Connect?

Imagine that all the computers in your neighborhood are connected to each other. That collection of computers is a network. Now imagine that that network of computers is connected to another network of computers, and so on. That's the Internet.

You can connect to the Internet using an Internet Service Provider (ISP) or through one of several online services, such as the Microsoft Network or America Online. You'll learn more about both of these options, including the merits of each, later on in this chapter. For now, let's define what the Internet is and why you should be using it.

For a long time the hardest thing about using the Internet (which includes sending and receiving electronic mail) was making that first connection and actually getting online. That's become somewhat easier in recent years. And Windows 98 makes it even simpler by including all the necessary software. Online services such as America Online, AT&T WorldNet, CompuServe, Prodigy Internet, and the Microsoft Network offer simple installation procedures through Windows 98 that help you sign up for the service and get connected to the Internet quickly.

E-Mail

The Internet and online services are often used for electronic mail or *e-mail* (see Figure 9.1). Just as you exchange postal mail with a friend or business associate across the United States or across the world, you can exchange e-mail without ever placing a pen to paper.

You can create e-mail messages using an e-mail program such as Outlook Express. Designate the electronic address (for example, `njs@williams.edu`), type the subject for the message, and type the message in the corresponding areas, press Send, and it's off.

The World Wide Web

Another very popular feature of the Internet is the *World Wide Web*. The Web (as it's commonly called) is a collection of locations (called Web sites or home pages) that offer an attractive and easy-to-use interface. Figure 9.2 shows the home page for the Microsoft Corporation.

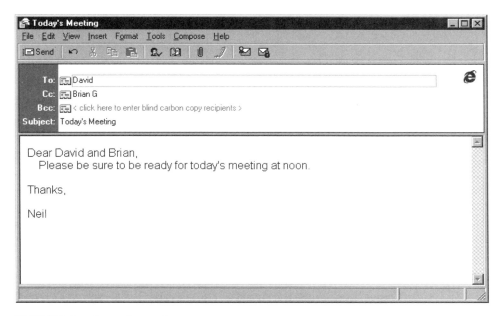

FIGURE 9.1: A sample e-mail message

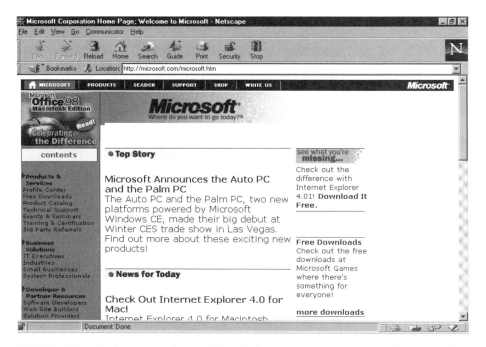

FIGURE 9.2: The home page for the Microsoft Corporation is one example of the many Web sites you can visit on the World Wide Web.

To view Web sites you need an Internet browser. Currently, the two most popular browsers are Netscape Navigator and Internet Explorer.

Newsgroups

There are thousands of discussion groups or *newsgroups* available on the Internet. This is where discussions take place about topics ranging from what type of goggles are best for swimming to the authenticity of a document signed by Quantril before he burned Lawrence, Kansas to the ground. These groups are electronically sitting around a table and discussing topics with others who have the same interest. In Figure 9.3 you can see the types of messages contributed to a newsgroup about swimming.

You may have heard about chat groups. A chat group and a newsgroup are similar in that they usually focus on one topic, but a chat group takes place in the present (or "real time") where you are more or less "talking" with others through the use of the computer. Newsgroup discussions are not in real time. The messages are stored on a network where they can be retrieved, read, and responded to.

You need a news reader (like the one that comes with Office Express) to participate in newsgroups. Participating means responding to messages or postings that other people have created and left, or even submitting a posting of your own. It's a very simple process. In fact, it's the same process you use for creating mail.

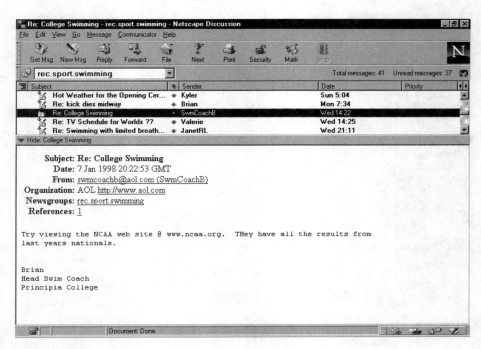

FIGURE 9.3: Discussing swimming in an online newsgroup

What You Need to Connect

To get online, whether you are connecting using an ISP or an online service, you must have the following:

- A modem that modulates and demodulates the digital signal and transfers it over the phone line. A modem can be internal or external. Make sure the modem is plugged in everywhere it's supposed to be. Believe it or not, that's often the reason why people cannot connect. The ISP or online service you are connecting to also has a modem, so digital signals can be converted back and forth between you and your provider. The faster the modem, the faster the information can be transferred. Modems started off operating at 300 bps (bauds per second) and are now up to 56Kbps. Currently, a good connection speed is 33.6Kbps. Be sure your ISP or online service will allow you to connect at your modem's speed. It's also a good idea to make sure your provider will allow you to connect at higher speeds as well (in case you get a faster modem).

- Telecommunications software that connects you to the ISP or online service. Windows 98 comes with all you need to connect to an online service. You can use the Dial-Up Connection in My Computer (covered in Chapter 5) to connect to an ISP.

- Adequate space on your hard drive. A significant part of online activity involves transferring files, such as a new Windows 98 utility or a game you want to try out, to your computer. A hard drive that is at least 1GB in size (which is almost the standard for new computers these days) should be able to handle your needs. You can check on the amount of space that is available on your hard drive by right-clicking the icon that represents the hard drive in My Computer and then selecting Properties.

TIP

Now there's an alternative to using your phone lines to go online. More and more cable companies (yes, the same people who bring you *ER* and *The X-Files*) are offering cable-modem hookups. You will need a cable running from your computer to the cable service. You also need what's called an *Ethernet card*. This allows the online service or ISP to connect and communicate with your computer. Ethernet cards cost about $50, and many new computers come with them already installed. While more expensive than connecting by phone, connecting by cable provides a more direct and much faster connection (anywhere from 100 to 1,000 times faster). Interested? Call the people who supply your TV cable service.

An Internet Service Provider or an Online Service?

There are two ways to connect to the Internet. The first is through an Internet Service Provider (ISP). An ISP is a local or national company that you connect to via phone using a phone or cable modem, and in turn they connect you to the Internet. They usually provide only a connection, although they may provide an Internet browser and even an e-mail program.

WARNING   **Not every ISP's software will work flawlessly with Windows 98. It's often your job to configure Windows 98 to work with that provider, as well as to find and configure a browser and an e-mail service to use. On the other hand, some providers may give you everything you need and show you how to set it all up. Find out before you sign up.**

If you're an absolute novice (called a *newbee* by Internet know-it-alls), you should consider either an ISP that will give you connecting support or one of the all-in-one-package-get-connected-and-start-paying-us-right-now online services such as AOL, AT&T, CSi, Prodigy Internet, or MSN. They each provide you with a connection to the Internet, immediate and direct access to their own e-mail system, a Web browser, and lots of other features such as news, discussion groups, games, and entertainment.

Either an ISP or an online service will get you online and onto the Internet. It's just a matter of convenience, and in some cases, cost. Most ISPs charge a flat rate (around $20 per month for unlimited connection time), while the online services offer several different plans. See the section "Connecting to an Online Service" later in this chapter for information about how to choose an Internet Service Provider.

Choosing an Internet Service Provider or Online Service

There are a few things you should find out from any company whose service you are considering using. Here are the top ten subject areas that you should ask any ISP or online service about before you sign up:

Account options   Are there different types of accounts available, such as for a family or a small business? Do you offer any kind of discount if I'm online for only a certain number of hours per month?

Connection software   Do you offer software for connecting to the Internet?

Cost   How are users charged for the service? Hourly? Monthly? Is there a setup fee? Are there different costs for different speed modems?

Local connection   Is there a local phone number for me to use to connect to the service? If not, how can I connect from a remote location and what are the charges? (This is a very important question. Connecting to the Internet from a long distance number can be very expensive.)

Modem speed   What modems speeds are available? (This is a good question to ask if your system doesn't have a modem and you're planning to buy one.)

Services   What basic services (e-mail, Web browser, discussion groups) are provided?

Storage space   Do you offer storage space for files that I download? Are there any costs for this?

Technical support   Is technical support available? And if so, is it available online, over the phone, or both? Does technical support have a toll-free number? What are the hours for technical support?

Trial period   Is there a trial period when I can use your service for free?

Tutorials   Are there tutorials available so I can learn how to use the system?

And the Cost?

Rates for both Internet Service Providers and online services can change at any moment. But over the past few years there has been enough business that the rates are fairly stable. And the market competition has kept things in check, so the rates are also fairly reasonable.

Most Internet providers charge a flat rate of around $19.95 per month for unlimited access. They usually throw in three to five e-mail addresses (usually enough for the whole family) and enough storage space for you to create a pretty cool Web page. Some providers also provide an hourly plan that costs about $5 per month, plus an hourly charge. Choose a plan that you think will work best for you, but keep in mind that you can always change plans.

WARNING   **If your connection is a toll call, you'll run up phone bills of ferocious dimensions very quickly. Make sure you check the access numbers you can use and select the one that is the closest and cheapest for you to use. Also, if you live near the border of another state, an access phone number in a different area code may be cheaper than one that is in the same area code. Strange but true.**

Using Passwords

No matter how you connect to the Internet, you will need a password. And, in many cases, you will have to provide the password each time you connect.

Passwords are a good idea because they prevent other people from signing on to your account and running up a tab that you might learn about only when you get your monthly credit card bill. Most systems also allow you to easily change your password, a practice that some users regularly exercise.

Here are some golden rules about using passwords. Some of them may be obvious, but they also seem to be the rules that people forget most easily.

- Don't give your password to anyone else. If you want to let someone connect using your account, sign on for them.
- Change your password every month or so, or when you suspect that someone has been trying to learn what it is.
- Be sure that your password does not make sense and isn't obvious. For example, if your name is Lew, guess what you shouldn't use? (Lew, that's right.) Also don't use your phone number or house address or your honey's first name. Combine letters and numbers such as edr435tgh or 857tn8es. Some systems won't let you use anything other than letters and numbers mixed together as a security measure.
- Write your password down and keep it in a safe place out of public view. But don't keep it near your computer where someone could easily find it if they were looking. Passwords are sometimes easy to forget, and while online services require only a phone call to get a new one, some ISPs make it very difficult to make any changes.
- Be sure you know whether your service is case sensitive. If it is case sensitive, Ef56ti is not the same as ef56ti.

We're sure you're not packing plans for a nuclear weapon on your hard drive, but knowing and using a password only makes good sense in any setting, especially when you want access to the Internet guarded.

The Nine Online Commandments

You now know what you need to access the Internet, so it's time to briefly review how to behave. What's so remarkable about the Internet is that in spite of attempts by government regulators to impose rules for the Internet's use, the Internet has very few rules. What it does have are standards.

The following nine commandments are not as impressive as the real ones (or as numerous), but you would be well served to read and follow them. As more people get online, there's more chance that things won't go exactly as planned. So, keep the following in mind as you begin your online activities.

Commandment 1: Be sure you're connected.   For beginners, it is not always clear whether you are actually connected to the Internet even when you think you may be. If you don't see any onscreen activity or you don't get a message that you are connected, close the application and try again.

Commandment 2: Once you press the key, it's gone.   There's no recalling keystrokes. Once you press Enter or execute a command, such as send e-mail, it's done. There's no going to the mailbox and fishing that angry letter out. You need to be extra careful and extra sure of what you say before you send it electronically.

Commandment 3: Typing counts, and sometimes case does as well. One of the idiosyncrasies of some operating systems on the Internet and the computers connected to it is that uppercase and lowercase characters have different meanings. Many Internet connections require you to use uppercase letters to sign on. If your password is SARA, then Sara or sara may not work. Also, type carefully. The Internet often demands long names and addresses. It's easy to type **njs@falcon.cc.ukans.eud** rather than **njs@ukans.cc.edu** and spend the next hour trying to figure out why you couldn't connect.

Commandment 4: Be flexible about when and how you use the Internet.   The Internet is a very busy place, especially if you try to locate or download a file during regular business hours (8AM to 5PM). If you choose to work during these hours, you will have to be patient, since it will take longer to do almost everything. If you can, use the Internet after dinner, during the late evening hours, or on weekends. Fewer people are online at these times because businesses and other facilities that operate during standard work hours are not open, and the people who work there are not online.

Commandment 5: There's more stuff out there than anyone can know about.   When you get on the Internet for the first time, you probably will not be able to contain your enthusiasm for what's ahead of you. That's great, but don't get carried away. There are thousands and thousands—maybe even millions—of Web sites, files, and resources for you to access and use. Take a little bit at a time rather than surfing all over the place. You'll find that you're more successful that way.

Commandment 6: Be considerate of others and play by the rules.
There is no central Internet authority that controls every network on the Internet.
Many think this lack of a central control is what's best about the Internet and
what makes it especially unique. Unless there were some self-imposed rules or
etiquette to follow, it's likely that the Internet would self-destruct, as would any
large organization that had no guidelines. For that reason, a set of informal and
unendorsed rules have evolved. These rules are called *netiquette*. We'll discuss
this topic in the next section of this chapter, "Netiquette: Behaving Online".

Commandment 7: Practice, practice, practice; but take it slow.   The
more you practice, the more you will learn and the more useful the Internet will
be for you. When you first get started, however, take your time and limit your
efforts to an hour or less. This will prevent you from becoming fatigued and
frustrated.

Commandment 8: Be patient with yourself.   Learning to use the Internet
is not like learning a new word processing program or a new game. There is no
documentation and no one program to run everything. If you have difficulty at
first, be patient and don't quit.

Commandment 9: Ask others for help and help others.   A tremendous
amount of valuable information comes from other users rather than from user
manuals, write-ups, and technical papers. Ask others for help, and pay back that
debt by sharing new and interesting things you learn with others.

Netiquette: Behaving Online

Behavior online is, above all, the responsibility of the user. You own your own
words, so say what you mean and mean what you say. Always reread what you type
before you send it, making sure it comes across how you intended. This is especially
true with e-mail and newsgroup contributions. Here are a few tips for getting along on
the Internet:

- Individual differences are to be fostered and respected. You might disagree
  with someone's opinion about a book, their view of a raging philosophical
  debate, or their political viewpoint, but remember that the free exchange of
  information is one of the foremost goals of the Internet.
- *Flaming* is an Internet term for being nasty in words or in spirit. Don't
  intimidate, insult, or verbally abuse anyone.

- What's yours is yours, and what is not is not. Don't appropriate other people's materials (either intentionally or unintentionally) as your own. Taking something that someone else wrote and claiming it's your own is plagiarism, even though it's not written material.
- The key to success online is self-regulation. Even if it's 3AM, you are still using resources. So playing Kung Wung Fu for five straight hours may not be the best idea. Give other people wanting to use the system the opportunity to do so. This is especially true if there is a limited number of phone lines.
- Avoid sending junk mail. Announcing a meeting to your staff is quite different from sending a chain letter or a commercial message to 5,000 e-mail addresses. Junk mail ties up valuable resources.
- If you need to download a substantial number of files, do it during off-hours (generally, 6AM to 8AM) when traffic is a bit slower. But remember, the online world is a global community. What might be 1PM in your warm house on Main Street in Lawrence, Kansas, is 7PM in London.

Connecting to an Online Service

The easiest way to connect to the Internet is through an online service, such as the five we mentioned earlier. The software for signing up for any of these services is located in the Online Services folder on the Desktop.

Whether you want to use AOL, AT&T, CSi, Prodigy Internet, or MSN, signing up with any one of them involves the following steps:

1. Select the online service you want to use from the Start menu, or open the Online Services folder on the Desktop (see Figure 9.4) and the icon representing the service you want to use.

2. Follow the setup directions for whatever service you chose, and provide personal information requested from the online service. This will include at least your name, address, and phone number. You might also have to provide information about where you heard about the service or personal information such as your mother's maiden name (used for identification verification purposes later on).

3. Provide billing information (including a credit card number and expiration date). Keep track of the credit card number you used. Some services, such as CompuServe, require the last four digits of the card number to change your password.

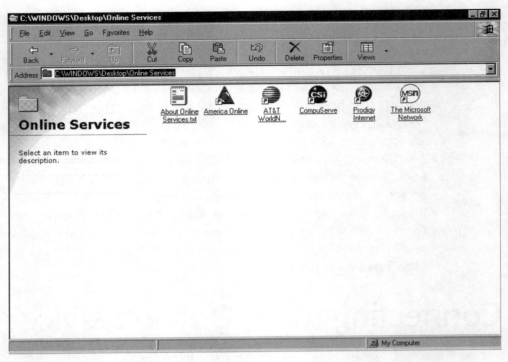

FIGURE 9.4: Select the Online Services folder on the Desktop to access online services available through Windows 98.

TIP Some online users have a credit card (usually with a very low credit limit to avoid misuse of the card) they use only for their online charges. That way, they can easily check their statement to see if the charges are correct.

4. Read the entire agreement and check the button that indicates you understand and agree to the terms.
5. Complete any additional sign-up steps.
6. Once you're done, you'll get an account number and you'll be ready to use the service.

All five of these services provide you with a certain number of free hours or a free trial period (for instance, AOL provides up to 50 free hours). You should consider signing up with all five services and taking some time to decide which you like most. After the trial period (which varies from service to service), you can then ask to be disconnected with no future charges.

WARNING Don't forget to cancel any services that you don't want; they'll keep charging you even if you forget. When your free trial period is up AOL, AT&T, CSi, Prodigy Internet, or MSN will probably not notify you. Instead, they'll begin to charge you for your time used and assume that you are a happy customer. Try to make a decision about whether you want to stick with a service after using it for a few hours so you can get out of the agreement without accruing any charges if you are not satisfied. And keep in mind that almost the only way to unsubscribe to a service is by calling them. E-mail often won't do.

NOTE Don't forget that when you're online your phone line is tied up (unless you have a cable modem connection). Also, if you have call waiting, you'll want to turn it off while you're online. Otherwise, an incoming call could disconnect you from the Internet.

America Online

AOL

AOL is best known for its size (more than 10,000,000 subscribers), its chat groups (or what they call their People Connection), and its vast collection of entertainment forums. If you like the idea of chatting online, there are always lots of people talking live in the many chat rooms on AOL.

America Online's Internet connection software is easy to use (see Figure 9.5.). Moving from page to page on the World Wide Web is fast, though connecting to the Internet through AOL in the evenings can be frustrating. (Some people refer to AOL as America Onhold because you may experience lots of busy signals.) Like other growing online services, AOL is trying to deal with their rapid growth.

Here's how to sign up for AOL:

1. Click the Online Services folder on the Desktop.
2. Click the AOL shortcut button.

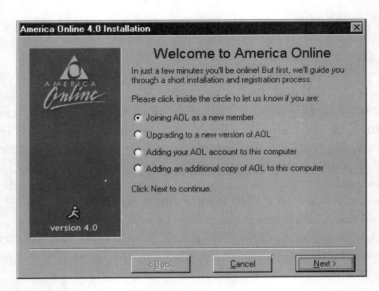

FIGURE 9.5: A sample AOL screen

3. AOL will connect you to an 800 number, which will allow you to connect and then select local access numbers.
4. Complete all the onscreen steps until you see the opening AOL screen.

Want to talk to someone at AOL? Call them (in the U.S.) at 1-800-827-6364. AOL is the king (and queen) of the voice mail system, so listen carefully and get ready to push lots of buttons before you can get to a human.

AT&T WorldNet

AT&T WorldN...

AT&T WorldNet has the power of the huge telecommunications company AT&T behind it and has won several awards for its offerings. To connect to AT&T WorldNet:

1. Click the Online Services folder on the Desktop.
2. Click the AT&T shortcut button.
3. Follow the onscreen instructions. Throughout the sign-up process, you will be asked to restart your computer as AT&T fine tunes the installation.

Want to talk to an AT&T WordNet representative? You can reach them at 1-800-967-5363.

CompuServe

CompuServe

CompuServe (see Figure 9.6) is the oldest of these online services and the second most popular. Their most notable feature is access to reference materials through the forums they host. There are special interest forums on everything from investments to horses to genealogy to women in aviation. They also have what has been rated as the easiest to use and most comprehensive e-mail system available by several personal computer magazines. CSi has also just been purchased by America Online. Steve Case, chair of AOL, has made assurances that the CSi service won't change at all, but it's still something to look into. To sign up with CompuServe:

1. Click the Online Services folder on the Desktop.
2. Click the CSi shortcut button.
3. Follow the onscreen instructions.

FIGURE 9.6: The opening CSi screen

You can reach someone at CSi at 1-800-848-8990.

Prodigy Internet

Prodigy Internet

Prodigy was one of the first Internet services, but it has not been very strong in either membership or online presence over the past few years. It's been reincarnated as Prodigy Internet, and some new and interesting features have been added. To sign up with Prodigy Internet:

1. Click the Online Services folder on the Desktop.
2. Click the Prodigy Internet shortcut button.
3. Follow the onscreen instructions.

You can reach someone at Prodigy Internet at 1-800-213-0992.

The Microsoft Network

The Microsoft Network

Of all the online services, the Microsoft Network, the newest of the online services, is the most closely integrated with the Windows 98 operating system (since it's a Microsoft product this should come as no surprise). That makes it the easiest of all the online services to install. It does almost all of the work for you using an installation wizard. Microsoft has been very aggressive in trying to get new members, so you'll probably be seeing their fancy advertisements in print as well as other media. To sign up with MSN:

1. Click the Online Services folder on the Desktop.
2. Click the MSN shortcut button.
3. Follow the instructions. When complete, you'll see the opening screen shown in Figure 9.7.

You can reach someone at the Microsoft Network at 1-800-386-5550.

TIP Other tech support numbers and contact information can be found in the ABOUT THE ONLINE SERVICES.TXT file in the ONLINE SERVICES folder.

Connecting to the Internet

The most difficult thing about using the Internet used to be connecting to it. The process included so many different steps and so many different system settings that unless an expert showed you how it was almost impossible to figure out on your own.

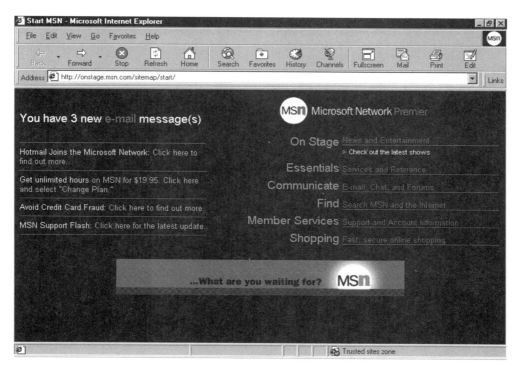

FIGURE 9.7: Getting started with MSN

That's no longer the case. Now the Windows 98 Connection Wizard walks you through each of a relatively short number of steps. The only thing you need to do is follow the steps and make sure that you have the necessary information about your Internet Service Provider. To use the Connection Wizard, follow these steps:

1. Click Start ➤ Programs ➤ Internet Explorer. Then click Connection Wizard.
2. When you see the Get Connected! Opening screen, click Next.

You have three options from which to chose as to how you are going to connect (see Figure 9.8). The first is to have the Connection Wizard search for an Internet Service Provider based on your area code. Select this if you have not already established an account with an ISP. The second is to set up a connection to an existing account through a phone line or through a network connection. The third Connection Wizard option is where you can indicate that you already have an account and don't need to change it. Since most people will be setting up a new connection (the second option), that's the path we'll follow here.

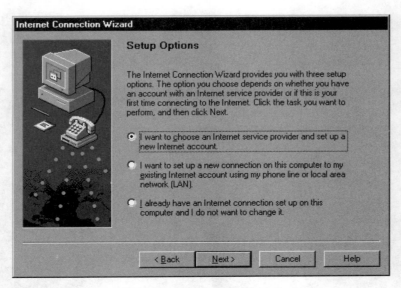

FIGURE 9.8: Selecting how you will be connecting to the Internet

To set up a new account with the Connection Wizard:

1. Click Next and then tell the Connection Wizard whether you will be connecting through your phone line (with a modem) or through a network (such as a cable modem) connection. Then click Next. If you connect through the phone line, you need to select the modem you'll be using and then provide the phone number that you use to access your Internet Service Provider. Click Next after you provide the phone number.

2. Follow the screens that require you to provide information about your e-mail address, password, and settings. You will need the following information to complete the sign-up process.
   - Your e-mail name (for instance, `njs@falcon.cc.uakns.edu`)
   - Your password
   - The name of the e-mail server (for instance, `falcon.cc.ukans.edu`)
   - The name of the news server (for instance, `news.cc.uakns.edu`)

Figure 9.9 shows you a screen that confirms the settings that have already been entered during the wizard sign-up.

Once you have provided all the information, click the Finish button and the Connection Wizard will establish a connection to the Internet through Windows 98. You're ready to go with e-mail, news, or exploring the World Wide Web using the correct applications.

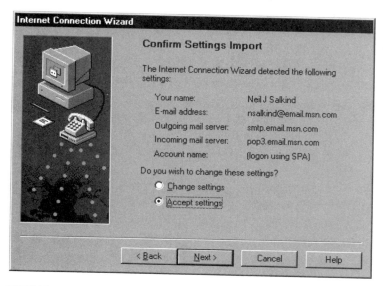

FIGURE 9.9: The information provided during the Connection Wizard

What's Next?

Now that you're connected to the Internet, the fun really begins. In the next chapter, we'll show you how to send and receive e-mail, keep a personal address book of important e-mail addresses, and even attach files to your e-mail messages.

Chapter 10

USING OUTLOOK EXPRESS

FEATURING

- **Using Outlook Express**
- **Working with e-mail attachments**
- **Adding entries to the address book**
- **Finding and subscribing to newsgroups**
- **Working with the Outlook Express newsreader**

Now is your chance to start using the Internet to communicate with friends, neighbors, and business colleagues across the street and across the world.

You can send and receive e-mail through CompuServe, AT&T WorldNet, America Online, Prodigy Internet, the Microsoft Network, or another online service. You can also use the new Windows 98 Outlook Express to monitor your mailbox without having to subscribe to an online service such as AOL. All you will need is an Internet Service Provider.

This new mail program for Windows 98 is easy to use, quick, and can help you perform many otherwise time-consuming tasks easily. With Outlook Express, you can:

- Exchange e-mail messages
- Create and use an address book for storing e-mail addresses
- Read and contribute to newsgroups

TIP **By this time, you should have already established an Internet connection using the Internet Connection Wizard presented in Chapter 9. When you established the connection, you told Windows 98 whether you were connecting by phone or through a Local Area Network (or LAN). You also indicated your e-mail and news server addresses. Outlook Express will use that information to help you create, send, and receive mail and news.**

The Outlook Express Opening Screen

Outlook Express can be found on the Internet Explorer menu. To start Outlook Express, select Start ➤ Programs ➤ Internet Explorer ➤ Outlook Express, or click the Outlook Express icon on the Desktop. You'll see the Outlook Express screen shown in Figure 10.1. When this dialog box opens, you will have to specify where you want your Outlook Express messages stored.

The button bar for Outlook Express contains the following buttons:

- The Compose Message button is used to create a message.
- The Send and Receive button is used to send mail and to check on mail that might have been sent to you.
- The Address Book button opens the Address Book, where you can keep a record of e-mail addresses you want easy access to.
- The Connect and Hang Up buttons let you do just that—connect when you want to check your mail and hang up when you are finished.

With its two-pane view, Outlook Express looks very similar to Windows Explorer. In the right pane is the content of the screen. The left pane lists the various receptacles of

Outlook Express information, including the Inbox (where mail sent to you is located) and the Outbox (where mail that you created but have not yet sent is located).

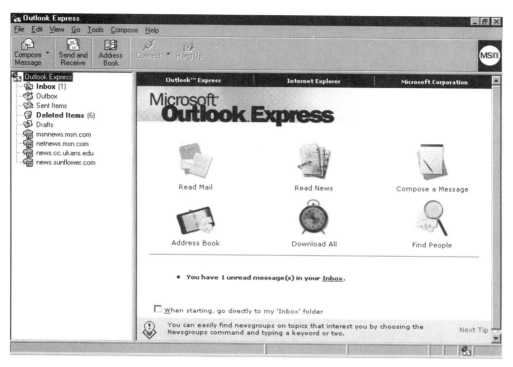

FIGURE 10.1: The Outlook Express opening window

TIP

You can always tell if you have new mail by opening the Outlook Express screen and then checking for a message at the bottom of the screen indicating you have unread message(s) in your Inbox, or by the number that appears next to the Inbox in the left pane. Just a click on the Inbox will take you there to read them.

You can change the look or the layout of the opening screen by selecting Layout from the View menu to open the Layout Properties screen shown in Figure 10.2. You can choose to hide parts of the Outlook Express window, move the location of the toolbar to any one of the four edges of the Outlook Express window, and preview messages without opening them.

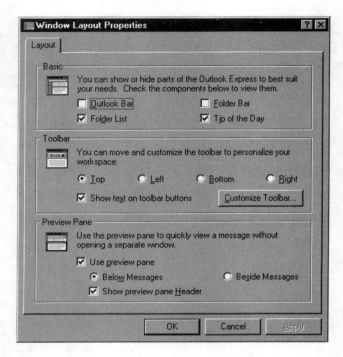

FIGURE 10.2:
You can change the layout of Outlook Express on the Layout Properties screen.

Creating and Sending Mail Messages

To send a message in Outlook Express, click the Compose Message button on the Outlook Express toolbar. You will see the New Message window shown in Figure 10.3. To create a message once you are in the New Message screen:

1. In the To field, type the e-mail address of the individual or individuals to whom you want to send a message. If there is more than one person, separate the addresses by a comma. For example, `sarababe@smith.edu`, `mfc@farralon.com`, `eddyboy@uk.org`.

2. In the Cc (carbon copy) field, enter the e-mail address of the person to whom you want a copy of the mail to also be sent (if necessary). This field can be thought of as an "FYI" field. You want the people or persons listed here to know something, but you don't necessarily want them to respond or act on your message. Below the Cc field is the Bcc (blind carbon copy) field. Other recipients of the message won't see that a copy of your e-mail message was sent to this e-mail address.

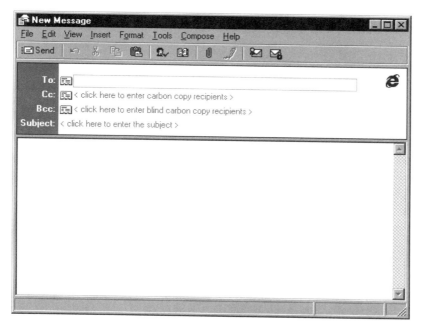

FIGURE 10.3:   The New Message window for composing a message in Outlook Express

3.   Enter a subject in the Subject line. This should be a brief description of the message's content. This information is a help to the recipient, who will know about the content of the message before they open and read it.

4.   Type the content of the message in the lower pane on the screen.

5.   Click the Send button. The message is on its way.

NOTE   If you want to be a little fancy, click the down arrow to the right of the Compose button. Here you'll find a nice collection of pre-designed e-mail messages that you can adjust as necessary. These pre-designed message helpers include formal announcements, birthday cards, ivy, holiday letters, and a balloon party invitation, among others.

TIP   Be sure you use the spell checker after you complete your message to check for any spelling mistakes. The spell checker can be found under Tools ➢ Spelling or by pressing the F7 function key.

Attaching Files to Your Messages

You may need to attach a file to a mail message. For example, you might be sending an e-mail message to a business colleague and want to also send a report that is saved as a separate file.

To attach a file to a message:

1. Create the e-mail message, including the e-mail address of the recipient.
2. Click the Insert Attachment (paper clip) button on the Outlook Express toolbar. You will see the Insert Attachment dialog box shown in Figure 10.4.
3. Highlight the file you want to attach to the e-mail message and click Attach. You will end up back in the e-mail message screen.
4. Click Send. The e-mail message and the selected file are sent as one package to the person specified in the To field. (The selected file will still be on your computer; only a copy of it was sent with the mail message.)

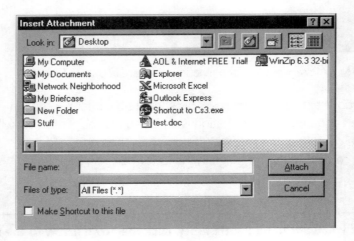

FIGURE 10.4: The Insert Attachment dialog box is where you specify the file you want to attach to an e-mail message.

NOTE   You can also just cut and paste the contents of a file into your e-mail message. However, you may lose some formatting features when you do this.

Reading Mail Messages

To retrieve new mail, click the Inbox button. The Outlook Express window will look like the one shown in Figure 10.5, listing the sender, the subject, and the date and time the message arrived.

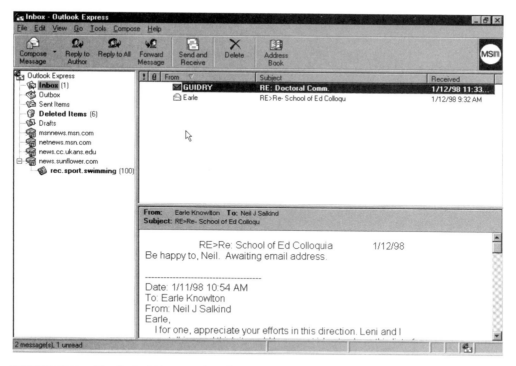

FIGURE 10.5: The Outlook Express Inbox shows mail that has arrived.

In the top pane of the Inbox is a list of mail that has been received. The envelope icon to the left of the name of the sender is closed if the mail has not been read and opened if the mail has been read.

You have two options for viewing a message. You can single-click a message to display the contents in the lower pane on the Outlook Express Inbox. This is a good way to get a quick view of what the mail message contains. To see the message in its own window, double-click the message in the upper pane. The message will be displayed as shown in Figure 10.6.

Once a mail message is read, it remains in the Inbox until you delete it. To delete a message, either select the message and click the Delete button, or right-click the message and select Delete from the pop-up menu. If you decide you still want to read a message after it's deleted, you can always click the Deleted Items option in the left pane of the Outlook Express window and read the message there. Deleted messages will stay in this folder until you move them or delete them for good. To retrieve a message from this folder, simply drag it to the Inbox. To delete all of the messages, right-click the Deleted Items option and select Empty Folder.

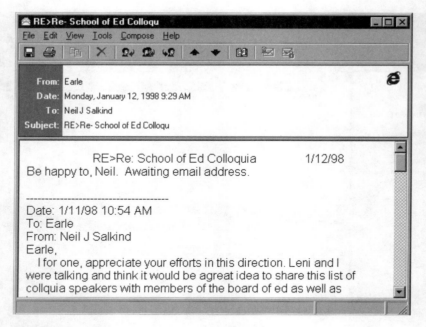

FIGURE 10.6: Reading an e-mail message in its own window

NOTE To have all messages in the Deleted Items folder deleted when you exit Outlook Express, select Tools > Options. On the General tab, check Empty Messages from the Deleted Items folder on Exit.

Replying to a Message

Once you've read a message, odds are that you will need to answer it. The nice thing about the way most mail programs (including Outlook Express) are designed is that your answer is automatically sent back to the person who sent you the original e-mail when you choose to reply.

To reply to an e-mail message in Outlook Express:

1. Be sure that you have opened the message to which you want to reply. The message should appear in its own window with the title of the message in the title bar.

2. Click the Reply to Author button. You'll see the reply screen shown in Figure 10.7 containing the original message with the vertical insertion point blinking at the location where your entry will begin.

Reply to Author

3. Type your reply. You can make other adjustments such as adding another recipient to the To, Cc, or Bcc field and deleting portions of the original message that are not relevant to your response.

4. Click the Send button.

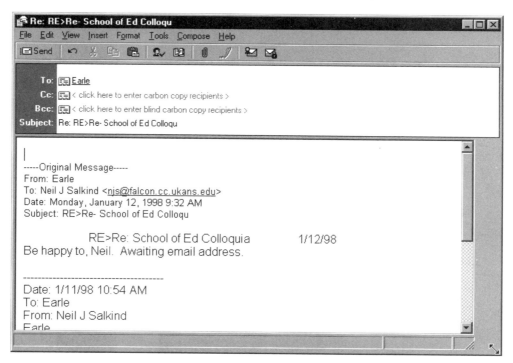

FIGURE 10.7: Getting ready to reply to a message

NOTE   There are three delivery options you can choose from when responding to mail. You can send it back to just the person who sent it to you or all the people that the original message was sent to, or you can forward it on to another person. Each of these options is represented by an icon on the toolbar in the Outlook Express opening window.

Formatting Mail Messages

Once a mail message is created, it can be easily formatted using all of the tools that you probably know about from working with a word processor. In fact, the Format menu in the Reply and New Message windows may even contain more formatting options than your word processor.

Here's a summary of the different Format menu options and what they do:

Style   allows you to add features such as heading sizes, bulleted lists, and numbered lists. It also allows you to define paragraphs.

Font   allows you to change the font, style (italics, bold, etc.), and size of the font used in the reply message.

Align   aligns text left, center, or right justified.

Numbers   assigns numbers to the items in the reply mail text by paragraph.

Bullets   assigns bullets to items in the reply by paragraph.

Increase Indent and **Decrease Indent**   let you increase or decrease the indent space from the left margin for the paragraph in which the cursor is located.

Background   allows you to add a color or a picture to a mail message.

Language   lets you select the alphabet you want to use.

Rich Text and **Plain Text**   let you decide whether you want a plain text file or one that is created in HTML format and can be read as a Web page.

Apply Stationery   allows you to use any of the different pre-made stationery designs that we talked about earlier.

A Few E-Mail Precautions

Here are some simple guidelines to make your mail experience more enjoyable.

- While you might think e-mail is private, it may very well not be.
- Only send e-mail that you could stand everyone in the neighborhood, office, and school knowing about.
- Check your mail on a regular basis. If you have an e-mail account, your friends and colleagues will assume that you check your mail.
- Once that Send button is clicked, the mail or news contribution is gone. There's no way to go into the mailbox and take it out. Be sure before you send a message that it says what you want.

Using the Address Book

As you send and receive mail, you will want to keep track of the e-mail addresses of your correspondents. These addresses, plus other information, can be stored in the Address book. Why store this information? It's much easier to automatically enter your correspondent's name than his or her e-mail address when you want to focus on writing the e-mail message.

Adding an Address to the Address Book

Let's say that rather than waiting for your friend to e-mail you so you can automatically record her e-mail address, you want to enter it right when you start using Outlook Express.

To enter a new e-mail address in the Address Book, follow these steps:

1. Click the Address Book button or select Tools ➤ Address Book. You'll see the Address Book screen shown here (except yours will probably be empty).

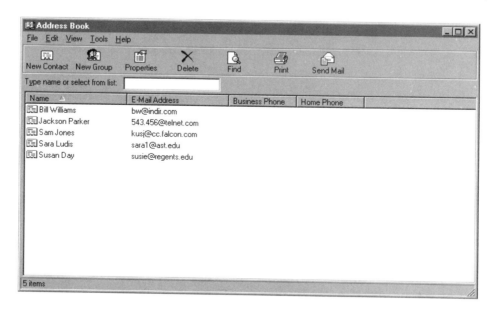

2. Click the New Contact button on the toolbar. The Properties screen shown here will open with lots of tabs and fields for you to fill in. Fill in as much or as little as you want, but you must at least enter a name and an e-mail address for each entry.

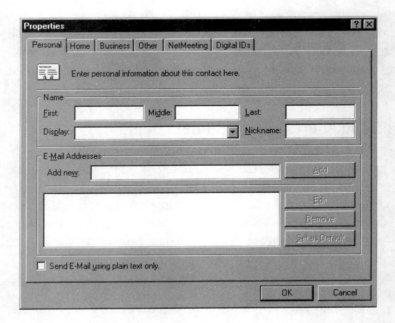

3. Click OK after you complete each new entry and it will be added to the Address Book. How do you know? Try clicking the Address Book button and opening up the current address file. You'll see your entry.

NOTE   **When you enter the name for an address book corespondent in a new e-mail message, you will not see that person's e-mail address. Rather, you'll see only the name you typed.**

Other Important Outlook Express Features

The more you use Outlook Express, the more comfortable you will feel creating, sending, and replying to mail. Besides the features we have already discussed, there are some others that you should know about:

- If you want to send an e-mail message to a group of friends or colleagues, click the New Group button in the Address Book dialog box, name the group, and then select the members you want to be part of the group. When you enter the name of the group in the To field of a message, the mail will be sent to all the members of that group.

- You can alphabetically sort your messages based on any column in the Outlook Express dialog box by clicking a column name. For instance, to sort your mail alphabetically by sender, click the To column heading.
- The Find People button in the opening Outlook Express window helps you find information (such as the e-mail address) for anyone whose name you enter by searching through the Address Book.
- If you want to go directly to the Inbox (where you can see what mail you've received), check the When Starting, Go Directly checkbox on the opening Outlook Express screen.

Starting the Outlook Express Newsreader

The Outlook Express newsreader, which you need in order to read and interact with newsgroups, is found on the Outlook Express opening screen. Click the Read News icon and you'll see the opening news window shown in Figure 10.8.

When the newsreader opens for the first time, it will ask you if you want to view the newsgroups that are available to you. The system administrator at your Internet Service Provider is the one who decides which of the 6,000 or so newsgroups you will have access to. This download may take a few minutes, especially if your system is slow. Once the download process is finished, you'll see an alphabetical list of all the newsgroups available to you (see Figure 10.9).

TIP

To find a newsgroup that you are interested in, click the News Groups column button and type the words that you want to search for in the Display Newsgroups Which Contain box. If a specific newsgroup you are looking for does not come up, it may only mean that your news server might not make that newsgroup available to you, not that it does not exist.

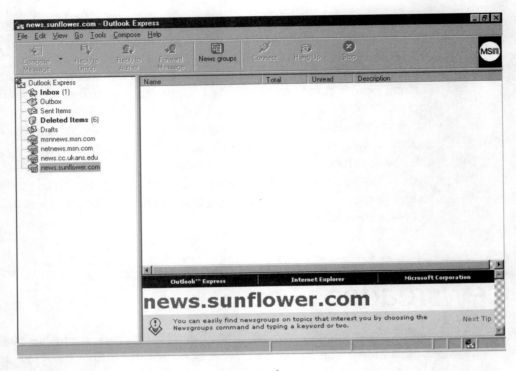

FIGURE 10.8: Starting the Outlook Express newsreader

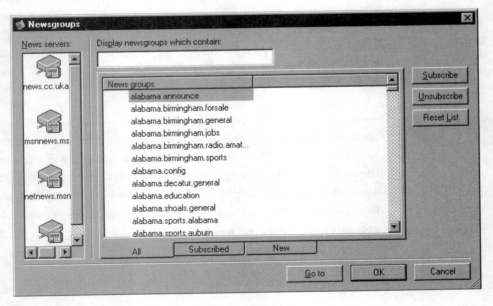

FIGURE 10.9: A listing of newsgroups that are available to you

All newsgroups belong to a specific group and you can tell what group that is by the set of characters that appears at the beginning of the newsgroup's name. For example, all newsgroups that begin with the characters "rec" deal with topics in the general area of recreation. Here's a listing of some of the major newsgroups and what areas they represent.

Newsgroup Name	Newsgroup Focus
comp	Information about computers
news	Information about newsgroups
rec	Information about recreation, the performing arts, and sports
sci	Information about science and scientific research
soc	Information about the social sciences
alt	Information about everything else that does not conveniently fit into an existing newsgroup category

How a Newsgroup Works

A newsgroup is no different from a bunch of people sitting around a table discussing a particular topic, except that the discussion doesn't happen in the present (or what newsgroup folk call real time). And of course, a newsgroup discussion takes place electronically over the Internet, not at a table.

A newsgroup begins with someone putting forth a statement or a *post* (in the form of a message) about a particular topic. This message resides in the newsgroup listing. Someone on the Internet interested in that topic might read the initial contribution and then choose to make a contribution as well. In turn, someone else might read these two news messages and then make their own contribution. It's a very democratic way to do things since anyone can participate in any newsgroup, whether they be an active participant or just someone who wants to drop in and see who's saying what about what.

Subscribing to a Newsgroup

It's not difficult at all to become part of a newsgroup and read and make your own contributions. When you are interested in a particular newsgroup, you subscribe to it. When you subscribe, you are telling your news server to send you the latest news generated in that newsgroup. After you subscribe, you can see all the activity that takes place in the newsgroup and make your own contributions as you see fit. Contributions can be posted to the newsgroup so everyone in the group can see them, or they can be sent only to the person who posted the newsgroup message you are responding to.

Some news programs allow you to respond to both the group and the individual at the same time. Outlook Express allows you to reply to the author or the group, but not both.

To subscribe to a newsgroup:

1. Open Outlook Express.
2. Click the Read News icon.
3. Click the News Groups column button. You will see a listing lof all the newsgroups that are available to you through your server.

News groups

4. Scroll through the list of newsgroups and highlight the newsgroup to which you want to subscribe.
5. Click the Subscribe button and click OK.
6. Once you are subscribed to a newsgroup, each time you open that newsgroup to read its contents, it will be automatically updated with the news that is sent from your news server to your computer and on to Outlook Express.

TIP   It may take some time, but eventually you will find the newsgroups that interest you most. Obviously the name of a newsgroup is help-ful in determining if it interests you, but so is talking to friends and coworkers and reading some of the popular computer publications.

Unsubscribing to a Newsgroup

If you are no longer interested in receiving information from a newsgroup, just high-light it in the Newsgroups list window, click the Unsubscribe button, and then click OK. You can also unsubscribe in the main window. Just right-click the newsgroup and then click Unsubscribe. You'll be asked to confirm the deletion.

Opening a Newsgroup and Reading Messages

The reason you subscribe to a newsgroup in the first place is to be able to read the messages that other people leave and to respond to a message should you see fit. In order to see those messages, you have to first open the newsgroup. You can do this by simply double-clicking the title of the newsgroup in the Outlook Express newsreader. The contents of the newsgroup will become visible, as you can see in Figure 10.10.

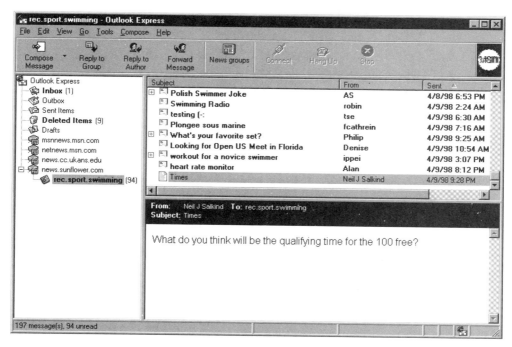

FIGURE 10.10:   What a newsgroup message looks like when it is opened for reading

Once you see the messages listed, you can read any message by clicking that message. This reveals the contents of the message in the preview pane in the bottom half of the newsreader window shown in Figure 10.10.

> **TIP**   If you want to find out everything there is to know about any particular message, such as who sent it, when it was sent, and how big it is (among other information), right-click the message and click Properties from the drop-down menu.

Posting New Messages and Replying to Messages

There are two times that you may want to make a contribution to a newsgroup. The first is when you want to reply to an already posted message. The second is when you want to start your own thread of messages. In other words, you have something important or interesting enough to say that it shouldn't be lumped with a bunch of other messages.

To post a new a message to a newsgroup:

1. Select the newsgroup that you want to post a message to.
2. Click the Compose Message button on the toolbar.
3. Type a subject for your message in the Subject line and type the content of your message in the content area (see in Figure 10.11). Outlook Express will not post a message without a subject header.
4. Click Post and the message will be sent to the newsgroup. Now it's your turn to sit back and see how people react to your posting.

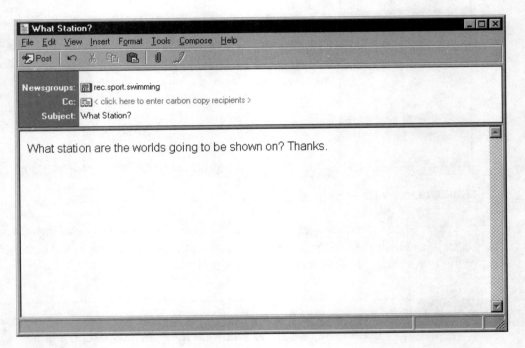

FIGURE 10.11:   The content of a news message

If you want to reply to a message in a newsgroup:

1. Click the message to which you want to reply.
2. Click the Reply to Group button if you want to reply to the entire newsgroup. This is usually the first choice people make since they want their contribution to be part of the public discussion. The alternative is to designate that the message go just to the author. This is an acceptable alternative as well, especially when the content might be of a private nature.

3. Type the message.
4. Click the Post Message button on the toolbar.

Working with News Offline

You might be able to tell from your early excursions into news how very much information there is out there in so many, many groups. It would be great if there was a way for Outlook Express to automatically download news messages that you are interested in so that you can read them offline at your leisure—especially if you're paying your online service by the hour. Luckily, Outlook Express has that very capability.

To set up news for reading offline:

1. Select the newsgroup for which you want to read news offline.
2. Click the File menu, then click Properties.
3. Click the Download tab, then click When Downloading This Newsgroup, Retrieve, and click the option you want.
4. Repeat steps 1 through 3 for any other newsgroups you want information automatically downloaded for.
5. Once you have completed the above four steps, click Download All from the Tools menu and Outlook Express will download the messages from the newsgroups you specified.

What's Next?

News and mail get to us via the Internet. Wouldn't it be great to explore what else might be in store for us on that network of networks? That's just what the next chapter is about, browsing the Internet and seeing what's on it and how to find what you need.

Chapter 11

BROWSING THE WEB

- **Understanding Internet Explorer**
- **Navigating the World Wide Web**
- **Learning about Web pages**
- **Working with Channels**
- **Using FrontPage**

The World Wide Web is out there for you to explore. All you need to begin your journey is a Web browser. Windows 98 provides you with Internet Explorer, a newly-designed and greatly-improved tool for accessing Web sites.

This chapter will introduce you to Internet Explorer and teach you how to use it to navigate the World Wide Web. You'll also learn how to send and receive e-mail using Internet Explorer. While you'll probably use Outlook Express for your e-mail, the convenience of being in Internet Explorer and being able to create and send e-mail is important.

Introducing Internet Explorer

If you've been living in a cave for the past couple of years and haven't heard of the World Wide Web, you're probably better off. That way you don't have to unlearn how to use a Web browser. You can jump right in and enjoy the Web the easy, Internet Explorer way. If you connect to the Internet using CompuServe, Microsoft Network, Prodigy Internet, or AT&T WorldNet, you'll be using Internet Explorer as your Web browser. (America Online uses its own software.) In all cases, you will join a commercial service and use their software to get to their server. Each service provides you with their own group of diversions such as discussion groups, reference materials, news, and so forth. It's when you pass through these services to get to the Internet that Internet Explorer comes in.

TIP

You can find new versions of Internet Explorer as they come out by visiting http://www.microsoft.com/msdownload **and downloading a copy.**

NOTE

If you use just a generic Internet Service Provider, there won't be any amusements or other services on their servers. These providers connect you directly to the Internet with no hoopla in between.

To start Internet Explorer, click the Internet icon on your Desktop. Once you are in Internet Explorer, you can travel around the Web as you'd like.

In your Internet Explorer explorations, you will surely come across links to other sites. Just click those and you'll be taken to that site. Another way to surf is to click in the Address box and type the URL (Uniform Resource Locator) of the site to which you'd like to be transported. For example, you could type **http://www.microsoft .com** and you'd end up at the main Microsoft site on the World Wide Web.

TIP

Many browsers (Internet Explorer among them) allow you to travel to a site without typing the full address in the Address box. For instance, in the example we just gave, you could type microsoft and press enter and you would go to the Microsoft site just as if you'd typed http://www.microsoft.com.

Fortunately, once you've typed in one of these unwieldy addresses, you can open the Favorites menu and add the Internet address. From then on, you need only select the site from the Favorites menu to return. And the Favorites menu comes with some interesting sites already installed.

TIP If you were at a site recently but failed to add it to your Favorites list, you can find it again by clicking the arrow to the right of the Address field to open a drop-down list of recent URLs.

Navigating the Web with Internet Explorer

Once Internet Explorer is opened and you are connected to the Internet, it's simple to navigate your way around the Internet. At first, you will have to enter the addresses of those Web sites you want to visit, but after a while, you will have created and saved a collection of your favorite spots, and a simple point-and-click will take you to all the old familiar places.

The buttons on the Internet Explorer toolbar are designed to help you navigate quickly and easily. Here's an overview of what each one does:

Button Name	Function
Back	Returns you to the document from which you just came. This button is grayed out if you've just started surfing—that is, if the document you're looking at is the first one you've visited during this session. Clicking the Down arrow lists all the pages you've visited in this session, and you can select any URL to return to that page.
Forward	Takes you one document forward (to the next item) in the sequence of pages or sites you've already visited. This button is grayed out if you're on the last item on your History list (the list of pages and sites you've visited). Clicking the Down arrow lists all the pages you've visited in this session, and you can select any URL to go forward to that page.

Button Name	Function
Stop	Halts transmission of the document at which you've pointed the Internet Explorer. This button is especially useful if a connection is painfully slow and you've decided you'd rather bail out than wait.
Refresh	Refreshes the current document. You may want to do this if, for example, you believe the information on the displayed Web page has been updated since you last loaded it, or if you have a temporary communication problem with the Web server you're connected to and the document you want to see is not completely displayed.
Home	Returns you to the start-up home page.
Search	Connects you with a page full of Internet search engines. Using one of these programs, you can search the Internet for names, places, and ideas.
Favorites	Opens your own personal list of favorite documents. You can add a document to your Favorites folder by using the Add to Favorites option on the Favorites menu while you're viewing the document.
History	Reviews the Web pages you've visited in past Internet Explorer sessions and allows you to return to any one of them.
Channels	Provides Web sites, selected by your online service provider, that specialize in a particular area such as entertainment or business, plus those to which you can subscribe.
Fullscreen	Toggles between a full and partial Internet Explorer screen.

Button Name	Function
Mail	Click here to send or receive e-mail, read newsgroups, or send a URL address to someone.
Print	Prints the active Web page.
Edit	Opens FrontPage Express and allows you to create or edit a Web page.

As you move the mouse pointer around a Web page, the arrow pointer will sometimes change to a hand. When it does, it means that the location on the page is a link to another location on the Internet.

About Web Pages

A Web page (as you've probably already figured out) is a collection of information. All Web pages have certain characteristics in common. For example, clicking a particular word, image, or even sound on many sites takes you to another Web page linked to the original one. How do you know which Web page elements are "hot" (Web lingo for a spot that links to another Web page) and will lead you to another location? When you place the mouse pointer on such a link, the pointer turns into a hand. When you click while the hand is displayed, another page linked to that spot on the current page will open. There may also be some visual cues to let you know when you've hit a "hot spot." For example, text links are likely to be underlined and perhaps displayed in a different color, and image links may have a different color border around them. It's hard to be more specific about how this feature works because different pages use many different linking methods, but once you encounter a link, it will become obvious.

TIP When the pointer changes to a hand, you can see that a URL is displayed in the lower-left corner of the status bar.

Visiting Other Web Pages

There are several ways you can move from one Web page to another. The first, and easiest, is by clicking an established link from the current page to another page. In Figure 11.1 you can see the Web page for Online Epicure. If you place the pointer on any link shown on this page (all of different arrows, the buttons across the top, and some of the text are links) and click, you will be transferred to the Web page for that link.

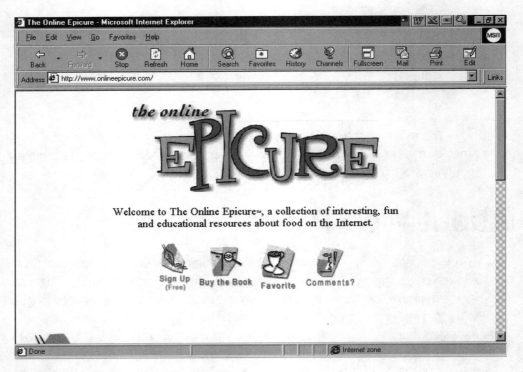

FIGURE 11.1: The opening Online Epicure page

Besides clicking a hot link to another page, you can also enter the address for a Web page you want to visit in the Address box. Once you do this (being very careful to type the name correctly) and press the Enter button, you will be delivered to that site as fast as your equipment allows.

WARNING No one home? You're sure you entered the correct URL, but your browser tells you that it can't connect. There are a few possibilities. Your Internet Service Provider could be down. The location you are trying to connect to could be down. Or the site to which you are trying to connect could no longer be active. That is, the site may no longer be hosted. Try again in a few minutes. If the problem is related to site management, it might very well be fixed when you try again. If it's an ownership problem, you won't be able to connect at all because the link is "dead."

Saving Your Favorite Sites

You certainly have a favorite flavor of ice cream and a favorite book. Why not a favorite Web site? It might be a news site such as *The New York Times* (www.nytimes .com) or a food site such as Online Epicure (www.onlineepicure.com). As you work with Internet Explorer and visit new and wonderful sites on the Internet, you will want to revisit those same sites in the future. Rather than having to retype a URL (which is time consuming and can be long and difficult), just store it as a favorite and go to the Favorites list the next time to recall the URL you want.

When you open the Favorites folder for the first time, you'll notice that Internet Explorer already has a suggested list of Favorites it thinks you might like taking a look at. That list includes the folders and files that appear on the Start menu under the Favorites option.

If you want to reorganize your folders, select Favorites ➤ Organize Favorites. Using the Organize Favorites dialog box (see Figure 11.2), create folders you want to appear on the Favorite list, move files from one location to another, and design a set of folders and files as you see fit. These new folders and their contents will appear on the Favorites menu.

To add a Web page to your collection of favorite pages:

1. Go to the Web page you want to add to the collection.
2. From the Favorites menu on the Internet Explorer toolbar, click Add to Favorites.
3. If you want to, type a new name for the page as shown in Figure11.3.

Once you have created a list of favorite home pages, just click the Favorites button on the Internet Explorer toolbar and then click to add the page as shown in Figure 11.3.

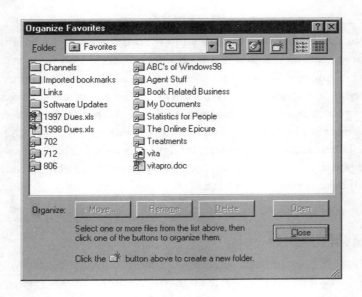

FIGURE 11.2:
The Organize
Favorites
dialog box

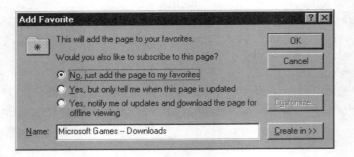

FIGURE 11.3:
Adding a new
Web page to the
Favorites list

TIP   One very handy feature of Internet Explorer and other browsers is that you need not enter the full URL. You can omit the http:// prefix and the suffix (for example, .com or .org) from the Address box. When you enter a URL name such as **onlineepicure**, Internet Explorer knows that http:// goes before it. It then tries all the domain names (suffixes) until it locates the site.

To delete a favorite site, just right-click the sight and click Delete from the pop-up menu. The reference to the Web page appearing in the Favorites folder will be deleted.

Using History

Clicking the History button shows you what activities have taken place in Internet Explorer today, yesterday, and over an even longer period of time, which you can define. As with the Favorites bar, you can click any site listed under History and return to that site immediately.

The big difference between clicking the History button and clicking the down arrow on the Back or Forward button (to see where you've been) is that the History feature records your activity from sessions other than the current one. So if you remember that you found a particularly useful site two weeks ago and forgot to add it to your Favorites list, the History list might do the trick.

When you click the History button or Favorites button on the toolbar, the list appears on the left side of the screen. When you click one of the links, the Web page will appear in only the right portion of the screen. To close either the Favorites list or the History list so you have more room to view Web pages, click the X button at the top of the list.

TIP   **To set the number of pages that appears in the History list, click View ➤ Internet Options. Then click the General tab, and in the History area, change the number of the days that you want Internet Explorer to keep track of your pages. Then click OK.**

Finding What You Want on the Web

When the World Wide Web first become popular, it was like visiting a library that had all the information you could ever need. The only problem was that all the "books" were not on shelves or organized in any particular order. Many people found the Web frustrating, and the chaos probably drove many potential users away.

Today, there are several search engines (such as Yahoo!, Infoseek, Excite, and Lycos) that make the chaos that is the Web a little more organized. You can use a search engine to search the Web for a particular item or topic. Each search engine tends to work in a different way from the others, but they all have a basic premise in common: You enter search terms (the more specific the better) and the search engine comes up with a selection of Web pages that it thinks closely approximates to what you entered as your search term.

You can use a specific search engine to do your search, or you can save some time and click the Search button on the Internet Explorer toolbar. Internet Explorer uses Excite as its default search engine. Once the terms you want to use are entered, just click Go Get It and the next thing you'll see is the results of your search.

Excite tells you how many URLs or Web pages it found. As to how useful each of those is, you will have to be the judge. The nice thing is that clicking any one of the listed URLs will take you to that new page. Convenient!

Should you not want to use the Excite search engine, here's a list of some others that you can enter directly. Note that the All-in-One Search page lists individual engines as well as categories of search tools.

Search Engine	Where to Find It
All-in-One	`http://www.albany.net/allinone/`
Alta Vista	`http://www.altavista.digital.com`
Excite	`http://www.excite.com/`
Yahoo!	`http://www.yahoo.com/`

Using the Mouse

Internet Explorer has a multitude of handy features that you can access armed with nothing but your right mouse button. You can right-click while on a page to bring up a pop-up menu. From that menu you can pick all sorts of fun options. Want to be able to get to that page again quickly? You can make a shortcut to the page or add it to your list of favorite pages. Come across a beautiful picture on a Web page? Just right-click and select Save Picture As to save it as an image file, or select Set As Wallpaper to turn it into wallpaper for your Desktop.

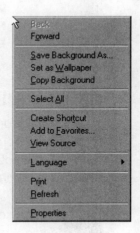

NOTE   **Be aware that pictures and text you download from the Internet are protected by copyright law. For more information, search for copyright law sites on the Internet.**

Tuning In Channels

Channels is a wonderful new Windows 98 feature offered through Internet Explorer. A channel is a Web site that automatically delivers content to your computer. The categories of channels that are available are listed in the Explorer bar in the Internet Explorer window. All you need to do to see the content of any channel is click the category (such as Disney or Entertainment) and then click the channel button you want to visit. In Figure 11.4, you can see the opening screen for the Channels plus a map of all the content within the Entertainment category.

What's neat about the Channels feature is that the information is updated regularly according to the provider's schedule. So, while the Entertainment channel one day contains the AudioNet Channel, Hollywood Online, and the Comics Channel, the next day it might include a new set of Web sites or even different Web content within already existing sites.

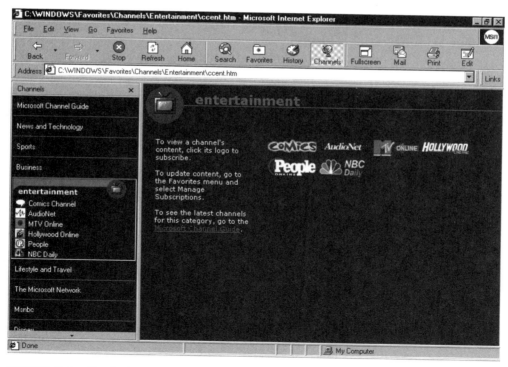

FIGURE 11.4:   The Explorer toolbar with the Channel categories

Adding a Channel to the Channel Toolbar

You are not limited to the channels listed in the Channels toolbar. You can view others by adding them to the toolbar.

To add a channel:

1. Click the Channels button on the Explorer toolbar.
2. Click the Microsoft Active Channel Guide button at the top of the Explorer toolbar. You'll see a list of channels that are new as well as some that are being previewed and should be available shortly.
3. Click the category of channels you want to add (for instance, Sports or Business).
4. Click the particular channel you want to add.
5. Click the Add to Active Desktop button. The channel will be added to the category and will appear on your Desktop in the Channels toolbar.

Once a channel is added to the Explorer toolbar, it is available with a click and will be updated on a regular basis by the information provider.

Subscribing to a Channel

Subscribing to a channel is the next step up from simply viewing a channel. When you view a channel, the content changes as a function of the information provider's actions. When you subscribe to a channel, Internet Explorer will check your favorite Web sites (defined as channels) for any change in the content. Internet Explorer will then notify you that the content has changed (and offer you the option to see it) or automatically update the content and have it loaded to your hard drive so you can view it offline at your convenience. The content of a channel is server-based, while a subscription is user-defined. With a subscription, you make the decision about what information you see, when it will be delivered, and where it will be delivered to.

For example, you might want to subscribe to a Web site where business news about a particular company is delivered to you each morning. And you can have these updates completed daily, weekly, monthly or on whatever schedule you choose. Beware, however, that the more channels you subscribe to, the more precious memory is used by your computer to stay current. So, look and enjoy, but when it comes to subscribing, be selective.

To subscribe to a channel:

1. Click the Channels button on the Explorer toolbar.
2. Right-click the channel you want to subscribe to and then click Subscribe.
3. Click OK to confirm the subscription.

WARNING If you subscribe to too many channels your computer may be slowed down, so make sure you only subscribe to ones that really interest you.

Creating and Sending Mail Using Internet Explorer

You already know that Windows 98 has an easy-to-use mailing program named Outlook Express (discussed in Chapter 10) that you will probably use for most of your mail business.

But, should you be working in Internet Explorer and want to send mail without starting Outlook Express, you can easily create and send messages in Internet Explorer in much the same way you do in Outlook Express.

To send a mail message through Internet Explorer:

1. Click File ➢ New ➢ Message. You'll see the New Message Window shown in Figure 11.5.

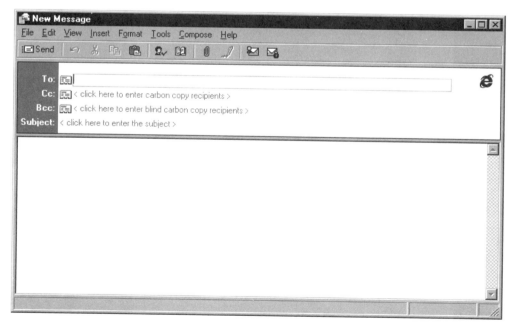

FIGURE 11.5: The New Message window

2. Enter an e-mail address in the To line. This is the address where the mail will be sent.

3. Click in the Subject field and type a subject to accompany the message so your reader will know what the message is about.

4. Use the Tab key to move down to the message area and compose the message.

5. Click Send.

NOTE If you are in Internet Explorer and want to read mail, click the Read Mail option that appears when you click the Mail icon on the Internet Explorer toolbar, and Outlook Express will automatically open.

Creating Your Own Web Page Using FrontPage

By this time you have probably seen several different Web pages. You may be thinking that some of the pages you've seen are very difficult and time consuming to create. That's not necessarily the case. In fact, you can use Windows 98 FrontPage Express to design your own page in just a few minutes. Admittedly, complex pages do take more time to create, but it can be done. You can start FrontPage by clicking Start ➤ Programs ➤ Internet Explorer ➤ FrontPage Express.

HTML: The Basis of All Web Pages

All Web page are written in a special markup language called Hypertext Markup Language (HTML). This language includes the use of tags that surround text, images, or references to other files or other Internet sites. For example, the tag <i> before text indicates that italics is turned on. The tag </i> at the end of text means that italics is being turned off. Whatever appears between the two tags will appear in italics.

In Figure 11.6, you can see how a simple home page appears when viewed in Internet Explorer.

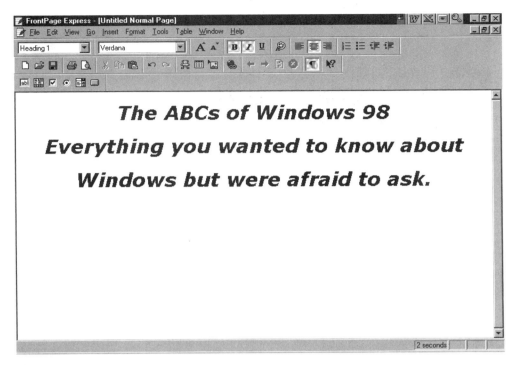

FIGURE 11.6: A simple home page

Here's the actual HTML code for the Web page:

```
<head>
<meta http-equiv="Content-Type"
content="text/html; charset=iso-8859-1">
<meta name="GENERATOR" content="Microsoft FrontPage Express 2.0">
<title>Untitled Normal Page</title>
</head>
<body bgcolor="#FFFFFF">
<h1 align="center"><font face="Verdana"><em><strong>The ABCs of
Windows 98</strong></em></font></h1>
<h1 align="center"><font face="Verdana"><em><strong>Everything
you wanted to know about</strong></em></font></h1>
<h1 align="center"><font face="Verdana"><em><strong>Windows but
were afraid to ask.</strong></em></font></h1>
</body>
</html>
```

HTML files can be created using a word processor. The HTML content can be saved as a simple text file. But since the development of Web pages has become so popular, many different applications have been created so that you don't have to trouble yourself with learning HTML. All you need to do is click what you want, enter text, and indicate where the images that you want to appear are stored; and like magic, you've got a home page.

Creating a Web Page

Creating a Web page using FrontPage is really a matter of entering the text and images and using the various available toolbars (on the View menu) to make the formatting changes you want. For example, the first line of the Web page shown in Figure 11.6 was typed in, then the Center button was clicked to align it. Next the size was changed using the Change Style drop-down menu, and italics and bold were added by clicking the Italic and Bold buttons on the Format toolbar. No actual HTML commands were entered.

NOTE **Want to see what your document looks like in HTML? Click View ➤ HTML and you will see the source code or the official HTML commands that produce the Web page you are working on. Click OK to get back to the main FrontPage window.**

The FrontPage Window

Creating a FrontPage file is similar to using a word processor. You enter text and references to other elements, such as images, and format them as you choose. Once the Web page is created, it is saved and then sent via the Internet to your Internet Service Provider, who will then make it available to others through the World Wide Web.

NOTE **Not all ISPs offer space for a Web site. Contact your ISP for details on the services they provide.**

The FrontPage window you saw in Figure 11.6 contains all the tools you need to create your own Web page. From left to right, here's what each tool on the standard toolbar does:

   Provide a blank document for creating a new Web page.

   Open an existing FrontPage file.

Save a FrontPage file.

Print a FrontPage file.

Preview a FrontPage file.

Cut FrontPage material from a file.

Copy FrontPage material.

Paste cut or copied material in a new location.

Undo the last action.

Redo the last action.

Insert a WebBot component, which is a self-starting file or Web activity.

Insert a table on the Web page.

Insert an image on the Web page.

Create a hyperlink to another Web site.

Move back one page.

Move forward one page.

Refresh the screen.

Stop loading the page.

Show or hide formatting marks.

Get help.

What's Next?

Up until now, we've talked about Windows 98 as a graphical environment—and an excellent one it is. In the next chapter, we'll see how Windows 98 runs DOS programs better and faster than plain DOS ever did—and many, many times better than any previous version of Windows.

Chapter 12

DOS AND WINDOWS 98

- **DOS: better than ever**
- **Fine tuning DOS settings**
- **Making DOS programs run**
- **Working with the DOS prompt**
- **DOS commands in Windows 98**

You usually won't have much to do with DOS when working in Windows 98. There are times, however, when a knowledge of DOS commands and how to run DOS-based programs will be valuable. In this chapter, we'll talk about the simple way to run DOS programs and how you can cajole even the most poorly behaved DOS program to run without any complaints. We'll also discuss some of the more important DOS commands that you might find useful—even if you work mainly in Windows 98.

DOS Lives On

If you're new to personal computers, you may not even know what DOS (Disk Operating System) is. It was the primary operating system used with millions of personal computers before the introduction of Windows (and other user-friendly operating systems). DOS was Microsoft's first big success and was the standard for years.

DOS programs aren't automatically placed on the Programs menu the way Windows programs are when you first install them. But you can create a shortcut to a DOS program and put the shortcut either on your Desktop or in one of the folders that make up the Programs menu by using the same technique you would use for creating any other shortcut (covered in Chapter 3). Just open the Windows 98 Explorer and find the folder that contains the .EXE file for the program. Right-click the program name and drag it to the Desktop to make a shortcut, or put it on your Start menu or in a folder.

In other words, DOS programs are handled exactly the same way as Windows programs. Almost every DOS program *should* open with a simple click on the icon. But what if it won't? Or what if it opens in a window and you'd like it to run full screen? Fortunately, every DOS program has a very extensive collection of Properties sheets that you can use to tweak your DOS performance. We'll get to those later in this chapter.

Why Use DOS?

You can run a DOS program through Windows 98 or restart your computer in the DOS mode. To do this, select Shut Down on the Start menu and then select the Restart in MS-DOS Mode option.

There are several reasons why running a DOS program within Windows 98 makes more sense that running it in DOS mode:

- Windows 98 is designed to make certain resources, such as sound and video, more accessible, and DOS applications have the same accessibility.
- More memory is available for DOS applications because Windows 98 uses less memory than DOS to run such things as the mouse and the CD-ROM driver.
- Finally, graphics run better in Windows 98 than in DOS. And there are so many graphics in DOS applications (many of which are games), you're sure to get better results.

TIP You can switch back and forth from DOS to Windows programs using the Alt+Tab key combination. This is very useful if you run a favorite utility in DOS, yet Windows 98 is the system within which all the other programs you use are run.

Running DOS Programs in Windows

There are three ways you can start a DOS program while in Windows 98. Which way you use depends on your work habits and your computing needs. Your three options are:

- Find the DOS object (such as an icon representing an .EXE file) and click it. The program will start in a DOS window.
- Open the MS-DOS prompt window and type the name of the program on the command line, such as **c:\wordper\wp.exe**.
- Use the Run option on the Start menu, enter the full name of the program, and then click OK to open it.

Here's the easiest and fastest way to run a DOS program inside of a Windows 98 window:

1. Click the Start button and point to Programs.
2. Click the MS-DOS prompt. When you do this, a small DOS window like the one you see in Figure 12.1 will appear.
3. Type the command line to start the DOS program you want to run (such as **c:\wordperf\wp.exe**).

When you have finished with the DOS program, exit it and close the DOS window using the File ➤ Exit command (just as you would for any other open window). You'll be returned to a DOS prompt. Type **exit** to return to Windows 98.

NOTE You must know the exact command line in order to run a DOS program. There is no Browse button that lets you look for the location of the .EXE program. If you are having difficulty, use the Alt+Tab key combination to go to Windows 98 Explorer (or to get back to a place where you can get to Explorer) and either use Find to determine the path or search through Explorer's folders and files manually.

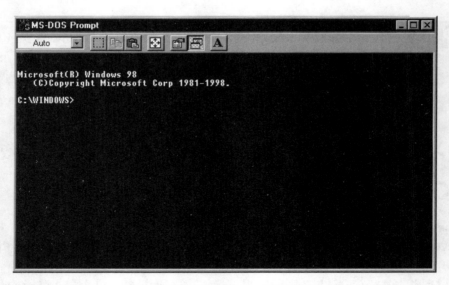

FIGURE 12.1: You can use a DOS window inside of Windows 98 to start a program.

Setting DOS Program Properties

More often than not, your DOS programs will run fine from within Windows 98. And, when you run a DOS program, you have access to a wide variety of properties for the program. As elsewhere in Windows 98, you get to those properties by right-clicking the icon or the shortcut for the program in any of three different places.

- Right-click the program's executable (or .EXE) file in Explorer or My Computer.
- Right-click a shortcut to the program.
- Open a DOS window and click the little icon in the upper-left corner once.

In all cases, you'll select Properties from the menu that opens. This will open up a Properties sheet for the DOS program like the one in Figure 12.2.

There are at least six pages on the Properties sheet. The number depends upon how your computer is configured. The six you're sure to find are:

General shows information about the file and file attributes. Such information as the size and location of the file are valuable when creating shortcuts and deleting files.

Program sets command line options and allows you to define the icon that is used to represent the program.

Font   sets the font design and the size of the font to be used when the program is run in a window.

Memory   sets how much and what kind of memory is made available to the DOS program.

Screen   changes whether the program runs full screen or in a window, and chnages the characteristics of the window.

Misc   like miscellaneous files everywhere, sets stuff that doesn't fit in any other category, such as Windows shortcut keys that you want to keep.

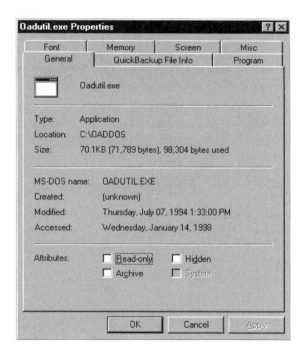

FIGURE 12.2:
A DOS-based program Properties sheet

Depending on your computer's configuration (such as the programs that have been installed), you may have other pages as well. The default settings are adequate for most programs, but if you need to fuss with one or more of these pages, read on.

General Properties

The General tab shows information about the program, as well as allowing you to set the attributes of the underlying file. As you can see in Figure 12.2, this tab shows you the type of program or file, its location and size, the DOS file name associated with it, and when the file was created, modified, and last accessed.

If you're looking at a shortcut, the information about the file size, location, and type will refer to the shortcut and not to the original .EXE file. If you are looking at an open DOS window or program, you won't see this page.

On this tab, you can change the MS-DOS attributes of the program, including whether the archive bit is set, whether the file can be modified or not (read-only bit), and whether the file is a hidden or system file. You won't want to change these settings except in very special circumstances— and then only if you're sure you know why you're making the change.

Program Properties

The Program tab of the Properties window (see Figure 12.3) lets you change the command line, which defines where the executable file is located. It also allows you to change the name and icon associated with the program and to assign a shortcut key. In addition, you can define whether you want a program to run in a normal-sized window, minimized, or maximized.

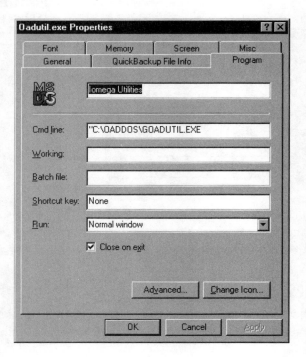

FIGURE 12.3:
The Program tab of the Properties sheet for a DOS program

Some Basic Settings

Here's what those settings mean:

Cmd Line   This box shows the actual command line that is executed when the window runs. Here you can add any command line parameters that you need.

Working   If your program has a favorite working directory, set that here. This isn't common any more, but some older programs need to be told this information. If there's already an entry in this box, Windows 98 and the program have figured out that it's necessary. Don't change this setting unless you're sure you know why you're changing it.

Batch File   If you want to run a batch file either before or as part of the program, place the name (and full path, if necessary) for that batch file in this box. A batch file is a file that automatically runs when DOS detects this particular type of file.

Shortcut Key   This box lets you add a shortcut key. (Some DOS programs may not work well with this option, but there's no harm in trying.)

Run   You can decide whether the program will run in a normal window, maximized, or minimized. Some DOS programs may pay no attention to this setting.

Close on Exit   When this box is checked, the DOS window will close when you close the program.

Advanced Settings

Use the Advanced button only if you have a very specialized, hardware-dependent program—such as a game that seems not to work properly under normal conditions. Click Advanced to open the Advanced Program Settings dialog box shown in Figure 12.4.

If really drastic measures are required, you can set the program to run in MS-DOS mode. This closes all your applications, restarts your computer in DOS mode, and may reboot your computer.

NOTE   It's not necessary for you to guess whether your game needs DOS mode to run. Go ahead and run the game. By default, the system will suggest DOS mode when the program requires it. So except in unusual situations, the system will let you know when a particular program needs DOS mode to run.

FIGURE 12.4:
The Advanced
Program Settings
from the Program
page of the DOS
Properties sheet

In MS-DOS mode you can only run a single program, and when you exit from that program, the system may automatically start Windows 98 or you may have to type **exit** to return to Windows. Again, this may well mean a reboot, so don't be startled.

The Last Resort

Running programs in MS-DOS mode should be a last resort. Almost everything should run fine in a full-screen DOS session or a DOS window. It is unlikely you will want or need to run anything in MS-DOS mode. Even DOOM and Flight Simulator run fine without it.

A primary reason for not running anything in DOS mode is that you lose the multi-tasking advantages of Windows 98. Plus, since a reboot may be required, the whole process takes a substantial amount of time.

Changing the Icon

Click the Change Icon button on the Program page to change the icon for the program. You can accept one of the icons offered or use the Browse button to look elsewhere. Icons are available aplenty on the Internet. Just use one of the search tools we talked about in Chapter 11, download the file, and be sure that the Properties sheet has the file properly located.

Font Properties

The Font tab of the Properties sheet (see Figure 12.5) lets you set which fonts will be available when the program is running in a window on the Desktop. You can select from either bitmapped or TrueType fonts, or you can choose to have both available.

Bitmapped fonts are fonts that are made up of hundreds of small squares arranged together to form a character. That's why when you increase the size of a bit-mapped font, you may see the dreaded "jaggies" or rough edges. TrueType fonts use a mathematical formula to generate a smooth and very clean looking font, regardless of the size.

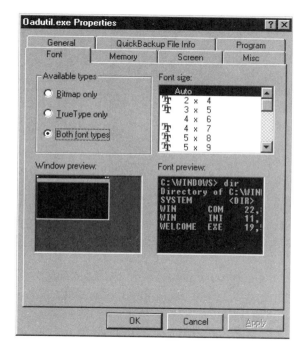

FIGURE 12.5:
The Font tab on the DOS Properties sheet

Resizing the DOS Window

The size of the font in the DOS window depends in part on how much room there is in the window. To change the size of a DOS window, go to the program's Properties sheet and try setting the font size to Auto. Then click and drag the edge of the DOS window. Sometimes setting the font to a fixed size and then dragging the edge of the window will work also. Different programs have different abilities to shrink and expand.

Memory Properties

The Memory tab of the Properties sheet (see Figure 12.6) lets you control how much and what kind of memory DOS programs have available when they run.

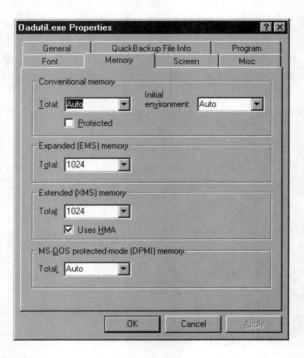

FIGURE 12.6:
Working with different types of memory in the DOS Properties sheet

On this tab you can make sure your program has a specific amount of conventional, expanded, and extended memory. You can also let Windows 98 automatically determine how much to make available. Generally, it's best to leave the settings here on Auto because fooling with memory can make a program run erratically and even make it crash. If you know you have a program that has specific memory requirements (which is often true of DOS games because of the vivid graphics and constant action), you can set that here.

And Memory Problems

If you have a program that has a habit of crashing occasionally, and you want to be sure it doesn't cause problems for the rest of the system, check the Protected box in the Conventional Memory section. This may slow down the program a little, but it will provide an additional layer of protection.

Some programs can actually have a problem with too much memory. Older versions of the Borland database Paradox, for example, have difficulty coping with unlimited extended memory. If you leave the Expanded and Extended sections set to Auto, programs like this may not run reliably. Try setting expanded and extended memory to some reasonable maximum number, such as 8192, which should be enough for most programs.

Screen Properties

The Screen tab of the Properties sheet (shown in Figure 12.7) lets you set your program's display. If you're running a graphical program, set it for Full-Screen. Most text-based programs (such as a DOS word processor) run better in a window. Unlike earlier versions of Windows, Windows 98 handles windowed DOS programs extremely well, and there is no real gain to running them full-screen unless you need the extra space for the program to look good.

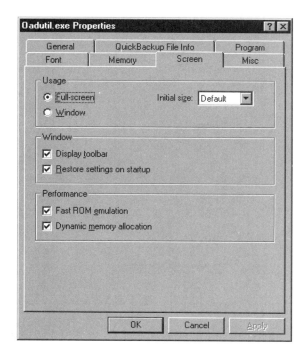

FIGURE 12.7:
The Screen tab
on the DOS
Properties sheet

Except for the Full-Screen versus Window option, the options on this page are best left alone unless you know why you're changing them. If you're sure you need to make a change, right-click an item and select What's This? If you understand what's in the box, you're hereby authorized to make the change.

Switching from a Window to Full Screen (and Back Again)

To switch a DOS program window to full screen, just press Alt+Enter. Press Alt+Enter a second time to return to the window.

To switch from a DOS program running full screen to the Windows 98 Desktop, press Alt+Tab and cycle through the open windows (by continuing to press Tab while holding down the Alt key) until you reach the Desktop.

Miscellaneous Properties

The Misc tab of the Properties sheet (shown in Figure 12.8) lets you tweak several characteristics that don't fit in any of the other categories.

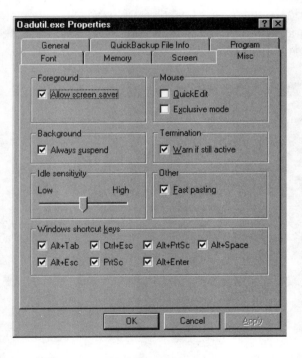

FIGURE 12.8:
The Misc tab on the DOS Properties sheet

The properties you can set here include:

Allow Screen Saver   When this box is checked, the Windows screen saver is allowed to come on when this program is in the foreground. If this box isn't checked, an active DOS program will keep your screen saver from kicking in.

Quick Edit   Allows you to use your mouse to select text for cut-and-copy operations. If this box is cleared, you must use Mark on the Edit menu of the program to mark text.

Exclusive Mode   Lets the mouse work exclusively with this program. This means that when this program is open, the mouse won't be available outside this program's window.

Always Suspend   When this box is checked, no system resources are allocated to this program while it's in the background (open, but not the active window). If this is a communications or other type of program that you want churning away in the background while you do something else, don't check this box.

Warn If Still Active   Some DOS programs (such as WordPerfect for DOS) are very fussy about being closed properly. When this box is checked, you'll get a warning message if you try to close the window without closing the program first.

Idle Sensitivity   When this slider is set too high, the DOS program will release resources and processing time more quickly to other, foreground tasks. For communications programs, however, you will probably want to set this to the low side.

Fast Pasting   This allows a faster method of pasting, but if you have trouble with pasting correctly in this application, clear the box.

Windows Shortcut Keys   Generally you will want to leave these alone unless your DOS program absolutely needs to use one of these keystrokes. Clear the appropriate box or boxes if there are special keystrokes normally used by Windows 98 that you want passed on to your DOS program instead.

Getting DOS Programs to Run

If your favorite DOS application is having trouble running in Windows 98, there are a variety of ways to get it going. They are presented here in approximately the order you should try them—from addressing the relatively mild to addressing the seriously serious. You should try these only if you have problems running a program after you have installed it, and after you have tried to reach the tech support line for the program.

NOTE The default settings in Windows 98 are excellent for the vast majority of DOS-based programs and should only be messed with if you're having problems.

- Run the program full screen. You can do this by pressing Alt+Enter when the program is active, or from the program's Properties sheet. Select Full-Screen from the Screen page. This should be all that most graphical programs need, and with text-only programs this step can usually be skipped.
- Give the program only the kind of memory it absolutely needs. From the Memory page of the Properties sheet, select None for any memory types that you know the program doesn't need. Most DOS programs will not use Extended (XMS) memory or DPMI memory, so those are good choices to try turning off first. You can usually find out exactly what type of memory is needed by reading the documentation that came along with the program.
- Give the program the exact amount of memory it needs. If there's a minimum amount of memory that you know the program requires, set the conventional memory setting of the Memory page of the Properties sheet to some figure slightly above that. This will ensure that the program will only attempt to run when there is sufficient memory available.
- Protect the memory that the program uses. On the Memory page of the Properties sheet, check the Protected box in the Conventional Memory section.
- Turn off Dynamic Memory Allocation on the Screen page. If the program uses both text mode and graphics mode (an example would be Symantec's TimeLine), this will prevent Windows 98 from trying to change the amount of memory allocated when there's a mode change.
- Turn off Fast ROM Emulation on the Screen page. This may make the program run a bit more slowly, especially in text mode, but if the program is having problems writing text to the screen, this may help.
- Turn off the Windows 98 screen saver by clearing the Allow Screen Saver checkbox on the Misc page.
- Turn the idle sensitivity down to the minimum by moving the slider for this option on the Misc page all the way to the left.
- If your program refuses to run from within Windows, try lying to it. Click the Advanced button on the Program page, and check the Prevent MS-DOS–Based

Programs from Detecting Windows box. Do this as a last trick before you resort to trying the DOS mode.

- OK, everything else failed, so it's time to get serious. Run the program in MS-DOS mode. This is the last resort for reasons we have already gone into. If nothing else works, this will. From the Advanced Program Settings dialog box of the Program page of the Properties sheet, check the MS-DOS Mode box. If the program needs special CONFIG.SYS and AUTOEXEC.BAT files, type them into the appropriate boxes, or use the current versions by checking the Use Current MS-DOS Configuration box.

TIP

This list of troubleshooting tips should help you get that recalcitrant DOS program to behave. But a word of warning: Never change more than one thing at a time! If you try something and it doesn't work, return to the default settings and try the next one on the list. If you try to change too many things at once, you're likely to make the situation worse—and even if it does work, you won't be sure which setting was the important one.

MS-DOS Prompt

As you've probably noticed by now, there's an MS-DOS Prompt listing on your Start ➤ Programs menu. Select it and you get a DOS window on your Desktop. You can use this window to run most DOS commands.

If you're the sort of person who uses a DOS window a lot, you can put a shortcut to the DOS prompt on your Desktop or in the Startup folder so it'll be ready and waiting on the Taskbar each time you start the computer. To make a shortcut to the DOS prompt window:

1. Right-click the Start button in the Windows 98 Explorer, and select Open.
2. Click the Programs folder.
3. Locate the MS-DOS Prompt icon.
4. Right-click the icon and either select Create Shortcut to create a shortcut in the current location or drag-and-drop the icon to another location and select Create Shortcut(s) Here.

Important DOS Commands

The DOS commands that come with Windows 98 are fairly few in number compared to earlier version of DOS (which contained well over 100). All the external DOS commands are in the COMMAND folder inside your WINDOWS folder.

This table lists the commands and a brief description of what each one does.

COMMAND NAME	Displays or changes file attributes, and starts new copy of Windows Command Interpreter
CHKDSK.EXE	Reports on disk status and any errors found. Superseded by SCANDISK.EXE
CHOICE.COM	Allows for user input in a batch file. Waits for user to select choice
DEBUG.EXE	Hexadecimal editor and viewer
DISKCOPY.COM	Makes a full copy of a diskette. Same function also available in Explorer
EDIT.COM	New version of older file editor
EXTRACT.EXE	Extracts files from a cabinet (.CAB) file
FC.EXE	Compares files
FDISK.EXE	Makes and removes hard drive partitions
FIND.EXE	Locates text in a file
FORMAT.COM	Formats disks
LABEL.EXE	Adds, removes, or changes a disk label
MEM.EXE	Displays total memory, amount in use, and amount available
MODE.COM	Configures system devices
MORE.COM	Displays output one screen at a time
MOVE.EXE	Moves and renames one or more files
NAMEDOSKEY.COM	Beloved of all DOS-geeks, edits command lines, makes macros, and starts new copy of Windows Command Interpreter
SHARE.EXE	Sets file locking. No longer needed in a DOS window, but can be used in MS-DOS mode
SORT.EXE	Sorts input
START.EXE	Runs a program

SUBST.EXE	Associates a drive letter with a particular path
SYS.COM	Copies system files to a disk, making the disk bootable
XCOPY.EXE	Copies files and whole directories, including subdirectories
XCOPY32.EXE	A juiced-up version of XCOPY with more functions, plus the ability to copy long file names

These commands are rarely used by Windows 98 users. In fact, several of them (such as FORMAT) have their own counterpart in Windows 98. But, should you need to perform specialized commands (such as FDISK or DEBUG), they're there for you.

What's Next?

Now that we've covered many of the software issues of Windows 98, it's time to cast an eye toward hardware. This is where Windows 98 stands out from earlier versions of Windows. In the next chapter, we'll talk about adding and removing hardware, and—if Windows 98 is reluctant—getting it to recognize all the pieces of your system now and in the future.

Chapter 13

HARDWARE CHANGES WITH WINDOWS 98

- **Adding new hardware to Windows 98**
- **Making a modem work**
- **Adding or removing a printer**
- **Troubleshooting the troublesome**

Changing hardware on a PC has always been a challenge (to say the least) because most PCs are made up of a hard drive from one manufacturer, a video card from another, a sound card built somewhere in Asia, and a modem manufactured by someone you never heard of. And once everything was functioning, changing your system by installing a new hard drive or a different modem was more grief than most could bear. But now with Windows 98, getting all these disparate parts to work together is easy.

Getting different hardware components to work together began to get easier with the wide adoption of what's called the *Plug-and-Play* standard. Any hardware built to this is recognized and installed by Windows 98 without fuss or muss. But even older hardware—like that modem handed down to you by your annoyingly techie brother-in-law—can be installed in just a few steps. In this chapter, you'll see how easy it is to get Windows 98 to recognize your new hardware as well as how to troubleshoot any hardware that gets flaky.

Adding New Hardware in Windows 98

With hardware built to the Plug-and-Play specification, you can shut down the computer, install the new hardware, and, when you turn the computer on again, Windows 98 will detect the new hardware and do whatever is necessary to make the device work.

This is, of course, the ideal situation. You do nothing. Windows 98 does everything. Always try this approach first.

WARNING   **Be cautious of phrases such as "works with Plug-and-Play" or "works with Windows 98." Neither phrase is very meaningful because practically everything works with both Plug-and-Play and Windows 98. What you're looking for when you buy new hardware is a device that's built to the Plug-and-Play standard. Also watch out for anything that's a too-good-to-be-true bargain. It may well be from a company dumping the last of their non–Plug-and-Play stock. You don't want to buy old technology.**

Other devices (most notably modems) sometimes have to be pointed out to Windows 98, which is where the Add New Hardware Wizard comes in.

Start this Wizard using Start ➤ Settings ➤ Control Panel ➤ Add New Hardware. The first screen of the Wizard opens.

Click Next to get to the following page of the Wizard. You can select Cancel at any time in the Wizard to stop the installation process, or Back to change an option you've already chosen.

On the second page of the Wizard, Windows 98 will tell you that its next step is to search and detect the hardware on your system. Carefully read every page of the Wizard so you know what's going on.

You'll see the page shown in Figure 13.1 with a bar across the bottom showing how near you are to finishing. The bar will sometimes look as if it's stalled and nothing's happening, but be patient. Unless the computer is completely silent for at least five minutes, there's still activity going on.

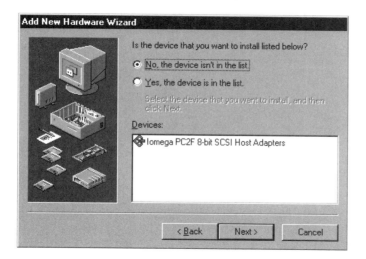

FIGURE 13.1: Specify devices you want installed in this dialog box, and Windows 98 will search for and install them.

After the search, the Wizard will tell you what it found and ask you to confirm if the device you want to install is listed in the Devices area. If it's all correct, click Next and the installation process will be completed.

If the Wizard finds some hardware but it's *not* the hardware you just installed, click No, the Device Isn't in the List. Then click Next and follow the instructions in the next section.

When You Have to Help

But what if, at the end of the search, Windows 98 comes up empty and can't find the hardware you want to install?

Don't worry, this just means that you have to provide some help. When you determine that the device you want to install is not listed, the Add New Hardware Wizard will then search for hardware that is not Plug-and-Play compatible, which is exactly what you want it to do (see Figure 13.2). Click Yes (Recommended) and then click the Next button. The Wizard will search for non–Plug-and-Play compatible devices (which may take a few minutes) and then allow you to finish the installation process by clicking the Finish button.

FIGURE 13.2: Getting ready to search for non-Plug-and-Play compatible devices

If you click No, I Want to Select the Hardware from a List in the screen you see in Figure 13.2 and then click Next, you are telling Windows 98 that you want to select the hardware from a list of what's available. You'll be presented with a list of hardware types. Let's say you're adding a sound card to your system. Scroll down until you see Sound, Video, and Game Controllers and click it once. Then click the Next button.

The Wizard will compile information about these devices and show a box with two panes. The left one is a list of manufacturers. Find the name of the company that made your new piece of hardware and highlight it by clicking once on the name. That will open a list of models on the right (as shown in Figure 13.3).

NOTE

The name or number of your hardware model may be on the hardware itself; it certainly will be in the documentation or on your purchase receipt. Don't have the documentation? Call the manufacturer's technical support line (or find the information on the Web). If you guess and you're wrong, no harm done. You'll just have to run the Add New Hardware Wizard and try again.

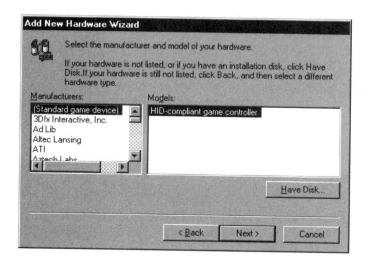

FIGURE 13.3:
Picking the manufacturer and the model

TIP

The Have Disk button is used only when you know that the hardware in question requires some files (called *drivers*) that Windows 98 doesn't provide. These files would be on a disk that came with the hardware. This doesn't happen very often. Most of the time, the Windows 98 drivers will work best.

Highlight the model and click the Next button. What happens then depends on the hardware being installed. Just be sure to read all the instructions you receive.

TIP

Modems and printers can be installed from the Add New Hardware Wizard, but installation is easier using other methods that we will describe later in this chapter.

Continue following the Wizard's instructions until the installation is complete.

Still Not Working?

If you've tried the above steps and your system still can't see the hardware in question, there's plenty more you can do before calling in an expert. Of course, you can go for the expert now and forget the rest of this if you're too uncomfortable messing around with your computer. But you're unlikely to do any harm trying these steps, and you might actually fix the problem yourself!

Checking for Conflicts

Open the System Properties dialog box (Start ➤ Settings ➤ Control Panel ➤ System), and click the Device Manager tab. Click the plus sign (+) beside the type of device you are having trouble with, then right-click the particular device. Click Properties, then click the Resources page, and see if there are any conflicts shown at the bottom of the page (See Figure 13.4). If there are, you'll probably want to run one of the Troubleshooting Wizards from the Windows 98 Help system.

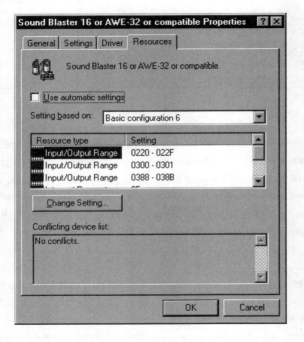

FIGURE 13.4:
Looking for conflicts among hardware

External Devices

If the thing that isn't working is attached to your computer, as opposed to something inside the box, here are a few things to check:

Power   Check that the power is on to the device. (Examples of devices include printers and external backup drives such as Jaz or Zip drives.) Even if the power is on, try turning the power off and back on. This single step will clear an amazing percentage of all hardware problems.

Cable connections   Make sure that the cable that connects the device and the computer is solidly attached at both ends, with all the screws that lock the connectors screwed in.

Cable integrity   Check the cable and make sure that your cat hasn't decided that it looked like a tasty supplement to her kibble. If you are in doubt, use another cable to test the hardware.

Internal Devices

If the problem is with something inside the computer box, it gets trickier. First, shut down Windows 98 completely and turn the power off. Then carefully remove the screws that hold your computer's box together and put them somewhere safe. Remove the cover to your computer. Here are a few things to check:

Cables   Check that all the cables are firmly attached and that there is no obvious physical evidence of problems (a worn spot or burn mark).

Cards   Make sure that all the cards are firmly placed in their slots. It's easy to install a card in such a way that it's sort of loose. This will cause the device to work intermittently or not at all.

Dirt   Over time, the amount of dust and dirt that builds up inside your computer's box is astounding. This can actually degrade performance or cause a device to stop working since the dirt can provide a conductive path. Remove dirt either by using a small amount of compressed air or one of those tiny computer vacuums. Or you can just do what everybody else does, huff and puff and blow the dirt loose.

When you have checked everything you can inside the computer box, before you put the cover back on, power the computer back up and see if you have corrected the problem. Be sure to turn off the computer again before you put the cover back on.

Video Problems

Most video problems can be traced to a driver problem and are out of your scope of control. But here are a few things to look at:

Distortion   If your picture is highly distorted, especially along one edge, you may be suffering from interference with other equipment or monitors in the area. Check where your cable is running, and try moving it to see if that helps. If not, you may need to figure out which piece of equipment is causing the interference and move either it or the computer.

Setting defaults   Your video card needs to have its options set from DOS and won't let you just run the utilities in a DOS window from inside Windows 98? Well, in the first place, shame on the manufacturer! But to get around this problem, select Shut Down from the Start menu. Then select the option Restart the

Computer in MS-DOS Mode. Once you've run the utility that the video card requires, you can exit and reboot into Windows 98 again. With video problems, it's almost always fruitful to get in touch with the manufacturer of the card and ask about "new drivers." Don't be shy; this is one inquiry they're *very* used to getting.

Modems

In the past, modems (along with printers, discussed in the next section) have been the worst possible pains-in-the-neck to get installed. There has been some steady improvement over the years, and Windows 98 is a big step forward. Modems are still quirky animals, but Windows 98 gives you a lot of help in solving whatever problems might occur.

All the steps for getting a modem up and running are included in the Modem Properties sheet you see in Figure 13.5. You can open this sheet by clicking the Modems icon in the Control Panel.

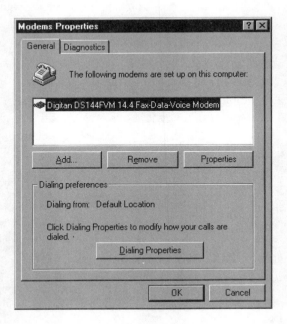

FIGURE 13.5:
The Modem Properties sheet

As you can see, in the window that opens, you'll see which modem (or modems) are set up on the computer.

Adding a Modem

If no modem is listed and you need to install one:

1. Shut down Windows 98 (click the Start button and select Shut Down). Then turn the computer off. Install the modem.
   - If it's an external modem, you need to plug it into a serial port on the back of the computer box. You'll also need to plug the modem's electrical cord into an outlet, then make sure to turn the modem *on* before proceeding.
   - For an internal modem, you'll need to open the computer box. The instructions that came with the modem should help. Be sure that you firmly seat the modem card into the motherboard.
2. Turn your computer back on and let Windows 98 start. If Windows 98 does not automatically recognize the new installation, click the Modems icon in the Control Panel.
3. In the Modems Properties window, click the Add button.
4. Windows 98 will volunteer to find the modem for you and install it. Take advantage of this offer and click Next.
5. The system will search the communications ports and report its findings.
6. If the finding is correct, click the Next button. If Windows 98 came up with the wrong information, click the Change button and select the right manufacturer and type from the list provided and *then* click Next. The process will continue and you'll be notified of a successful installation.

Removing a Modem

If you change modems (or install the wrong one), it's easy to correct the situation.

1. Open the Modems icon in the Control Panel.
2. On the General page, highlight the modem name.
3. Click the Remove button, and it's gone!

TIP   **Some modem problems in Windows 98 arise when pre–Windows 98 communications software intervenes and changes a modem setting without your knowledge. If you repeatedly get a "modem will not initialize" message, try removing the modem from the General page and adding it again. Sometimes just shutting down the computer and starting it up again will do the trick. You may even need to switch software or upgrade your existing software to a Windows 98 version.**

Modem Settings

To find the hardware-type settings for your modem, click the Modems icon in the Control Panel. Highlight your modem (if it isn't already) and select Properties. What opens is the Properties sheet for this particular modem (see Figure 13.6).

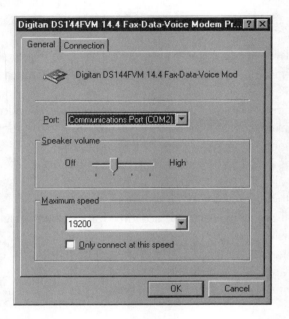

FIGURE 13.6: This is the place to check modem settings.

On the General page you'll find:
- The full name of the modem
- The port the modem is connected to
- A slider for setting the volume of the modem speaker
- A drop-down box for setting the maximum speed

NOTE These settings (except for volume, which is strictly a matter of preference) rarely need to be fooled with. That's because they come from what Windows 98 knows about your specific modem. Only change the settings when you've had some difficulty with your modem being recognized or you're sure a particular setting is wrong.

The Connection Page

On the Connection page are more of the hardware settings. Again, unless you have a good reason for changing the Connection preferences, leave them alone. The Call Preferences can be changed if you find the default ones unsuitable.

Advanced Settings

If you click the Advanced button on the Connection page, you'll see the window in Figure 13.7. These settings are rarely anything to be concerned about. They're just here for those odd and infrequent times when it might be necessary to force error correction or use software for error control.

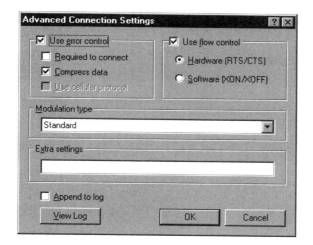

FIGURE 13.7:
The Advanced settings can sometimes help with a difficult installation.

Dialing Properties

In addition to centralizing the modem's hardware and software settings, you also want to enter information about how you're dialing and where you're dialing from. Windows 98 allows multiple dialing locations to be configured, so if you travel with your computer, you can make calls from your branch office (or the ski resort in Gstaad where you take your vacations) without making complex changes.

Click the Modems icon in the Control Panel, then click Dialing Properties on the General page and fill out the information for your location. Click the New button to supply additional locations. When you change physical locations, you need only tell

Windows 98 where you are (see Figure 13.8) and all your necessary dialing information will be loaded.

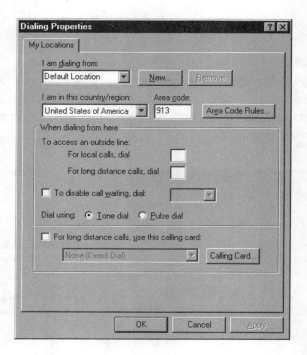

FIGURE 13.8: When you travel with your computer, you don't have to redo your communications settings when you change locations.

Modem Solutions

As a general rule, when your modem is uncooperative, it's for obvious reasons:

- It's not plugged into a phone line. Or, the wall and phone lines are plugged into the wrong modem receptacles at the back of the modem.
- The modem is turned off or it's not plugged into an active electrical socket (external modems).
- One or more programs have confused the settings.

This usually happens when an older communications program is used with Windows 98. Suffice it to say, communications programs written for earlier versions of Windows and not updated for Windows 98 can change your modem's settings. Not all older programs do this—just some. If this happens, you'll try to use another communications program and get an error message that says something like "Initialization failure" or "Modem not recognized." The problem can usually be fixed by removing your modem (as described earlier in this chapter) and then adding it again. This isn't really difficult, but it is a pain and a delay. More permanent solutions include:

- Upgrading to the Windows 98 version of the software.
- Changing to a communications program that doesn't cause other programs to fail.

Another problem in Windows 98 is that most programs can't share a communications port. You become aware of this when you are ready to receive a fax and then try to connect to America Online or CompuServe or your Internet Service Provider. In this case, you'll get a message such as "The modem can't be found" or "The modem is not responding." The immediate solution is to close the fax software before starting another communications program. The long-term fix is to upgrade all your communications programs to ones that are TAPI-aware.

Printers

Working with printers is generally a lot easier in Windows 98 than in any previous version of Windows. As in Windows 3.1 and Windows 95, printers are set up to use a common set of drivers so you don't have to configure each program independently for printing. Adding or removing a printer is as easy as point and click, and sharing printers over a network is painless. And again, especially if you buy a new printer, the Windows 98 Plug-and-Play feature should be able to recognize and install your printer with no extra effort on your part.

Printers are accessible through the Printers folder inside My Computer, off the Start menu under Settings, or in the Printers folder in the Control Panel. And, of course, you can drag a shortcut to the Printers folder (or any of the printers in the folder) to your Desktop. Open the Printers folder to see what printers are installed for your system.

Adding a Printer

Setting up a printer is part of the installation routine. But if your printer isn't installed or you want to add another printer or a network printer, it's very easy to do.

For a printer that's connected directly to your computer, click the Printers folder and follow these steps (clicking the Next button after each entry):

1. Select Add Printer.
2. When the Add Printer Wizard starts, click Next, and check the Local Printer entry. (This step will be skipped if you're not on a network.)
3. Highlight the name of the printer's manufacturer and the model name.
4. Indicate whether you want to keep the existing driver (which is the recommended choice) or use a new one. In almost all cases, you will want to keep the existing one.
5. Select the port you want to use. Unless you know of some special circumstances, choose LPT1.
6. Type in the name you want the printer to be known by.
7. Print a test page to verify all is well. Then click Finish.

Adding a Network Printer

A network printer is plugged into someone else's computer—a computer you have access to via a network.

To install a network printer so you can use it, click the Printers folder and follow these steps (clicking Next after each entry):

1. Click Add Printer. When the Add Printer Wizard starts, click Next Then, select Network Printer, and click Next again.
2. You'll need to tell the system the address of the printer, so click the Browse button to look for available printers. Highlight the printer and click OK.
3. If you expect to print from DOS programs, click Yes so the system can add the necessary information to the printer setup.
4. Enter the name you want to call the printer and check whether you want this printer to be the default printer. Only check Yes if you expect to be using the network printer for the majority of your printing.
5. Print a test page to make sure everything's running properly, and then click Finish.

TIP   To be able to use a printer set up this way, both the printer and the computer it's connected to must be switched on.

Removing a Printer

Sometimes you may need to uninstall a printer, which is quite easily done. Just right-click the printer's icon in the Printers folder and select Delete. You'll be asked to confirm the deletion. You may also be asked if you want to delete files that are associated with this printer that won't be necessary if the printer is gone. If you're getting rid of the printer permanently, select Yes. If you're planning on reinstalling the same printer soon, select No.

Printer Settings

To get at the settings for a printer, you need to right-click the printer's icon and select Properties. On the Properties sheet that opens, you can set details as to fonts, paper, how the printer treats graphics, and so on.

Most of these settings are made by the printer driver that Windows 98 installed to run the printer. Change ones that you need to change, but avoid changing settings if you're not clear what the setting does. You can inadvertently disable your printer. If this happens, you can usually cure it by deleting the printer (see the previous section) and then installing it again.

Printer Solutions

Besides the usual paper jam problems that we all hate, you can easily run into subtle conflicts between your application program and the printer drivers, as well as downright bugs in either. Here are some things to try, in roughly the order to try them:

Printer Online   This happens all the time, especially if the printer's not right next to you where you can see it. Make sure the online light is on.

Power   Turn the power off and back on. This does two things. It forces you to check that the power is actually on, and, more to the point, it causes the printer to do a complete reset, getting back to the known starting point that Windows 98 expects to find it in. Some printers allow you to press and keep down the power or online switch which forces the printer to cycle through, clear its memory, and reset itself.

Cable   Check the cable connections on both ends.

Switch Boxes, "Buffalo Boxes," Spoolers   There are all sorts of ways to share a printer that are left over from the bad old DOS days. With networking built into Windows 98, these probably won't last long, but if you have one of these boxes, temporarily connect the printer directly to your computer with nothing in between except the actual cable (preferably a nice short one). Now try printing. If you can print now, you know the problem isn't the printer itself. It's the device between your computer and the printer.

Network Print Servers   Same approach as for switch boxes. Try connecting directly to the printer without the intervening network connection.

Test File   Print a simple test file from Notepad—a few words are enough to know if the printer is being recognized by Windows 98. If the test file prints, but you have a problem with more complicated printing from your application, chances are you have a problem with the application or possibly the printer driver. Check with the company that makes the application for a newer version, or check with the manufacturer of your printer to see if there's a newer driver.

If none of these help, try the print troubleshooter that comes with Windows 98. Select Help from the Start menu. On the Contents page, click Troubleshooting and then on Windows 98 Troubleshooters and select Print. The guide is interactive in that you select the problem you're having, and then you're stepped through the process of finding a solution.

Solving Hardware Conflicts

No matter how much Windows 98 does to let you simply plug in your new hardware and play with it immediately, sooner or later you're going to have problems with either a new piece of hardware or an existing one. Sometimes the source of the problem is a subtle conflict between two (or more) pieces of hardware, but much more often the root cause is something fairly simple and straightforward.

Open the System Properties dialog box (Properties of My Computer or System from the Control Panel) and click the Device Manager tab. Click the type of device you are having trouble with and see if there are any conflicts shown. If there are, then you'll probably want to run one of the Troubleshooter Wizards.

You can reach the Troubleshooter Wizards by clicking Help on the Start menu and then clicking Troubleshooting and then Windows 98 Troubleshooters. As you can see in Figure 13.9, you'll see an entire list of troubleshooters from which you can select the one that most closely matches your problem.

Troubleshooters will resolve the vast majority of any hardware problems you might have. For example, if you're having trouble with Sound, click the Sound Wizard shown in Figure 13.9. That Wizard will begin as you see in Figure 13.10. Just follow the directions, and click the buttons as required. We're not going to trace through every step of using this tool because there are just too many directions it could branch in, depending on what it finds and how you respond to its questions.

If your problem is a sort of general "it doesn't work" where "it" is some device, there are a few things to look for or think about. If none of these seem to fit the bill, start the Windows 98 Help system, and see if there's a Wizard for it in the Troubleshooting section. Figure 13.10 gives an example of a troubleshooter for problems with sound.

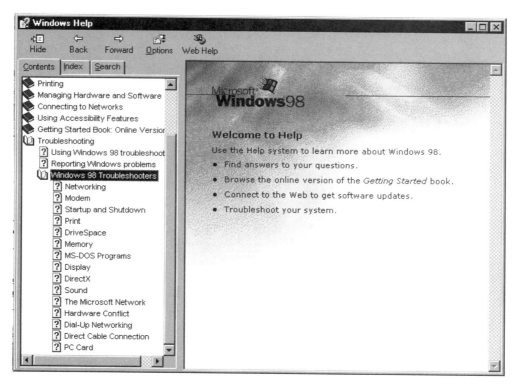

FIGURE 13.9:   The hardware conflict troubleshooter

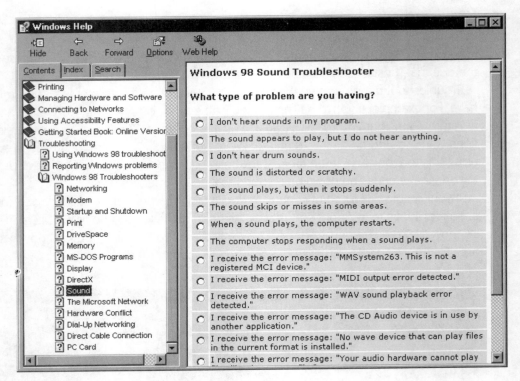

FIGURE 13.10: The Sound Troubleshooter

What's Next?

In this chapter, we've covered some of the most common hardware questions and answers. Next we'll move on to the features and programs that come with Windows 98, starting with some treats for your eyes and ears.

Chapter 14

SEEING AND HEARING MULTIMEDIA

FEATURING

- **Setting up multimedia**
- **Playing and programming CDs**
- **Playing video**
- **Recording and playing sound**
- **Turning the volume up (and down)**

The multimedia capabilities built into many computers and now implemented by Windows 98 may strike you more as toys than anything useful. People who use computers intensely, as writers, accountants, and computer consultants, are not looking for more ways to get distracted, but for ways to remove distractions. Who needs moving pictures or music to get a book written?

Turns out that's the wrong question. The fact is that publishing is different in the age of the computer, and so are accounting and data crunching. Books can be published online with animation, pictures, or music. Spreadsheets can include pictures of products or factories to make data more concrete. Databases can include pictures of clients and employees to make information more personal.

This chapter examines the CD Player, Media Player, ActiveMovie Control, and Sound Recorder built into Windows 98. The first can be used for your private enjoyment or to accompany a presentation with a soundtrack. The last three can be used to display and enhance multimedia presentations.

You'll find all the Multimedia applications by clicking the Start button and proceeding through Programs ➤ Accessories ➤ Entertainment.

Can't Find Multimedia?

You won't have a Multimedia menu in your Accessories menu if the Multimedia applications weren't installed at the time Windows 98 was installed. If this is the case, it's easily remedied:

1. Go to the Control Panel and click Add/Remove Programs.
2. Click the Windows Setup tab at the top of the Add/Remove Programs Properties dialog box.
3. Scroll through the list of options in the dialog box until you locate Multimedia.
4. Double-click Multimedia to see a list of multimedia programs available.
5. Click the checkboxes next to as many programs as you want to install. (For the purposes of this chapter, make sure CD Player, Media Player, Sound Recorder, and Volume Control are selected.)
6. OK your way out, and insert your Windows 98 CD-ROM as requested to complete the installation.

NOTE **You can associate sounds with different events—for example, a program opens and a particular sound plays. Chapter 15 covers how to do this.**

Working with the CD Player

The CD Player lets you play audio CDs using your CD-ROM drive, sound card, and speakers. If you want to listen through external speakers, a sound card is required. But even without a sound card, you can listen through headphones plugged into the CD-ROM drive itself.

To open the CD Player, follow these steps:

1. Click the Start button on the Taskbar.
2. Select Programs.
3. Select Accessories in the Program menu.
4. Select Entertainment in the Accessories menu. (Depending on the programs you selected when you installed Windows 98, you'll probably have several applications on this menu.)
5. Click the CD Player option. That will start the CD Player program (see Figure 14.1). You can then select options under the View menu to change the display.

FIGURE 14.1:
To change the look of the CD Player, select an option on the View menu.

All you have to do to start using the CD Player is supply a music CD. The player will play it through your sound card and speakers (plugged into the audio jacks on the back of the CD-ROM controller) or through the headphone jack in the front of your CD-ROM drive.

TIP

By default, the CD Player starts playing the CD the minute you put it in the drive. To overrule the automatic play for a particular CD, hold down the Shift key while you insert the CD. To turn this automatic play feature off completely (or back on), right-click the My Computer icon and select Properties. On the Device Manager page, double-click CD-ROM, highlight your CD-ROM drive's name, and click Properties. On the Settings page, click the Auto Insert Notification box. With a check in this box, CDs will play automatically. Without the check, you need to open the CD Player applet yourself.

How It Works

To try out the CD Player:

1. Put a music CD in the CD-ROM drive. (We recommend a Gipsy Kings CD, but if you don't have one available any old music CD will do.)
2. Click the large triangle (the Play button) next to the digital readout.
3. The CD Player will begin playing your CD. If you have Disc/Track Info enabled from the View menu, that information will appear in the display, as you can see in Figure 14.2.

FIGURE 14.2:
Here's what the CD Player looks like when its working and the Disc/Track Info option on the View menu is enabled.

Here is an explanation of the various buttons and options you'll find on the CD Player:

Play   The large right-pointing triangle is the Play button. In Figure 14.2, it is gray because the CD is already playing. (There's no reason to click the Play button when the CD is playing; but if you do, no harm is done.)

Pause   Next to the Play button is a button with two vertical bars. This is the Pause button. Click it to pause the music while you run to answer the door or the phone.

Stop   The last button at the right end of the top tier is the Stop button. Click it when you're tired of listening to the music or when the boss walks into your office. It will stop playing.

Previous Track   The first button at the left end of the second tier of buttons looks like a double arrowhead pointing left toward a vertical line. Click this button once to move to the beginning of the current piece, click it twice to move to the previous cut on the CD.

Skip Backwards   The second button on the second tier looks like a double arrowhead pointing left. This is the Skip Backwards button. Each time you click it, you will move back one second in the music. To move back through a track quickly, keep this button pressed until you get to the point you want to go back to.

Skip Forward   The third button on the second tier is the Skip Forward button. It looks like a double arrowhead pointing to the right. Each time you click it, you will move one second forward in the music. To move forward through a track quickly, keep this button pressed until you get to the point you want to go forward to.

Next Track   The fourth button on the second tier is the Next Track button. It looks like a double arrowhead pointing right toward a vertical bar. It will take you instantly to the next song. Click it twice to move forward two songs, and so on.

Eject   The final button at the right end of the second tier of buttons looks like a horizontal bar with an arrow pointing upward on top of it. This is the Eject button. It will cause your CD-ROM drive to stick its tongue out at you—which is what it looks like when a CD is ejected from most drives.

Setting Time and Play Options

Is that all there is? Certainly not. If you're an information freak, click the digital read-out. Before you click, the readout will tell you the current track number and the elapsed time for that track. The first time you click, you'll see the track number and the time remaining on the track. The second click will display the time remaining for the whole CD (shown in Figure 14.3).

FIGURE 14.3:
Getting instant information about the play time remaining on the whole CD

If you want to set time settings without clicking the digital display, pull down the View menu and select from:

- Track Time Elapsed
- Track Time Remaining
- Disc Time Remaining

The Options menu lets you opt for Continuous Play (plays tracks in sequence), Random Order (plays tacks in a random order), Intro Play (plays just the introduction of each track), or a combination of these (such as the introduction to each song in a random order). There is also an option called Preferences. Select the Preferences option. It allows you to set the font size for the digital readout as well as the length of Intro play (10 seconds is the default).

TIP Want a shortcut to the CD Player or the Media Player on your Desktop? Open the Windows folder and look for the file CDPLAYER.EXE or MPLAYER.EXE, then right-click and drag the file to the Desktop. Release the right mouse button and select Create Shortcut(s) Here.

Editing the Play List

And if that's not enough, there's an entire layer of the CD Player we haven't even touched yet. Here's how to access it:

1. Pull down the Disc menu.
2. Select Edit Play List. You will see the dialog box shown in Figure 14.4.

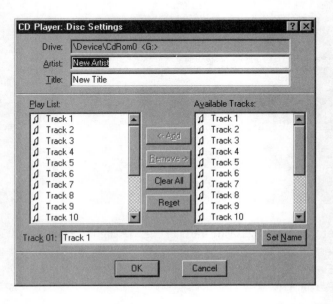

FIGURE 14.4:
The CD Player: Disc Settings dialog box lets you program a play list.

Using this dialog box, you can do something that owners of CD players often never get the hang of—programming your player to play specific songs in a specific order.

By Track Number

As an example, let's set up the CD Player to play Tracks 5, 12, and 3 on this particular disk. Here's how:

1. Click the Clear All button to clear all the entries on the Play List.
2. Double-click Track 5 in the Available Tracks list box. It will appear in the Play List.
3. Double-click Track 12 and then Track 3 in the Available Tracks list box.
4. Click OK and the CD Player will play the songs in the order you specified.

By Track Name

If you'd rather deal with track names than track numbers, you can insert names for each of the tracks (or just the ones you care about) as follows:

1. Click a track—for this example, we'll click Track 3 in the Available Tracks list.
2. Click the Track *x* text box (to the left of the Set Name button).
3. Refer to your CD packaging to get the name of the third song on the CD.
4. Type the name in the text box. (You can type it next to Track 3, or delete Track 3 and type the name instead.)
5. Click the Set Name button. In the Available Tracks list and in the Play List, Track 3 will be replaced with the name you just typed.
6. Just for the sake of completeness, click the text box near the top marked Artist and type the performer(s) name.
7. Highlight the text box marked Title and type the CD's title.
8. Click the OK button.

Once you've supplied your CD Player with this information, the program will remember it, recognize the CD, and follow your programmed instructions every time you play it.

TIP   If you have a CD-ROM player capable of playing multiple disks, Multidisc Play will be an option on the Options menu. Select it, and when you click the downward-pointing arrow at the right end of the Artist box, you will see each of the CDs available to you. Select the CD you want to play.

Playing Sounds with the Media Player

These days the word *media* conjures up images of talk show blather about how everything's the fault of the press. Not this media. The media in this section are fun—never trouble.

Let's begin, as always, by first opening the Media Player program:

1. Click the Start button on the Taskbar.
2. Select Programs ➤ Accessories ➤ Entertainment ➤ Media Player.

You will see something similar to the window shown in Figure 14.5.

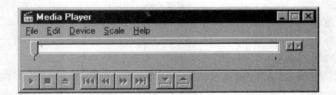

FIGURE 14.5:
The Media Player looks like this.

The Media Player will play Video for Windows animated files (.AVI), sound files (.WAV), MIDI files (.MID and .RMI), and many other files, on your audio CD. Yes, that's right. You can use Media Player to play your music CDs just like you use CD Player, except that Media Player offers fewer customization options.

Playing Files

Windows 98 comes with a variety of multimedia files. To play a file, follow these steps:

1. Pull down the Media Player Device menu and select the type of file you want to play.
2. Locate the file you want to play, double-click or highlight it, and select Open.
3. Click the right-pointing arrow (the Play button).

You can select sections of animation or movies just like you select recorded music tracks (see the "Working with the CD Player" section earlier in this chapter). Although the buttons are in different places than the ones on the CD Player, you should be able to identify them by their icons.

TIP   Can't find the type of file you want to play? Use the Find feature on the Start menu and search by the extension of the file, such as .AVI. If you still can't find any, use the Internet Explorer search tools and see what's on the Internet that is ready to download.

Copying and Pasting Files

You can copy and paste sound, animation, or movie files using the Select buttons, which look like tiny arrows pointing down (Start Selection) and up (End Selection) above a horizontal bar.

Selecting a Section

To select a section of either an audio or video file:

1. Listen (or watch) until you reach the point where the section begins.
2. Click the Start Selection button.
3. Continue listening or watching until you reach the end of the section.
4. Click the End Selection button. The Media Player will show you on its scale a visual representation of the file that you have copied, as you can see in Figure 14.6.
5. Pull down the Edit menu and select Copy Object. (The piece you have selected will be placed on the Clipboard for pasting into any document that supports sound or video files.)

FIGURE 14.6:
Copying part of a media file

Getting Looped

If you want a piece of music, film, or animation to repeat continuously:

1. Pull down the Edit menu, and select Options.
2. Click the option marked Auto Repeat. Your media file will play over and over until you turn off the media player, or you lose your mind and destroy your computer with a fire ax.

Playing Movies

Movies (files with the .AVI extension) can be played through the ActiveMovie Control.

To play a movie:

1. Click the Start button on the Taskbar.
2. Select Programs.
3. Select Accessories in the Program menu.
4. Select Entertainment in the Accessories menu.
5. Click the ActiveMovie Control option. That will produce a dialog box from which you can select the .AVI movie file you want to play.
6. Once the movie is open and ready to play, click the right triangle to start playing the movie (see in Figure 14.7).

FIGURE 14.7:
Playing an .AVI file

NOTE You should be able to find some movie files on the Windows 98 CD-ROM that was used to install Windows. Use the Find tool and search by the extension.

Recording Your Favorite Sounds

If you have an audio input device on your computer (either a microphone or a CD-ROM player), you can use the Sound Recorder to make a .WAV file you can associate with a Windows event or send in a message.

TIP   You can also use the headphones from your portable stereo as a microphone. Just plug them in and talk into one of the earphones. It really works!

Making .WAV Files

Here's how to create a .WAV file with the Sound Recorder:

1. Select Start ➤ Programs ➤ Accessories ➤ Entertainment.
2. Open Sound Recorder. You'll see the Sound Recorder window shown in Figure 14.8.
3. Select New from the File menu.
4. To begin recording, click the button with the dark red dot.
5. Start the CD or start speaking into the microphone.
6. Click the button with the black square to stop recording.
7. Select Save from the File menu and type in a name to save the sound clip.
8. To play the sound clip, just click the right triangle (Play).

FIGURE 14.8:
Create your own .WAV files from a CD-ROM with the Sound Recorder.

The Sound Recorder also lets you play other types of sound clips in the Media Player and record them as .WAV files. The .WAV files you make can be played back with the Sound Recorder or the Media Player.

> **TIP** To easily associate a .WAV file with an event in Windows 98, move the file to the Media folder (inside the Windows folder). See Chapter 15 for the specifics on how to use sound files in this way.

Special Effects and Editing

Use the Effects menu to change some of the sound's qualities—to add an echo or decrease the speed. The sound can also be edited using the menu controls.

Volume Control

The Volume Control panel not only lets you adjust the sound level but also individually tune different types of files. The easiest way to reach the Volume Control panel (see Figure 14.9) is to right-click the small speaker icon at the end of the Taskbar and select Open Volume Controls. You can also open the Volume Control panel from the Entertainment menu under Accessories.

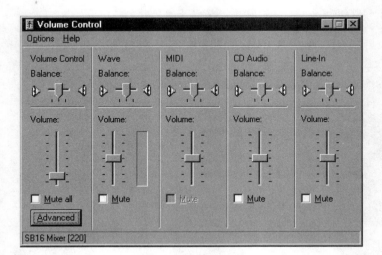

FIGURE 14.9: The Volume Control panel lets you make adjustments to your sound files.

Tone Controls

For tone controls (bass and treble), select Advanced Controls from the Options menu. This will put an Advanced button at the bottom of the Volume Control window. Click this button to open the page shown in Figure 14.10.

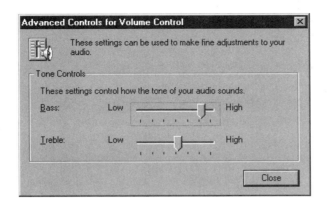

FIGURE 14.10:
Using advanced controls for adjusting different aspects of the volume

Use the slider controls to increase or decrease the treble and bass tones. These settings will affect all the sound files you play.

NOTE   **If Advanced Controls is dimmed on your screen, it means that your hardware doesn't support these functions.**

Setting Volume Control Display

Figure 14.10 shows the default settings for volume control, but you can decide which devices you want to show on the Volume Control panel. Open Volume Control and select Properties from the Options menu.

Select Playback and check the devices you want shown on Volume Control. Likewise, you can display recording levels. The choices will probably differ based on your specific computer hardware.

More Multimedia Settings

There's also a Multimedia icon in the Control Panel that contains mostly advanced settings but some basic ones too.

Click this icon and poke around, right-clicking anything you don't understand and selecting What's This? to get an explanation box. There are a lot of terms here that will be unfamiliar to anyone who's a novice at computer-based sound and video. Experiment, but also take care not to remove a device unintentionally. If you do, you may have to run the Add New Hardware icon in the Control Panel to get the device back.

What's Next?

This chapter hasn't exhausted all the features for eyes and ears. In the next chapter, we'll go on to some neat functions in the Control Panel that also affect how your computer looks and sounds, and you'll learn how to customize settings that make your computer truly your own. And if the computer is not 100 percent your own, you'll also see how to share with other users by creating User Profiles.

Chapter 15

CONTROLLING THE CONTROL PANEL

FEATURING

- **Windows 98 accessibility features**
- **Adding and removing programs and hardware**
- **Getting dates and times right**
- **Personalizing the display and working with fonts**
- **Modifying the keyboard**
- **Setting and using the password**

If you've fiddled around with the Control Panel at all, you can see that it acts as a sort of Mission Central for Windows 98. Some of the settings behind the icons can be reached from other directions, but others can be reached only by way of the Control Panel. Most of the items in the Control Panel help you customize Windows 98 even further. And if you share your computer with other people, the section on passwords will show you how each of you can have a unique Desktop.

You'll find a heading in this chapter for all the usual icons in the Control Panel (listed alphabetically). If the settings behind an icon are detailed elsewhere, you'll be pointed to the correct location.

> **NOTE** Many Windows 98 applications insert their own icons in the Control Panel when you install them. Consult the documentation that came with the programs for information on how to use these icons.

To open the Control Panel, click Start ➤ Settings ➤ Control Panel and you'll see the Control Panel window shown in Figure 15.1.

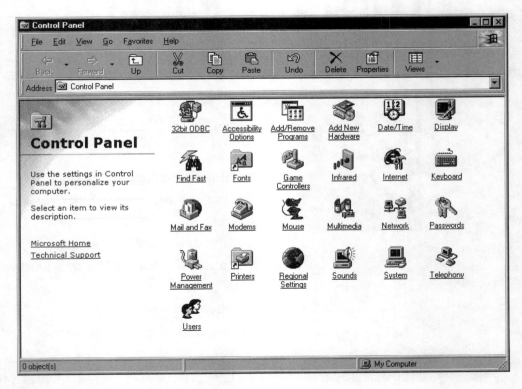

FIGURE 15.1: The Control Panel and its contents

Accessibility Options

The Accessibility Options are installed automatically when Windows 98 is installed. If you want them and they're not on your system, use Add/Remove Programs (covered later in this chapter) to add them. Click this icon and you'll find options for adding sound to the usual visual cues, adding visual cues to the sound ones, using high-contrast fonts and colors for easy reading, and making the keyboard and mouse easier to use for those of us with dexterity problems.

Not all the settings are obvious, so when you come across one that's unclear, right-click the text and then click the What's This? button for more information.

After you've set your settings, don't leave until you click the General tab and check the Automatic Reset section. Put a check next to Turn Off Accessibility Features After Idle For if you want the options to be turned off if the computer isn't used for the period specified in the Minutes box. Clear the checkbox if you want to make the selection of options permanent.

TIP | **The Use Toggle Keys option on the Keyboard page is of great help if you often hit the Caps Lock key inadvertently and look up to find your text looking like: cALL mR. jAMES IN cAPE vERDE. With Toggle Keys on, you'll hear a quiet but distinct warning beep when Caps Lock is switched on.**

Add New Hardware

Add New
Hardware

The functions behind this icon are covered in detail in Chapter 13, "Hardware Changes with Windows 98."

Add/Remove Programs

Add/Remove
Programs

Windows 98 provides a good deal of aid and comfort when it comes to adding or removing programs from your system, especially adding and removing parts of Windows 98 itself. Click this icon in the Control Panel.

The Add/Remove function has three parts, one on each tab:

- Installing or uninstalling software applications
- Installing or removing portions of Windows 98
- Making a Startup Disk to boot from if there's trouble

Install/Uninstall

Installing new programs is easy:

1. Just put the program's first floppy disk in the drive (or if the program came on a compact disk, insert the CD in the proper drive).
2. Click the Install/Uninstall tab.
3. Click the Install button.
4. The program prompts you to insert the first installation disk or the appropriate CD-ROM (see Figure 15.2) and then the install routine of the program takes over.

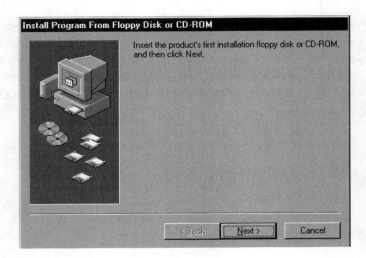

FIGURE 15.2:
The Installation program finds the file named INSTALL or SETUP and installs the program.

A software producer who wants the right to put a Windows 98 logo on a product is supposed to make sure the program can uninstall itself. And more and more Windows 98 applications come with an Uninstall icon that, when clicked, removes everything associated from the installation of the program.

Some programs that work with Windows 98, however, can actually be uninstalled and still leave bits of themselves cluttering your hard disk. How the major programs written for Windows 98 handle Add/Remove varies widely. Some just uninstall themselves without a fuss; others give you the option of removing all or just parts of the program. You'll have to click the program and select Remove to see. *Nothing* will be uninstalled without your OK.

Windows Setup

Click the Windows Setup tab to add or remove a component of Windows 98. The various parts are organized by groups (see Figure 15.3). You can highlight any group and click Details to see the individual components.

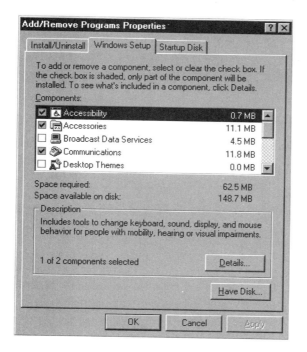

FIGURE 15.3: Here's where you can install and uninstall various parts of Windows 98.

As you click each item in a group, a description of the item's function displays at the bottom of the page. The rules are simple:

- If an item is checked, it's installed. Remove the check mark and it will be removed after you click the OK button.
- If an item is not checked, it's not currently installed on your system. Put a check mark next to it, and it will be installed after you click the OK button.
- If the checkbox is gray, a part of the component is selected for installation. Click the Details button to specify which parts you want installed.

If your Windows installation came on floppies, you'll be asked for one or more disks. If you installed from a CD, you'll have to return the Windows 98 compact disk to the CD drive.

Creating a Startup Disk

If your computer came with Windows 98 already installed, you probably don't have a startup disk. If you installed Windows 98 yourself, you should have one. But, if you lost the disk or made major changes to your system, it's wise to make a new one. Simply click this tab and select Create Disk. You'll be prompted for a floppy and the new Startup disk will be made.

A current Startup disk can be helpful (if not invaluable) to a technician if one day your system fails to boot on its own; so it's best to make a new Startup disk either monthly or whenever you make a major change in software or any change at all in hardware.

WARNING **When you create a Startup disk, the disk is first formatted so everything that was previously on the disk is erased and is not retrievable.**

Date and Time

Date/Time

To reset the day and time shown on your computer, click this icon. This function comes in handy when traveling and using Windows 98 on a laptop. You can use it to change the time zone or reset your computer clock. By default, Windows 98 will reset your clock for daylight savings time in the time zone you've selected. It even knows that Arizona and eastern Indiana don't use daylight savings time, but you have to be sure the time zone is set properly. Use the drop-down box on the Time Zone tab to select your time zone.

Other date and time information:

- Position the mouse pointer over the time display at the end of the Taskbar to see the current month, day, and year.
- For a shortcut to the Date/Time windows, right-click the time display on the Taskbar and select Adjust Date/Time (or just double-click the time display).
- To remove the time from the Taskbar, click the Start button and select Settings ➤ Taskbar & Start Menu. Clear the check mark from before the Show Clock option.

Display

Display

Behind the Display icon in the Control Panel are all the settings that affect your screen display, including colors, screen savers, type faces in windows and dialog boxes, and resolutions. See "Setting Up Your Desktop" in Chapter 2 for details on these settings.

Fonts

Fonts

TrueType fonts are managed in Windows 98 in a clear and understandable way. To see the list of fonts on your computer, click this icon in the Control Panel.

Selecting and Viewing Fonts

The Fonts folder is a little different from the usual run of folders in that the menus show some new items. In the View menu shown in Figure 15.4, you'll find, in addition to the choices for viewing icons and lists, an option called List Fonts by Similarity.

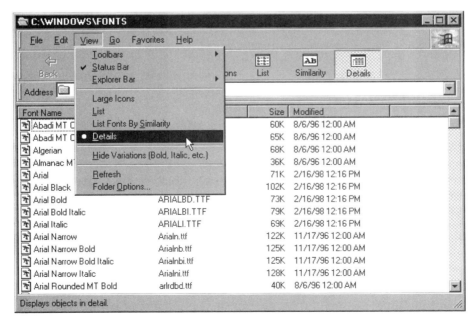

FIGURE 15.4: The View menu is a little different in the Fonts folder

TIP   **If your font list is very long and unwieldy, select View ≻ Hide Variations. That will conceal font variations such as italic and bold and make the list easier to look through.**

Select a font in the List Fonts by Similarity To drop-down box at the top and the other fonts will line up in terms of their degree of similarity. Before you make a commitment, you can right-click any of the font names and select Open or double-click the name of the font to see what it looks like. A window will open with a complete view of the font in question.

Fonts don't have to be physically located in the Windows/Fonts folder to be recognized by Windows 98. You can make a shortcut to a font in another folder and put the shortcut in the Fonts folder. The shortcut is all you need for the font to be installed.

Fonts that are identified with an icon **containing the letter A** are not TrueType fonts. They're not scaleable, which means that at large point sizes they tend to look quite crummy (see Figure 15.5). Many of these fonts should be used only in certain, limited point sizes.

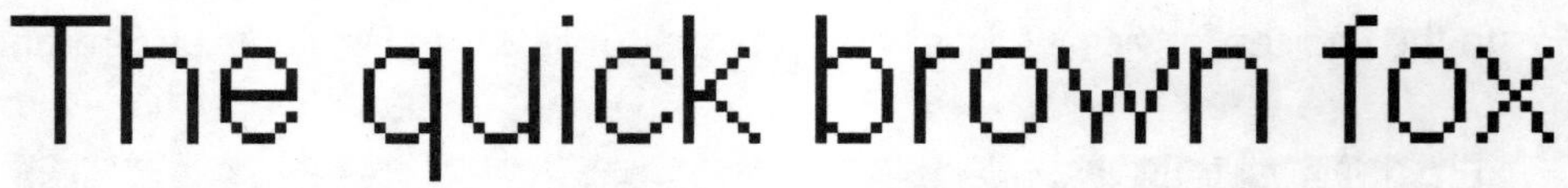

The quick brown fox

FIGURE 15.5:   The non-TrueType fonts are unattractive in larger sizes.

Installing New Fonts

Installing new fonts is a pretty easy project. Just open the Fonts icon in the Control Panel and select Install New Font from the File menu. In the Add Fonts window (see Figure 15.6) you can tell the system, the drive, and the directory where the font(s) reside. If there's one or more TrueType fonts at the location you specify, they'll show up in the List of Fonts window.

Highlight the font or fonts you want installed, and click the OK button. Programs that install fonts on their own may have to be installed on their own.

Other types of fonts, such as those installed by the Adobe Type Manager, will reside elsewhere on your hard drive, depending on the location you selected. You can't put them in the Fonts folder or view them by clicking. However, numerous applications can display fonts, and most font-installing programs have their own viewers.

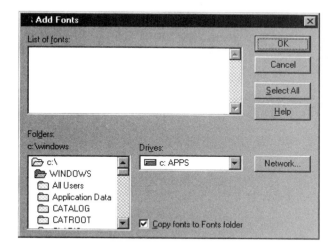

FIGURE 15.6:
Here's where you add new fonts to the folder.

Joysticks

Game Controllers

Click the Game Controllers icon to open a Properties sheet for calibrating your existing joystick or adding a second (or third or fourth) joystick to the setup. If you have a joystick (or game controller) attached to your computer when Windows 98 is installed, this icon will appear in the Control Panel.

TIP

To add a joystick at a later time, turn off your computer and plug the joystick in. Restart your computer. If the Joystick icon doesn't appear in the Control Panel, then Windows 98 was unable to detect it. Use Add New Hardware to install it.

After you click Add, you'll see there's a joystick type for all occasions (as shown in Figure 15.7).

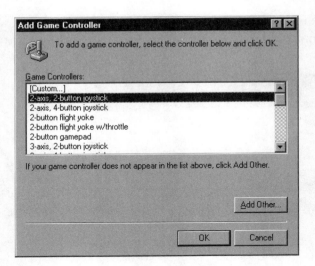

FIGURE 15.7:
Many different varieties of game devices are listed in the Windows 98 Control Panel, and you can select the one that's best for you.

Keyboards

The installation routine of Windows 98 finds the keyboard plugged into your computer and recognizes it, so you normally don't have to fuss with these settings. But if you need to change keyboards, adjust the keyboard's speed, or install a keyboard designed for another language, click this icon in the Control Panel.

The two tabs on the Keyboard Properties sheet cover these different types of settings—explained in the following sections.

Keyboard Speed

Click the Speed tab to adjust keyboard rates. Here are the available settings:

Repeat Delay   Determines how long a key has to be held down before it starts repeating. The difference between the Long and Short setting is only about a second.

Repeat Rate   Determines how fast a key repeats. Fast means if you hold down a key you almost instantly get vvvvvvvvvvvvery long streams of letters. (Click the practice area to test this setting.)

Cursor Blink Rate   Makes the cursor blink faster or slower. The blinking cursor on the left demonstrates the setting.

Keyboard Languages

If you need multiple language support for your keyboard, click the Language tab. Click the Add button to select languages from Afrikaans to Swedish—including 15 varieties of Spanish. If you have more than one language selected, the settings on the Language tab let you choose a keyboard combination to switch between languages (see Figure 15.8).

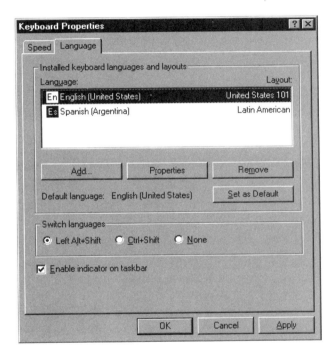

FIGURE 15.8:
Setting up your keyboard for more than one language

Highlight the language you want to be the default (the one that's enabled when you start your computer) and click the Set as Default button.

Mail and Fax

Mail and Fax

Mail and fax services have most of a chapter devoted to them. Check Chapter 10 for mail and other communications information.

Modems

Modems

The settings behind this icon are covered in the "Modems" section of Chapter 13.

Mouse

Mouse

Everything you ever wanted to know (and more) about mouse settings—including the use of settings connected to this icon—can be found in Chapter 4, devoted entirely to mouse use.

Multimedia

Multimedia

Read Chapter 14 for information on multimedia applications that come with Windows 98 and how to set them up. The settings behind this icon are covered there as well.

Passwords

Passwords

When you sign on to Windows 98 the first time, you're asked to provide a name and password. If you're the only one using a computer and you don't want to deal with a password every time you turn the machine on, leave the password blank. Then click the Network icon in the Control Panel, and under Primary Network Logon (on the Configuration page) make sure Windows Logon is selected. You won't be troubled with a request for a password again.

On the other hand, if you later want to start using a password or change the one you have, click the Passwords icon in the Control Panel.

Click the Change Passwords tab and enter the information requested. (If you had no previous password, leave the Old Password field empty.)

One Computer, Many Users

Everyone who sets up Windows 98 creates a Desktop that is unique. This is great—until you have to share your computer with another person (or even persons). Fortunately, Windows 98 allows you to set up a profile for each user. You'll each have to log on with your name and particular password, but once you do, the Desktop that appears will be the one you set up—programs, shortcuts, colors, and so forth, all just as you arranged.

Setting Up a User Profile

To allow user profiles, you'll need to follow these steps:

1. Click the Passwords icon in the Control Panel.
2. Select the User Profiles tab. Click the button for the second choice: Users Can Customize Their Preferences...
3. Select the kinds of settings you want individual users to be able to change and save:
   - Desktop icons and Network Neighborhood
   - Start menu and Programs groups
     You can allow either, both, or none of these. Any changes you allow the other users to make will affect their profiles only.
4. Click OK when you're finished.

After enabling user profiles, every time you restart Windows 98, you (and everyone else who uses the computer) will need to sign on with a name and password. The first time a new user signs on, the Desktop will look like it did at the time user profiles were enabled. But all changes, subject to the restrictions you set in step 3 above, will be saved for that user.

Removing a User Profile

To get rid of a user profile, sign on under a different name and password. Use the Find function to search for the user's name. For example, if the user signed on as Alfie, you should find ALFIE.PWL in the Windows folder and a folder named Alfie in the Profiles folder. Delete both the file and the folder to get rid of the profile and all things associated with it. (Don't be put off by the alarming message about deleting USER.DAT; it's just a copy and the original is still in the Windows directory.)

To eliminate all user profiles, log on and go back to the Passwords Properties sheet and change the User Profile setting.

You can also bypass all user profiles at startup by clicking Cancel in the dialog box that asks for name and password; so don't be misled into thinking these are *security* devices, they're strictly for convenience.

Security Issues

Windows 98 was not designed to be a high-security system, even though there are some security provisions. User profiles and passwords provide some security, though they can be bypassed. All someone has to do is boot in Safe Mode by pressing F8 at bootup and selecting Safe Mode from the menu.

You can prevent this by opening the file MSDOS.SYS in a text editor such as Notepad. Under Options, add the line

```
BootKeys=0
```

then save the file. Shut down and restart your computer.

TIP   **If you're in a situation where you absolutely, positively need maximum security, you should investigate running Microsoft Windows NT—a system that can be made very secure.**

Printers

This icon in the Control Panel is a shortcut to your Printers folder (also seen in My Computer and the Explorer).

Printers

Details on how to install, remove, or change the settings of printers are all in Chapter 11, "Hardware Changes with Windows 98."

Regional Settings

The Regional Settings icon in the Control Panel is where you set the variations in how numbers, time, and dates are formatted in different parts of the world. For example, if you're using a program that supports international symbols, changing the Regional Settings can affect how the program displays currency, time, and numbers. To change these settings, click the Regional Settings icon.

Regional Settings

First select the geographic area you want to use, then confirm or change the individual settings. Your system will have to be rebooted for the settings to take effect system-wide.

Sounds

Sounds

What with Windows 98's emphasis on multimedia, it's no surprise that using sound with your computer is easier than ever. Click the Sounds icon in the Control Panel to set and change sound schemes.

NOTE   **To play the sounds that come with Windows 98, you'll need a sound card and speakers (or wear headphones all the time).**

A Sheet Full of Sounds

The Sounds Properties sheet is shown in Figure 15.9. The Events window lists everything on your system that can be associated with a sound. Most are Windows events. For example, opening a program can cause a sound, as can maximizing or minimizing a window, and many other actions.

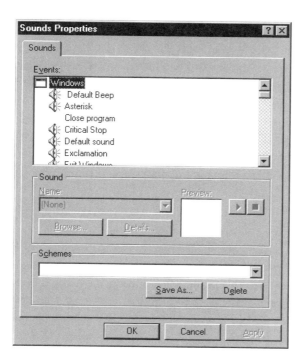

FIGURE 15.9:
The Sounds Properties Sheets is used to associate sounds with events.

Many of the new programs coming out include fabulously rich sound capabilities. Their sounds may not end up in the list shown on this sheet because they're configured in the program.

If there's a Speaker icon next to the event, a sound is associated with it. Highlight the event—the name of the sound file will appear in the Name window—and click the button next to the Preview window to hear its sound.

Sound schemes are included with Windows 98 (many more if you have the Plus! for Windows 98 package installed) and you can choose one of them from the drop-down list.

NOTE If sound schemes don't appear in the Schemes drop-down list, you'll need to install them. Go to the Add/Remove Programs icon in the Control Panel. Under the Windows Setup, click Multimedia and select the sound schemes you want. Select OK, and then follow the instructions.

Customizing a Sound Scheme

All the sound schemes that come with Windows are nice enough, but none of them is perfect. There are either too many sounds, not enough, the wrong sounds attached to various events, or whatever. Fortunately, there's a way to make as many customized sound schemes as you like. Here's how:

1. Click the Sounds icon in the Control Panel.
2. If there's a sound scheme that's close to the one you want, select it from the Schemes drop-down list. Otherwise, select Windows default.
3. Starting at the top of the Events list, select an item that you want a sound associated with.
4. Select a file from the Name drop-down list. To make sure it's the one you want, click the Preview button to hear it.
5. Select (None) in the Name list for events that you want to keep silent.
6. Repeat steps 3–5 until you've completed the list.
7. Select Save As to save this particular assortment of sounds under a specific name. (The new scheme will appear in the Schemes drop-down list.)

TIP **Windows 98 stores all its sound files in the Windows\Media folder. You'll probably want to move any additional sound files you acquire to that folder because using a single location makes setting up and changing sound schemes much easier.**

System Settings

System

The Properties sheet that opens when you click the System icon in the Control Panel can also be accessed by right-clicking My Computer and choosing Properties.

You won't use most of the settings if your computer is working properly. It's only when things go awry that you need to be changing anything here.

General

The General page only tells you the version of Windows 98, the registered owner, and a little bit about the type of computer. The main computer information starts on the next page.

Device Manager

The Device Manager page is where you can see what your system thinks is going on. Usually this is a reflection of reality, but when something is wrong with your computer, this is often the place you'll see it first.

The plus sign to the left of an item indicates there's more to see under that entry. To get the details of the setup for each item, highlight it and click Properties (or just right-click it and select Properties).

TIP **A list of hardware interrupts, DMA addresses, and memory addresses can be found by highlighting Computer and selecting Properties.**

Hardware Profiles

Hardware profiles are something you may need if you're using a portable computer with a docking station. In a limited number of circumstances, you may need to configure alternate setups when the hardware on your system changes.

If you think this might be your situation, consult the Windows 98 help files for instructions.

Performance

The Performance tab is used almost exclusively for troubleshooting. For example, Windows 98 is pretty good at figuring out what will work best on your system, but it's not always perfect. Because of the possible mixture of older (16-bit) applications in a newer (32-bit) system, there may come a time when you want to check that your system is running optimally (see Figure 15.10).

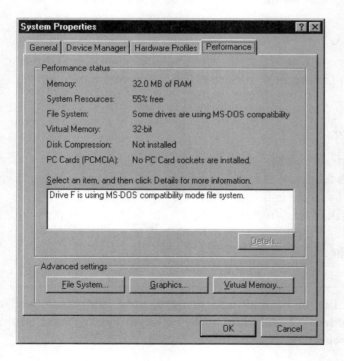

FIGURE 15.10:
The Performance tab tells you how your system is running.

Troubleshooting

Behind the File System button on the Performance page is a Troubleshooting page with options for changing some fundamental operations (see Figure 15.11). For example, let's say you have a piece of hardware that refuses to run properly under Windows 98. Sometimes, you can isolate the problem by disabling one or more of the options in Troubleshooting. In any case, the Performance entries are for solving problems. If you don't have problems, leave them alone.

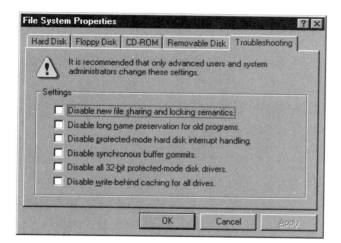

FIGURE 15.11:
Here are some troubleshooting options.

NOTE   **There's much more on hardware troubleshooting in Chapter 13.**

What's Next?

Now it's time to put to use all those junior applications that Windows 98 offers, ranging from a compact word processor (WordPad) to a painting program (Paint) to a tool to dial your most important phone numbers (Phone Dialer).

Chapter 16

A WORLD OF WINDOWS 98 APPLETS

From the first, graphical operating systems have come with a complement of smallish programs such as calculators and paint programs. Because of their usually limited capabilities, these programs are called *applets* rather than applications. In many cases, these programs are just as big as they need to be, so they actually *are* full applications. But the name applet has stuck and generally applies to programs that come with an operating system.

In this chapter, we'll discuss all the applets that aren't covered elsewhere in the book. The use of many of these programs is very simple, so we'll touch on some of the not-so-obvious functions (if there are any).

NOTE   Your computer may have more or fewer applets than what we've listed here already installed when you start using Windows 98. If you don't have the ones shown here, use the Add/Remove Programs icon in the Control Panel to add them to your system.

Using Notepad

Notepad is a simple text editor with very few charms except speed. Click any text file and it will immediately load into Notepad (unless it's associated with a word processing file installed on your system or it's bigger than 64K—in which case you'll be asked if you want to load it into WordPad instead).

To start Notepad, click Start ➤ Programs ➤ Accessories ➤ Notepad.

What Notepad Has

Notepad has the bare minimum of facilities on its menus. You can:

- Search for characters or words.
- Use Page Setup to set margins, paper orientation, customize the header and footer, and select a printer.
- Copy, cut, and paste text.
- Insert the time and date into a document.

Working with WordPad

WordPad, like Notepad, is a text editor, but it is more elaborate than Notepad. For one (important) thing, you can make format changes with WordPad, but not with Notepad. However, WordPad still falls way short of being a real word processing program. WordPad will read Write, Notepad, and Word for Windows 97 documents, as well as Text and Rich Text formats.

To start WordPad, click Start ➤ Programs ➤ Accessories ➤ WordPad.

TIP **WordPad can be uninstalled using the Add/Remove Programs func-tion in the Control Panel. However, if you use Microsoft Fax you'll need WordPad because it's the fax operation's text editor. If you use a different fax program such as WinFax or you don't fax from your computer at all, you can remove WordPad without worry.**

Opening WordPad

When you open WordPad, it looks like most other text editors (see Figure 16.1). On the menus you'll find the usual things one associates with text editors. Pull down the menus to see the various options.

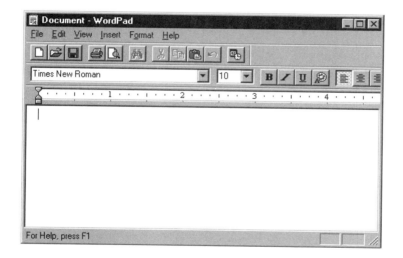

FIGURE 16.1:
The opening screen for WordPad

WordPad is completely integrated into Windows 98. You can write messages in color and post them to the Microsoft Network so recipients see your messages just as you wrote them—fonts, colors, embedded objects, and all. WordPad also has the distinct advantage of being able to load really big files.

Making and Formatting Documents

You can always click a document and drag it into WordPad. Documents made by Microsoft Word (.DOC) and Windows Write (.WRI), as well as Text (.TXT) and Rich Text format (.RTF), are all instantly recognized by WordPad. You can also just start typing away in the opening WordPad screen shown in Figure 16.1.

Formatting Tools

The toolbar (see Figure 16.2) and Format bar (see Figure 16.3) are displayed by default. You can turn either of them off by deselecting it from the list under the View menu.

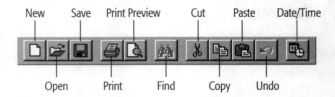

FIGURE 16.2:   Here are the various functions on the WordPad toolbar.

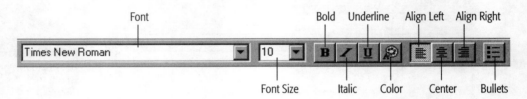

FIGURE 16.3:   The WordPad Format bar lets you manipulate text in all the basic ways.

Tabs are set using the ruler. Click the ruler at the spot where you want a tab. To remove a tab, just click it and drag it off the ruler.

Other Options

Other formatting tools are under Options on the View menu. This is where you can set measurement units as well as Word Wrap and toolbars for each of the different file types that WordPad recognizes.

Page Setup and Printing

The File menu has the usual Print command, but there's also a Page Setup item that you can use to set margins as well as paper size and orientation. WordPad can be used to print envelopes as well as work with varying sizes of paper.

It may take some fooling around to get envelopes lined up correctly, but fortunately there's a Print Preview choice (on the toolbar and also on the File menu). There you can see how the envelope or paper is lining up with your text. Adjust the margin in the Page Setup dialog box until you get it the way you want.

TIP

To change printers, select Page Setup from the File menu. Click the Printer button and you can select any printer currently available to you.

What's on the Clipboard

The Clipboard Viewer is not much different than the one shipped with earlier versions of Windows. When you copy or cut something, Windows needs to have a place to store it until you decide what to do with it. This storage place is called the Clipboard. And if you look in the Clipboard, you will see the material that has just been cut or copied.

Sometimes you want to see what's on the Clipboard and maybe save its contents. Clipboard Viewer makes it possible for you to do this.

Taking a Look

To see the Viewer, click the Start button, then select Programs ➤ Accessories ➤ System Tools ➤ Clipboard Viewer. You'll see a window like the one shown in Figure 16.4.

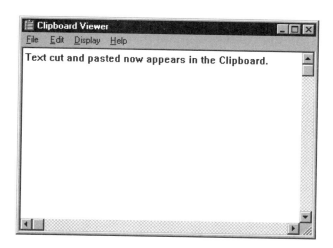

FIGURE 16.4:
The Clipboard Viewer

NOTE Immediately before snapping the screen shot of the Clipboard Viewer, we selected and copied the text you see in the figure. You can also press the PrintScreen keyboard button (which captures the entire screen to the Clipboard) or Alt+PrintScreen (which captures the active window to the Clipboard).

Saving the Clipboard's Contents

To save the current contents of the Clipboard, pull down the File menu and select Save As. You can save files under a proprietary format identified by the .CLP extension. These files are (as far as we can tell) only used by the Windows Clipboard Viewer.

Once you've saved the contents, you can use the Clipboard to copy and paste other material, and later, you can reload what you saved by pulling down the File menu and selecting Open. Pull down the Display menu and you'll be able to see all your options for viewing the data on the Clipboard.

The most important thing to remember about the Clipboard is that it can only hold one thing at a time, which is always the most recently cut or copied material. So if you copy a section of text (which goes to the Clipboard) and then copy an image, the image will replace the text on the Clipboard.

Drawing with Paint

As a drawing and painting program, Paint has its limitations, but it's fine for creating and modifying simple graphics. To find Paint, select Start ➤ Programs ➤ Accessories ➤ Paint. It may not be installed by default, so if you don't see it, use the Add/Remove Programs function in the Control Panel. (It's under Accessories on the Windows Setup page.)

Creating Original Art

Open Paint and, using the tools down the left side of the window, create a drawing and/or a painting. When you're done, you can:

- Select File ➤ Save and give the picture a name. You can save it as one of several different kinds of bitmaps (see the Save as Type list).
- Select File ➤ Send, which will open Exchange and let you select an e-mail recipient worthy of receiving your work.

- Select File ➤ Save as Wallpaper. This will let you tile or center your work of art as the wallpaper on your screen. (You must save the file before you choose this option.)

Modifying the Work of Others

Any file with the extension .BMP, .PCX or .DIB can be opened in Paint. Use the tools to make any modifications you want, and then do any of the things listed in the section above. Once a file is modified, it is saved as a bitmap (.BMP).

NOTE For a really good painting program at a very reasonable price, check out the excellent shareware program Paint Shop Pro. It's available for download on the major online services. Just search for Paint Shop Pro, download the program, and install it.

Entering New Characters

The fonts that show up in your word processor are very nice, but they often don't go beyond the characters found on your keyboard. What about when you need a copyright sign (©) or an e with an umlaut (ë)? With the Character Map you have access to all kinds of symbols, including Greek letters and other special signs.

To start the Character Map, click Start ➤ Programs ➤ Accessories ➤ System Tools ➤ Character Map and you'll see the opening screen shown in Figure 16.5.

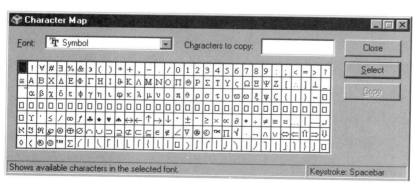

FIGURE 16.5: The Character Map shows all.

Entering Characters

Select the font you want to use by clicking the downward-pointing arrow at the right end of the Font list box. Each font represents a different set of symbols. To enter a character, double-click it in the window. It will appear in the text box at the top right of the window. Continue double-clicking until you have the entire string of characters you want in the text box. When you have all the characters you want in the text box, click the Copy button halfway down the right side of the window. Then return to your application using the Taskbar or by pressing Alt+Tab until your application is selected.

Position the cursor on the spot where you want to place the character, and select Paste from the Edit menu (or just press Ctrl+V).

Phone Dialing for Fun

Do you frequently have to make a lot of telephone calls? Has your dialing finger ever felt as if it were going to fall off? If you have Windows 98, you can turn over the grief of dialing to its capable, virtual hands. Phone Dialer is a handy little program that doesn't do a lot, but if you need it, it's terrific to have.

To start the Phone Dialer, click Start ➤ Programs ➤ Accessories ➤ Communications ➤ Phone Dialer. You'll see the opening screen shown in Figure 16.6 (without a phone number in the Number to dial box).

FIGURE 16.6:
The Phone Dialer window can help you put an end to the heartbreak of "Digititis."

NOTE   Windows uses your installed modem to dial your telephone. In order for this scheme to work, you need to have a telephone on the same line you're using for your modem. If you have a separate phone line for data, you'll need an actual telephone on that line to use Phone Dialer. You can pick up inexpensive couplers at Radio Shack so all your available phone lines can work in conjunction with your data line.

The Phone Dialer gives you two simple ways to make phone calls:

Speed Dial   If you have a number you need in an emergency or one you call constantly, you can enter it in the Speed Dial list.

The Telephone Log   If you have a long list of numbers you call periodically, you can simply type those numbers into the Number to Dial text box and they will be added to a telephone log. You can access your log by clicking the downward-pointing arrow at the right end of the Number to Dial box.

Speed Dialing

To create a speed dial number, pull down the Edit menu and select Speed Dial. You will see the dialog box shown in Figure 16.7.

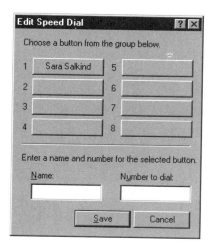

FIGURE 16.7:
Creating a Speed
Dial number

Here's how to set it up:
1. Click the numbered speed dial button you want to assign.
2. In the Name text box, type the name of the person or place that you will dial with that button.
3. Type the number to dial in the Number to Dial text box.
4. Click Save. (You'll be returned to the Phone Dialer dialog box and the name you entered in the Edit Speed Dial dialog box will appear on the numbered speed dial button you selected.)
5. To speed dial the number, just click the button and lift your telephone handset.

TIP When you enter a phone number in the Phone Dialer, don't forget to enter any numbers that are needed before the number, such as 1 or 70. Also, numbers can be entered separated by a dash or a space or nothing at all, such as 555-1212 or 555 1212 or 5551212.

The Telephone Log

As mentioned at the beginning of this section, there are two ways to use the Phone Dialer. The quick and easy way is to use the speed dialer, but as you may have noticed, the speed dialer is limited to a list of eight numbers. If you have more than eight numbers that you call on a regular basis, you'll have to use your log. Here's how:
1. In the opening Phone Dialer screen, either type the number in the Number to Dial box or use the telephone keypad in the Phone Dialer dialog box to enter the number.
2. When the number is completely entered, click the Dial button and pick up your telephone. In a moment, you will be connected to the number you are calling.
3. If you need to call the number again, pull down the Tools menu and select Show Log. This displays a list of all the numbers you have called.
4. To redial one of these numbers, double-click its entry in the log.

You can see how the Phone Dialer can be a terrific convenience if you spend a lot of time making calls.

Using the Calculators

You actually have two calculators in Windows 98: a standard calculator, the likes of which you could buy for $4.95 at any drugstore counter, and a scientific calculator.

Just the Basics

To start the Calculator, click Start ➣ Programs ➣ Accessories ➣ Calculator and you'll see the opening screen shown in Figure 16.8.

FIGURE 16.8:
The basic
calculator

Using the mouse, click the numbers and functions just as if you were pressing the keys on a hand-held calculator. Or, if you have a numerical keypad on your keyboard, press NumLock and then use the keypad keys to enter numbers and basic math functions.

Or One Step Beyond

To access the scientific calculator, pull down the View menu on the Calculator and select Scientific. That displays the calculator in Figure 16.9.

TIP

If you're unsure of the use for a function, right-click its button. You'll see a rectangle containing the words "What's This?". Click the text to see a short explanation of the function.

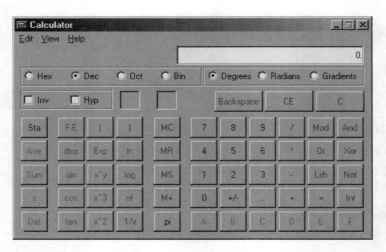

FIGURE 16.9: The much more sophisticated scientific calculator

Pasting In the Numbers

Both calculators can be used in conjunction with the Clipboard. Type a number in any application, and select it. Press Ctrl+C (for Copy). Press Alt+Tab until the calculator is selected (or click it in the Taskbar) and then press Ctrl+V (for Paste). The number will appear in the number display of the calculator as if you had entered it from the calculator keypad.

Work your magic adding, subtracting, multiplying, or deriving the inverse sine. You can pull down the Edit menu and select Copy, which places the contents of the display on the Clipboard—ready for you to paste into your document.

TIP

Here's a neat trick to transfer numbers from one calculator view to another. First, click the MS button to store the displayed number. Then, on the View menu, click the desired view. Finally, click the MR button to recall the stored number.

Communicating with HyperTerminal

HyperTerminal is the Windows 98 applet that accesses other computers, bulletin boards, and online services through your modem. For the most part, all of Hyper-Terminal's work will be done for you by your ISP or your online service. But, there may be special occasions where you need HyperTerminal to make a connection.

To start HyperTerminal, click Start ➤ Programs ➤ Accessories ➤ Communications ➤ HyperTerminal. Then click the HyperTerminal icon (HYPERTRM.EXE) and you'll see the opening screen shown in Figure 16.10.

All you need to do to create a new connection is select File ➤ New Connection. The New Connection window will appear where you assign a name to the new connection and specify an icon (see Figure 16.10).

FIGURE 16.10: The Hyper-Terminal screen where you begin the connection process

How to Use It

When you use HyperTerminal, each connection you make can be named and provided with an icon. That allows you to quickly identify connections so you can make them again. Once established, all it takes is a click on the icon to connect to where you want.

Let's create a fictional connection that will allow us to fill out the dialog box. Imagine you're a journalist working for a newspaper called *The Past Times* and you need to log on to the paper's BBS to file stories and columns.

1. Type **The Past Times** in the Name text box.
2. Scroll through the icons until you locate an icon that resembles a briefcase and an umbrella—what better icon for a reporter?
3. Click the OK button. You will see the Connect To dialog box shown here.

4. If the number you want to dial is located in a country other than the one listed in the Country Code list, click the downward-pointing arrow at the right end of the list box and select the correct country.
5. Enter the area code and phone number of the BBS in the appropriate text boxes. (For our example, enter 555-1212 as the number, and click the OK button.)
6. The Connect dialog box opens. Since this is the first time we've run this application, click the Dialing Properties button to confirm that the connection is made properly. Look over the options in this dialog box, and make sure that they're correctly set.

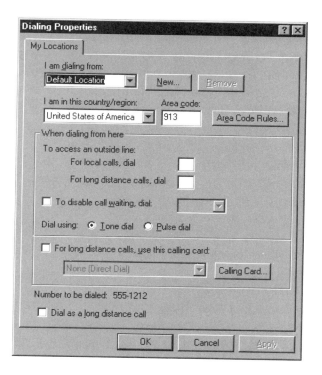

7. If you click the Calling Card button, a dialog box will open for you to enter your telephone credit card number.

8. If you have to dial a number to get out of your business or hotel phone system (typically 9 or 7), enter this number in the appropriate To access an outside line text box and enter the number (or numbers) you dial for long distance access in the text box below it.

9. When you are through filling out this dialog box, click OK. You will see the Connect dialog box again.

10. At this point, all you need to do is click Dial to make the connection. If all the settings you made in the previous dialog boxes are correct, the call will go through, and you can use the BBS software to upload your story to the newspaper. (We'll cover file transfers in a moment.)

11. When you're through placing your call, pull down the Call menu and select Disconnect, or click the icon that looks like a handset being hung up and the connection will be broken.

12. When you close the window, you will be prompted to save the session.

Sending Files

Once you have connected with a remote computer, you will probably want to upload or download files. This is the principal reason for making this sort of connection. The file transfer protocols (which are the rules for transferring information) supported by HyperTerminal are:

- 1K Xmodem
- Xmodem
- Ymodem
- Ymodem-G
- Zmodem
- Zmodem with Crash Recovery
- Kermit

Binary Files

To send a binary file, follow these steps:

1. After the connection is made, pull down the Transfer menu.
2. Select Send File. A dialog box will open.
3. Using the options in this dialog box, specify the file to send. Click the Browse button to locate and identify the file to be sent.
4. Select the protocol for file transfer from the Protocol drop-down menu. Zmodem is the best choice because it combines speed and good error correction (see Figure 16.11).
5. Click the Send button. The file will be transferred.

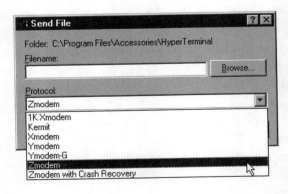

FIGURE 16.11:
Here's where you select a binary file and the protocol for sending it.

Text Files

Text files are a little different from binary files. Most file transfer software distinguishes between binary files and text files—sending one in Binary mode and the other in ASCII mode or Text mode. HyperTerminal is no different.

To send a text file, follow the steps for a binary file, except choose Send Text File from the Transfer menu. When you specify the file to send and click the Open button, the file will be sent as if you had typed it into the terminal program.

TIP
> Unless you're transferring files to a UNIX system, you're usually better off sending every file as a binary file. Even a little bit of formatting in the file can cause a text file transfer to fail, while *any* file can be sent as a binary transfer.

And Receiving Them Too

To receive a file being sent from another computer:

1. Pull down the Transfer menu and select Receive File. That will open a dialog box that looks similar to the dialog box (see Figure 16.12).
2. Click the Browse button to specify a file name and location for the received file.
3. Select a file transfer protocol.
4. Click the Receive button to start receiving the file from the remote location.

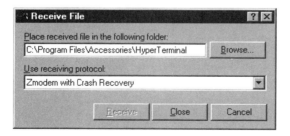

FIGURE 16.12:
Receiving files using HyperTerminal

NOTE
> Take the above steps when you hear the incoming call from the other computer. You have to do this yourself because HyperTerminal is not smart enough to answer the phone.

Saving a Session

To help you remember how to navigate the complexities of a service you don't use very often, terminal programs provide *logging*—a way to save everything you do in a particular session to disk and/or print it on paper.

To save everything to file:

1. Pull down the Transfer menu and select Capture Text.
2. By default, all the screen information in a session will be saved in a file called CAPTURE.TXT in the HyperTerminal folder inside the Accessories folder. Of course, you can use the Browse button to save the file in a different location. Click Start when you're ready.
3. Pull down the Transfer menu again. Now you will note that there is a tiny triangle next to the Capture Text option. Select it and you will see a submenu with Stop, Pause, and Resume options to give you control over the capture.
4. If you prefer to send the session to the printer rather than to a file on your disk, pull down the Transfer menu and select Capture to Printer.

Using a Connection

As you may recall, when we started using HyperTerminal, we created a connection with a name and an icon. This connection appears in the HyperTerminal program group. Any time you want to use this connection in the future, simply double-click its icon, and all the settings (telephone number and so forth) will be in place for you.

Any time you want to change the settings in a particular connection, open the connection, pull down the File menu, and select Properties.

Using the Briefcase

The Briefcase is not an applet in the usual sense. You won't find it listed under Accessories, but Briefcase should be on your Desktop from the original installation of Windows 98. If it's not, it is probably not installed. To install it, use the Add/Remove Programs option in the Control Panel (discussed in Chapter 15).

Briefcase is designed to help those with multiple computers keep a set of files synchronized. It may be your computer at work and your computer at home. Or maybe you have a desktop computer and a laptop where the same files are worked on.

When two computers are involved, it's only a matter of time before things get confused as to which version of a memo or a speech is the most current. Briefcase helps rectify that problem.

How It Works

When you open a Briefcase and copy a file into it, a link is made between the original and the copy in the Briefcase. This is called a sync link. After the link is made, you can work on the copy in the Briefcase or the original file and select Update All (from inside Briefcase), and the latest version will be copied over the earlier version, keeping both in sync.

To make use of Briefcase:

1. Drag the files that are important to the Briefcase folder on the Desktop of computer #1.
2. Copy the Briefcase to a floppy disk. Right-click and use the Send To command, which is particularly handy for this.
3. Take the floppy to computer #2. Open drive A either in Windows Explorer or My Computer.
4. Open the Briefcase. Work on the files inside the Briefcase on computer #2.
5. When you're finished, save and close the files on the floppy in the usual way.
6. Return the floppy to computer #1. Open the Briefcase on the floppy disk and select Update All from the Briefcase menu. Click the Update button.

What's Next?

As you can see, some applets are very valuable and others you'll never use. In the next chapter, we'll deal with other small applications that come with Windows 98. But in this case, they're known as system tools. No one uses them for fun, but like a smoke alarm in your house, they're not only necessary but also comforting to have.

Chapter 17

TOOLS FOR KEEPING YOUR SYSTEM HEALTHY

FEATURING

- **Tuning up Windows 98**
- **Keeping your hard disk healthy with ScanDisk**
- **Making things faster with Disk Defragmenter**
- **Backing up and restoring Files with Backup**
- **Compressing drives to gain more space**
- **Using the System File Checker and Disk Cleanup**

Some basic disk tools needed to keep your system healthy have always been included with Windows, but now Windows 98 offers just about a complete set. Of course, if there are other disk tools you want, such as Norton Utilities or McAffee Quickback (a backup program), you can use those too. Just make sure any utility programs you install are Windows 98-compatible so you don't damage any of your data.

In this chapter, we'll talk about disk tools—what they do, how best to use them, and how to schedule them so they automatically execute. You'll find your list of installed tools by clicking the Start button and then selecting Programs ➤ Accessories ➤ System Tools.

The Tune-Up Wizard

If you've ever been intimidated by specialty programs that fool with your hard drive or your system, the Windows 98's Tune-Up utility is just what you need. Once you set it up (which takes only a few minutes), the Tune-Up Wizard (see Figure 17.1) will do everything necessary to keep your hard drive(s) healthy and running at optimum performance.

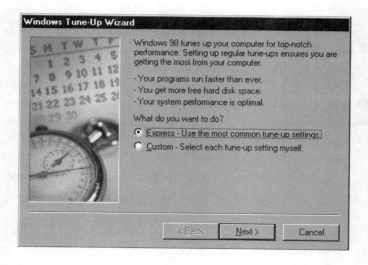

FIGURE 17.1: The Tune-Up Wizard

The Tune-Up Wizard can perform the following tasks:

- Optimize the hard drive to free up disk space and make programs run faster
- Scan the hard drive for disk errors and fix them
- Delete unnecessary or unused files
- Speed up the performance of your favorite programs

Now it's time to go through the steps of telling the Wizard which tune-up tasks to perform, and, if you choose, when to perform them.

To start the Tune-Up Wizard:

1. Click Start ➤ Programs ➤ Accessories ➤ System Tools ➤ Windows Tune-Up.

2. You'll see the opening screen shown in Figure 17.1.
   - If you select the Express options, Windows will automatically install the tune-up utility with the most common tune-up settings.
   - If you select the Custom option, you can make decisions about each setting.
3. For this exercise, select the Custom option and click Next.
4. Determine what time of the day you want to schedule a recurring tune-up and click Next.

TIP   **You can schedule the Wizard to do its magic when the computer is unattended, such as when you are sleeping. Do this in the Select a Tune-Up Schedule dialog box you see when you first start the Tune-Up Wizard.**

---

5. In the next screen, you can designate those programs you want to start immediately when Windows 98 starts. Click Next when you're done.
6. Now it's time to decide about optimizing your disk by running Disk Defragmenter, shown below. As with most Tune-Up tasks, you can have the Wizard complete the task now or schedule it for later. If you want to have the task performed now, click Yes, Speed Up My Programs Regularly. If you want to schedule the task for later, click the Reschedule a Later Time to Optimize button and set the date and time you want the task completed.

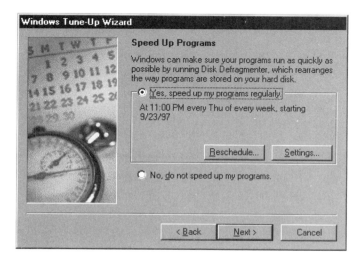

7. Continue to click Next until you get to the Scan Hard Disk for Errors screen shown in Figure 17.2. This screen requires you to work with settings. Designate a schedule for scanning the hard disk (if you want). Then click Next to move onto the next Tune-Up option in the Wizard.

8. Click Next until you get to the Delete Unnecessary Files screen. This screen requires you to define the type of files to remove. Clicking the Settings button provides you with a list of file types to select from. Once you have made your selection, continue to click OK until you get to the Finish button.

9. Click the When I Click Finish box and then click Finish. Windows 98's Tune-Up Wizard will convert any files necessary and perform the tasks that you define. If you don't click the When I Click Finish box, the Windows 98 Tune-Up will run right away, unless you scheduled it to occur at a later time.

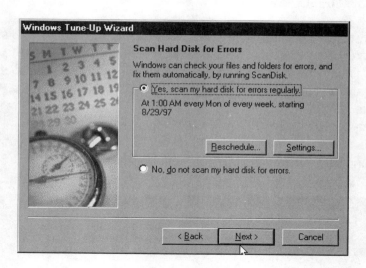

FIGURE 17.2:
It's a good idea to regularly scan for disk errors and correct them when they occur.

That's it for the Tune-Up Wizard. If you scheduled the tasks using the Wizard, they will each be performed when specified.

NOTE   **Keep in mind that your computer must be turned on for the Tune-Up to occur.**

WARNING In any of the Tune-Up Wizard screens, if you have already scheduled a task (by selecting it independently of the Wizard), the time and date will appear. To change it, you must click the Reschedule button.

ScanDisk

A computer is a very complex system. There's a lot of stuff going on all the time that you never know about. Like most complex systems, errors are made by the system itself, and if not corrected, will pile up into serious problems.

ScanDisk is protection against the accumulation of serious problems on your hard drive. It's a direct descendant of the CHKDSK utility in DOS with added features like those in the justly famous Norton Utilities.

NOTE You may have seen ScanDisk if you installed Windows 98 yourself, because in the installation routine ScanDisk does a quick check of the hard drive to look for errors.

Running ScanDisk

To run ScanDisk, follow these steps:

1. Select ScanDisk from the System Tools menu under Accessories. This will open the window shown in Figure 17.3.
2. Highlight the drive you want tested.
3. Select the type of test and whether you want ScanDisk to automatically fix all errors or not.
4. Click Start.

NOTE If the Automatically Fix Errors box is checked, ScanDisk will repair most errors without consulting you again. Such corrections are made based on settings you can review by clicking the Advanced button.

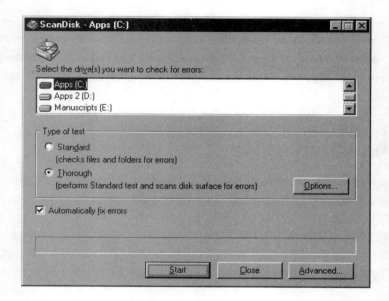

FIGURE 17.3:
The ScanDisk opening screen, where you can check and correct errors that might be on your hard drive

Changing ScanDisk Settings

Click the Advanced button to see (and change) the settings that ScanDisk uses (see Figure 17.4). Here's where you can fine tune ScanDisk settings.

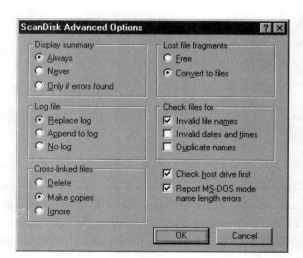

FIGURE 17.4:
Here's where you work with ScanDisk settings.

And here are the settings you can fine tune:

Display Summary   This setting controls when you see the summary of ScanDisk's findings after a check.

Log File   By default, ScanDisk creates a new log detailing its activities every time it's run. If you want one long continuous log or no log at all, change the setting.

Cross-Linked Files   A cross-link occurs when more than one file tries to use the same area (cluster) on the hard drive. Whatever information is in the cluster is probably correct only for one file (though it might not be correct for either of them). The default setting attempts to salvage order out of the mess by copying the information in the cluster to both files contending for the space. This is the best of the three settings—it may not save any of your data but the other two options definitely won't.

Lost File Fragments   File fragments are a fact of computer life. You can leave the default setting to convert them to files. They'll be given names like FILE0001 and FILE0002 and deposited in your root folder (that's the C: folder which contains a lot of folders but some files too). The odds are very high that these fragments aren't anything useful, and they do take up valuable disk space. We've changed our default setting to Free, but you can be extra cautious and leave it at Convert to Files. (Just remember to look at these files periodically and delete the junk.)

Check Files For   The default is to look just for invalid names, though you can add dates and times if you want. This will slow down ScanDisk's progress, but not dramatically.

Check Host Drive First   If you have a compressed drive, errors are sometimes caused by errors on the host drive. Leave this box checked so the host drive will be examined first. If you want to report naming problems with MSDOS, check that box as well.

TIP   You should run ScanDisk frequently. Once a week is a good idea. And at least once a month you should run its thorough testing procedure, so the hard disk surface is checked for problems in addition to the standard checking of files and folders.

Defragmenting Disks

Windows 98 is much like the operating systems that preceded it in that when it writes a file to your disk, it puts it anywhere it finds room. As you delete and create files over time, files start to be stored as a piece here, a piece there, another piece somewhere else.

This isn't a problem for Windows 98—it always knows where the pieces are. But it will tend to slow down file access time because the system has to go to several locations to pick up one file. When a file is spread over multiple places, it's said to be fragmented. The more fragmented files you have, the slower your hard drive will run.

As a matter of good housekeeping then, Disk Defragmenter should probably be run about once a month. Here's how it's done:

1. Select Disk Defragmenter from the Start ➤ Programs ➤ Accessories ➤ System Tools menu.
2. Use the drop-down list to choose the drive you want to defragment. If you click the Settings button you can decide on whether you want to rearrange files so everything runs faster and if you want errors fixed as the disk is defragmented. You can also decide if you want to use these options just once or every time. When you're ready, click OK.

NOTE **When Disk Defragmenter has found an error on your disk, run ScanDisk (described earlier in this chapter) to repair the problem, and then run the Defragmenter again.**

3. Click OK to return to the Select Drive dialog box.
4. Click OK. You can click Show Details to get a cluster-by-cluster view of the program's progress. Or you can just minimize Disk Defragmenter and do something else. If what you do writes to the hard drive, Disk Defragmenter will start over—but in the background and without bothering you.

Backing Up and Restoring Files

Your hard disk has (or will soon have) a lot of material on it that's valuable to you. Even if it's not your doctoral dissertation or this year's most important sales presentation, you'll have software (including Windows 98) that you've set up and configured just so.

Hard disk crashes are really quite rare these days, but if you are unlucky enough to have a crash, not having a recent backup can change your whole perspective on life. So resolve now to do frequent backups of your important files. If you are lucky and/or cautious enough to have a tape drive or other high-capacity backup system, you should also make less-frequent backups of your entire system.

NOTE   **Don't forget, there are two types of computer users. Those who have lost their data and those who backup their files! With Windows 98's Backup feature, you'll be able to tell Windows 98 what to back up, how to do it, where to back it up to, and when to do it. So make sure you are a computer user who backs up your files.**

Getting Started

To start the Backup program, click the Start button, then select Programs ➤ Accessories ➤ System Tools ➤ Backup. Your first decision is if you want backup to create a set of emergency disks for you to use should your hard drive crash. Creating an emergency set takes lots of disks and will take some time, but it's well worth the effort. Click OK if you want to create a set of emergency disks, and follow the on-screen instructions. Click No if you do not want to create such a set, and continue with the backup.

NOTE   **If the Backup program isn't on the menu, you'll need to install it. Go to Add/Remove Programs in the Control Panel and use Windows Setup to add Backup.**

Figure 17.5 shows the opening window you'll see when you open Backup the first time.

Tape Drive or Floppies

If you have a tape drive and it has been installed properly, Backup will find it and prepare to back up to it.

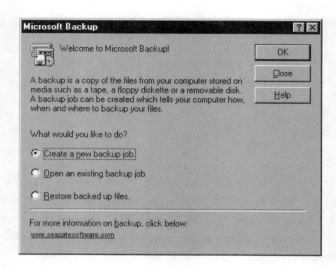

FIGURE 17.5:
Your introduction
to Backup

WARNING   **Not all tape drives are supported.**

If Windows 98 doesn't find a tape drive, it will present you with a message telling you that if you really do have a tape drive, it isn't working. It will also tell you what to do about it. If you really don't have a tape drive, just click OK. You'll be backing up to floppies (which you already know about).

NOTE   **If you have two hard drives, backing up from one to the other is as safe as any other method. But you must use two physically separate hard drives, not just different partitions on a single hard drive.**

Deciding on a Type of Backup

When you decide that you need to make a backup, it's important to know what you need to back up and where you want the backup to be created. There are three different ways to perform a backup. In the Microsoft Backup dialog box, you can create a new backup job (which you will if this is your first backup), open an existing backup job (which you created earlier), or restore files that were previously backed up that you no longer have immediate access to on your hard drive. Click OK when you're done.

Deciding What to Back Up

Before you create a backup, you should know that you don't have to backup your entire system at once. You can back up a set group of files or folders, or a specific drive on your computer.

NOTE When you backup, don't select applications. You should have them on disk or CD anyway. If your computer came with the programs already installed, you may not have the original disks. Contact the manufacturer and ask for a set, or you can make a set for yourself. Better yet, if you can afford it, buy a CD-ROM player you can write to and make your backups there.

Backing Up Everything

You can back up all the files and folders on the local drive, or back up just selected files. This means that everything that is on your hard drive will be duplicated on a set of disks or on whatever medium you back up to.

TIP If your hard disk suddenly sounds like it's full of little pebbles, there's nothing more comforting than having a Full System Backup on your shelf. You should make a Full System Backup when you first install Windows 98, after you install new applications, and occasionally thereafter. But keep in mind, if you do backup to floppy disks, the number of disks you use will be very large—possibly 30 or 40.

You need to tell Backup which folders need to be backed up every day or every week. Once you have a solid backup of your entire hard disk, you'll want to back up only certain folders on a regular basis.

Backing Up Selected Files

Regular backups involve less than the entire hard drive and will probably depend on how valuable certain files are, how difficult they would be to re-create (probably very if it's a document like a paper or a business plan), and how often they change.

Defining a File Set

If you want to backup up all the files and folders on your computer, you need not specify anything else. Backup will back up everything. There's no need to define a set of files or folders. But, if you just want to back up selected files, Backup will create a file set.

What is a file set? Backup is based on the idea that you have a large hard disk with perhaps thousands of individual files and perhaps hundreds of different folders. You don't usually want to back up everything on the disk. Usually you'll be backing up a few folders—the folders containing your Corel drawings, your Excel spreadsheets, your WordPerfect documents, your appointment book, your customer database, and so on. A file set is a collection of files that is backed up as a unit and has a unique name. When you use Backup, you create such file sets.

TIP	You might want to make several file sets for backups of different depths. Back up really important folders at the end of every work day (or at lunch) and less important ones at the end of major projects. How to create a backup file set is covered in the following section.

Creating a Backup

In this section we'll create a backup to demonstrate how it's done. If Backup isn't running, start it now. (See the instructions in the "Getting Started" section earlier in this chapter.) Once you get through the initial dialog boxes, you should see the window shown in Figure 17.6.

Clicking the objects in the section on the left tells Backup which device, folders, or individual files you want to back up.

NOTE	Each of the drives shown in the Backup window has a tiny checkbox next to it. If you want to back up the entire device—every file and folder from the root to the farthest branch—click this box to automatically select everything. This, in itself, may take several minutes.

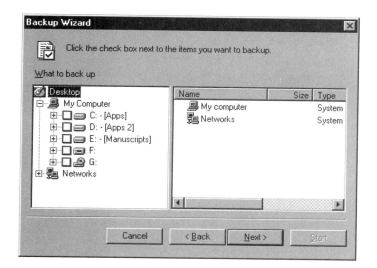

FIGURE 17.6:
Designing your backup

Backing Up Particular Files or Folders

Here's how you can back up particular files or folders. For the sake of this example, we'll back up a single file, but the principle is the same for a larger selection.

1. Click your hard disk's name in the list. That will make all of the folders in the root folder of your hard disk appear in the list at the right.

NOTE   When you look at the Backup window, it simply looks like a list of folders. Where are the files? The folders appear at the top of the list, so they may be the only thing visible to you. If you use the scroll bar at the right edge of the list to move to the bottom of the list, you will see the files in the root folder of the selected device. We'll get down to the file level shortly.

2. Search through the list of folders to find your Windows 98 folder. If you want to back up every file and folder in Windows, you should click the box to the left of the Windows folder name. Instead, we are going to select a single file to back up.

3. Click the Windows folder. You'll see even more folders; scroll down until you start seeing individual files like those shown here.

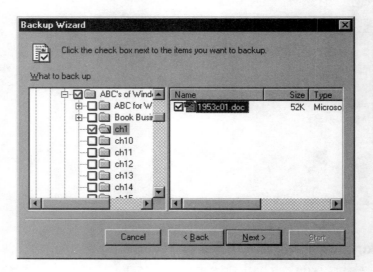

4. Scroll through the files in the folder until you locate the file called WIN. In the Type column, it will say Configuration Settings.

NOTE **If you have file extensions turned on, the file will be listed as WIN.INI.**

5. If the files are not in alphabetical order, you can click the Name block at the top of the list to list them alphabetically. Or you might want to click the Type block and search through the configuration files for WIN.

6. When you have located the file, click the tiny box to the left of the file name in the list.

7. Click the Next button. You will now decide whether you want Windows 98 to back up all the files that you have selected or only files that are new and have been changed.

8. Click Next and select where you will back up the files that you have designated.

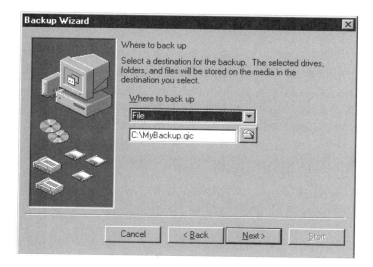

9. Select a media destination where the files will be backed up and click Start. For our example, we will pick the A drive.

10. Click Next and in the resulting dialog box, type the name WIN as the name of the file set. Here you can review the what, where, how, and when of the backup job. You can click the Back button to go back and change any decision you made earlier, but this is your last chance before the backup process begins.

11. Click Start and you'll see a progress report as Backup does its work. Once the backup is compete, click OK and then close the Backup dialog box.

TIP   If you want to keep this file set for future use, after you choose a destination for the backup, select Save from the File menu. Specify a name for your file set. When you next want to use it, start Backup and select Open File Set from the File menu.

Backing Up an Existing File Set

Let's do a backup of an existing file set. You'll do this once you've backed up files and folders and made changes that need to be backed up. Since we just created it, let's use the WIN file set. Here's what to do:

1. Begin by shutting down Backup. (You can do this by clicking the X icon at the extreme upper-right corner of the Backup window or by selecting Close from the File menu.)

2. Start Backup by following the instructions earlier in this chapter, in the section "Creating a Backup."

3. When you get to the Backup window, pull down the Backup Job drop-down menu and click the icon WIN (or whatever you used as the name of the file set we just created). The file set will open.

4. Click Start. Make sure your backup medium (floppy disk or tape) is in the device selected, and then click OK to begin the backup process.

Choosing Backup Options

To use Backup's options, pull down the Job menu and select Options. This will display a dialog box showing six tabs: General, Password, Type, Exclude, Report, and Advanced. Here is a description of each of the tabs:

General   This tab is used to set verification of the backup to the original, determine if data will be compressed to save space or time, and to decide whether backup files will be appended or written over.

Password   This tab is used to assign a password for any backup job.

Type   This tab allows you to set whether you want all selected files or only new and changed files backed up.

Exclude   This tab lets you set which files should be excluded from the backup. This is a very handy feature because it allows you to exclude hungry, space-eating files such as those with a .GIF or .AVI extension).

Report   This tab provides options for you to design how you want Backup to report the results.

Advanced   This tab allows you to back up the Windows Registry.

Drag-and-Drop Backup

You can also drag-and-drop files that you want backed up by first placing Backup on your Desktop as an icon. You can then back up a file by dragging it to the Backup icon and dropping it. Here's how to place Backup on your Desktop as an icon:

1. Right-click the Start button and select Open.

2. In the window that opens, select Programs ➤ Accessories ➤ System Tools.

3. Right-click the Backup icon and drag it to the Desktop.

4. Release the mouse button and select Create Shortcut(s) Here from the pop-up menu.

When you're ready to back up a particular file, you can find it in the Explorer or My Computer and then drag-and-drop it on the Backup icon on the Desktop. Another way to back up a file is to make a folder called Backup. Put shortcuts to your file sets and to Backup inside the folder. If you want, put a shortcut to the folder on your Desktop. Then all you have to do is open the folder and drag the appropriate file to the Backup icon to start a backup.

TIP   **Want some help backing up? Use the Backup Wizard on the Tools menu.**

Restoring Files

Restoring is useful for more than recovering from disaster. It's also a good way to restore large files that were backed up from your hard disk when they were no longer immediately needed. Now you can restore them and use them again.

Let's use Restore to restore the WIN configuration file we backed up earlier. (On the disk, it's called WIN.INI.) Specify where you want files restored from, what files you want restored, where you want the file restored to, and how you want the restore done. Here are the specific steps:

1.   Start Backup.
2.   When you get through all the introductory dialog boxes, click the tab at the top of the Backup window marked Restore.
3.   In the Restore From drop-down menu, click From Here the Backup Will Be Made. In this case it is from a file. Then, select the location of the backup file. In this case, the location is A:\BACKUP.QIC.
4.   Select the backup data set you want to restore.
5.   Select where you want the data restored to and how you want it restored.
6.   Click the Start button, and the restoration will begin.

Options for Restoring

Pull down the Job menu and select Options. You will see three tabs in the Restore dialog box (with names and functions similar to those listed in the "Choosing Backup Options" section earlier in this chapter). You can also click the Options button in the Restore dialog box to see the same set of tabs.

The tabs offer the following functions:

General   This tab lets you determine how and when you want files restored that already exist.

Report   This tab provides options for you to design how you want Restore to report the results of a restoration.

Advanced   This tab allows you to restore the Windows Registry.

Making More Room on Your Hard Disk

Compression is when all or a portion of your hard drive can be made to appear much larger than it actually is. When hard drives were running up to 5 dollars for each megabyte of storage space, the first disk compression programs were born. They were slow and not all that reliable. Now that hard drives are selling at maybe 20 cents per megabyte and compression is no longer a big issue, compression is very fast and very reliable.

DriveSpace 3 is the compression program that is supplied with Windows 98. Windows 98 works with drives that are compressed with Stacker, SuperStor, and AddStor, in addition to DriveSpace and DoubleSpace.

How Compression Works

Let's say you have one hard drive labeled C: and use DriveSpace to create a compressed drive D:. The compressed drive is not a separate partition of your hard drive. It's actually a file referred to as the CVF (compressed volume file) in the root folder of the C: drive. The C: drive is called the *host* drive for this CVF.

If you want to see the compressed volume file (named DRVSPACE.000), you'll have to turn off its setting as a hidden file. But we recommend that you not bother. There is nothing useful you can do with a CVF. Don't delete it, attempt to change it, or anything else. Only approach a compressed drive through DriveSpace. If you want to remove compression, use DriveSpace to do it.

Compressing a Drive

You'll need at least 2MB of free space on your C: drive if that's the one being compressed. If it's another drive or floppy disk, you'll need 768K of free space before compression. Follow these steps:

1. Click the Start button, then select Programs ➤ Accessories ➤ System Tools ➤ DriveSpace. You'll see the DriveSpace opening screen shown here.

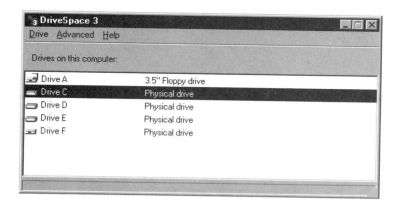

2. Click the drive you want to compress.
3. DriveSpace will check your system and report on what it finds.
4. Highlight the drive you want to compress and select Compress from the Drive menu.
5. The next window (see Figure 17.7) shows the current status of the drive and what the status will be after compression.
6. Click the Start button to compress files and free space on the drive.

At the end of the compression process, you'll see a window showing the amount of space you've gained by compressing.

Behind the Options Button

In Figure 17.7, you can see an Options button. Click it and you can see how Windows is planning to proceed. In the above example, we told Windows 98 that we wanted to compress drive C:—free space and files included. Figure 17.8 shows that the new host drive will be H: and it will be hidden.

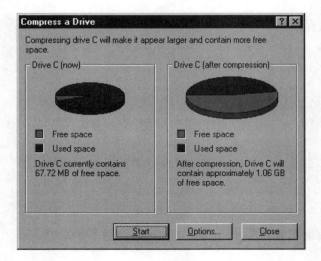

FIGURE 7.17:
The before and
after compression
comparison

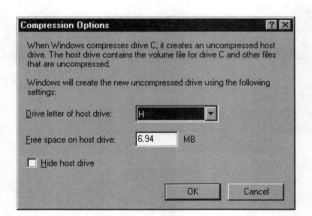

FIGURE 17.8:
Specifying the
host letter of the
compressed drive
and the amount
of space to be
left free

You can change these options: leaving more free space on H: and making it visible, or changing the drive letter designation for the host drive.

Changing the Size of a Compressed Drive

If there's free space on your compressed drive, you can add free space to the host drive by making the compressed portion smaller. Likewise, if you have free space on the host drive, you can make the compressed portion larger—as long as you keep within the 512MB maximum size for compressed drives.

To change the size of a compressed file, follow these steps:

1. Start DriveSpace, then highlight an existing drive. Select Adjust Free Space from the Drive menu.
2. Move the slider bar to adjust the free space.

Removing a Compressed Drive

A compressed drive can be removed (that is, returned to its pre-compression state) quite easily as long as there's enough space on the host drive for all the files once they're decompressed.

To remove a compressed drive, follow these steps:

1. Open DriveSpace and highlight the drive you want to uncompress.
2. Select Uncompress from the Drive menu.
3. A window will open and show you the current state of the drive and what it will look like after being uncompressed.
4. You'll see a warning notice advising that your computer will be unusable during the uncompress cycle and also advising you to back up important files first. Click Uncompress Now if you're ready to proceed.

A window with a progress bar will open so you can see how far along the process is. At the end you'll also get a window that shows the final results.

NOTE   Feel free to experiment with compressing and uncompressing drives and looking at other options on the DriveSpace menus. Microsoft has made DriveSpace very sturdy. You can even turn off the machine in the middle of a compress operation and when you turn the machine back on, DriveSpace will pick up right where it left off.

Resource Meter

The Resource Meter is a handy little device if you're keeping track of resources on your computer. It's pretty hard to run out of resources in Windows 98 but you can get awfully low if you have enough windows open. When you open the Resource Meter (Start ➤ Programs ➤ Accessories ➤ System Tools ➤ Resource Meter), an icon representing it is automatically placed on the end of the Taskbar, as you can see in Figure 17.9. To read the resources being used, place your pointer on the icon and a flyover box will open showing available resources. Or double-click the icon and the resource Meter will open. To close the Resource Meter, right-click the icon and click Exit.

FIGURE 17.9:
Reading the amount of resources available

There's no point in trying to describe what the different resources mean because the explanation would involve terms like *memory heaps* and *device contexts*. Suffice it to say that if any of these numbers starts approaching zero, it's time to close some open programs to give yourself more maneuvering room.

Scheduling Tasks

You read earlier in this chapter how many of the tasks that we have described (such as ScanDisk, and Disk Defragmenter) can be scheduled to run as part of the Window Tune-Up. But, you can use the Task Scheduler also to schedule individual tasks.

To open the scheduler, click Start ➤ Programs ➤ Accessories ➤ System Tools ➤ Schedule Tasks, or click the Task Scheduler icon on the Taskbar. You'll see the Scheduled Tasks window shown in Figure 17.10.

To schedule a specific task:

1. Click the Add Scheduled Task icon in the Scheduled Tasks window and the Add Scheduled Tasks Wizard will begin.
2. Click Next and select the program you want to schedule.
3. Click Next and assign a name to the scheduled task. It's usually best to use the same name as the task you are performing, such as Backup or ScanDisk.
4. Set the frequency with which you want to run the tasks as well as when you want the task to be performed.
5. Click the Finish button and the task will be added to the Scheduled Tasks window. In Figure 17.10, ScanDisk was added to run every Monday at 1AM.

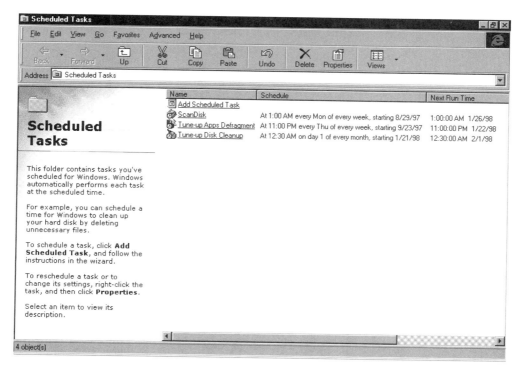

FIGURE 17.10: The Scheduled tasks window

What's Next?

After this chapter, what remains are two appendixes on installation and a glossary of computer terms you may encounter. Some of the terms aren't presented elsewhere in this book, but knowing their definitions can be helpful.

There's also a super-duper index, so you won't have any trouble locating sections you dimly remember seeing (but don't remember where)! That way, the book can continue to serve as a handy reference as you progress in your exploration of Windows 98.

Appendix A

INSTALLATION FOR WINDOWS 95 USERS

The designers of Windows 98 have worked hard to make the installation process for Windows 98 as simple and trouble-free as possible. If you use Windows 95 and you are satisfied with the way it's working for you, the preliminaries are minimal and the upgrade will probably proceed without problems.

On the other hand, if the performance of Windows 95 on your machine has you twiddling your thumbs, you may want to consider hardware improvements. Running multiple operating systems can also complicate matters, but there are easier solutions available now that weren't available in the past.

Hardware Requirements

One of the design goals for Windows 98 was to improve performance and, in some respects, this has been achieved. Windows 98 starts a bit faster than Windows 95, and application start-up is also a bit quicker. However, Windows 98 can't do much to reduce the demands made on hardware by ever-more-complex applications. In fact, new applications and technologies have raised hardware requirements substantially since the introduction of Windows 95.

Officially, Microsoft says that the minimum hardware required to run Windows 98 is:

- 486DX/66 or higher processor
- 16 MB or more of RAM
- 125 MB available hard drive space
- CD-ROM drive (3.5" disks may be available)

Windows 98 will work reasonably well at this level if you don't expect it to run the most demanding technologies, such as streaming video from the Internet.

The upshot is that Windows 98 itself is not likely to demand much in the way of hardware improvements for most users. If you are happy with the way your applications run under Windows 95, you should be just as satisfied with their performance under Windows 98. If you intend to take advantage of Windows 98's support for advanced technologies that place heavy demands on the processor, your hardware decisions should be based on those uses, rather than on Windows 98.

Before You Install

There are several things you need to do before installing Windows 98. Some depend on whether you want to install as an upgrade over Windows 95 or do a fresh installation. We will begin with the things everyone should do.

Backing Up Your Data

We've all heard how important it is to do backups, and we've all ignored those warnings (at times). That doesn't change our obligation to warn you yet again!

Please, make a backup of your system before you start this upgrade. We can not stress this enough. While the installation program of Windows 98 is remarkably good, and the number of systems that fail is small, you should never, never make changes to your operating system without doing a backup.

Choosing a Backup Program

If you haven't invested in a third-party program, the backup program included with Windows 95 is adequate. (It's available under Accessories on the Programs menu.) It's safe, easy to use, and reasonably fast. If you have another backup program you prefer, and are more comfortable with, by all means use it.

What to Back Up

If you have a tape drive or another high-capacity backup system, you can do a full system backup and be secure in the knowledge that everything is safe. You could even use it to return to your current Windows 95 setup, if necessary. If your backup device has a more limited capacity, you will probably only want to back up your data files. Even though it would take time, everything else could be re-created from the original disks.

Take your time and review all the directories and even subdirectories on your hard drive. Besides all the places that you have knowingly created files, check the directories of programs that save data without a specific command from you. These would include personal information managers, e-mail programs, and navigation programs for online services, among others. If you have any doubts about whether you should back up a particular file or group of files, it's best to err on the side of caution.

Upgrade or Make a Fresh Start?

One of the most important decisions you need to make is whether to install Windows 98 as an upgrade over Windows 95 or to do a clean installation from scratch. Generally speaking, an upgrade installation is satisfactory if Windows 95 and your applications are running well. If most of the programs you have ever installed are ones you still use, or if you can remove unused programs with Windows 95's Add/Remove Programs utility, upgrading should be fine. The same is true if you can remove unused programs using uninstall routines that came with them, or if you use a good third-party uninstaller. The advantages of installing Windows 98 as an upgrade are that it's faster and you won't have to reinstall your applications.

If Windows 95 or your application programs have not been running smoothly, you may be well advised to get a fresh start by doing a clean installation of Windows 98. The same is true if you suspect your hard drive of carrying a heavy load of application-related files you no longer use. Another reason to do a clean install is if you have already done an upgrade installation of Windows 98 and are experiencing problems. The advantage of a clean installation is that you get rid of anything old that might be causing trouble. The main disadvantages are the additional preparation required, and the fact that you will have to reinstall all of your Windows 95 applications. Also, you will lose Windows 95's built-in fax capability, because Windows 98 has no fax feature.

Fax

Windows 95 includes a program called Exchange, which can transmit faxes via your fax modem. Exchange is not a part of Windows 98 and there is no other fax capability included, either. If you use Exchange to send faxes from your computer under Windows 95, you have several choices:

- If you install Windows 98 as an upgrade, Exchange will be retained and you can continue to use it. If it has been working reliably for you, this is probably the best option. Just remember that if it fails you will not be able to reinstall it as you could when you were running Windows 95.
- Exchange is also part of Microsoft Office 95, and similar capabilities are included in Office 97. After installing Windows 98, you may be able to install Exchange or other Windows Messaging components from one of these sources, if you have them.
- You can purchase and install third-party fax software.

If Exchange is installed on your machine but you don't use it, you should remove it before upgrading Windows 95 to Windows 98. To do this:

1. Open the Control Panel, under Settings on the Start menu.
2. Open Add/Remove Programs.
3. Click the Windows Setup tab.
4. Remove the check mark in front of Microsoft Exchange.
5. Click OK.

More Housecleaning

Now is the perfect time to ponder which programs on your system are really needed and to clean up some of the clutter and debris that has built up on your hard drive. Windows 98 is going to need substantially more hard disk space than Windows 95, so this is an even better reason to clean house.

The first step is to take a look at installed programs you haven't used in the last year or two. Time to get rid of them. If they're DOS programs, just delete them. If they're Windows programs, you have to delete them and find all the files they've stuck in your Windows directories without telling you.

Your best bet here is to get one of the ingenious programs designed to remove all traces of ill-behaved Windows applications. One of the best is CleanSweep 3.0 from Quarterdeck.

TIP	If you have any doubts about removing a program from your hard drive, just save any data files to a floppy. You can always reinstall the program from the original disks if you suddenly need it.

Defragmenting Your Hard Drive

Once you have all the extraneous files cleaned off your hard drive, you should do a complete disk defragmentation. This will consolidate your existing files on the disk, creating the maximum possible room for Windows 98 Setup to do its thing. To defragment your disk:

1.   On the Windows 95 Start menu, go to Programs ➤ Accessories ➤ System Tools ➤ Disk Defragmenter.
2.   The default drive to defragment is C, so just click OK and let it do its thing.

Step-by-Step Installation

Windows 98 is a very clever operating system. You can just turn on your computer, put the CD in the drive, and start running Setup; and the system will install without a hiccup. Here's a step-by-step description of exactly how to do this.

Starting the Installation

Insert the Windows 98 CD in your CD-ROM drive. If Windows 95 is set up to automatically run a CD when it is inserted, you will see the screen shown in Figure A.1. Otherwise, open My Computer and double-click your CD-ROM drive to get to the same screen. Either way, click Yes and you will be on your way.

You'll see the Welcome screen and on the left side of the screen, the estimated time required to complete the installation. The time gauge will remain throughout the setup process to show your progress. Total time estimates vary from 30 to 60 minutes or more depending on how much you install and the speed of your system. Expect to spend somewhat more time than the estimate.

Read the information presented in the dialog box, then click Continue. Windows 98 will perform a quick survey of your system, prepare the Setup wizard, and ask you to read and consent to the license agreement. Click Next to move on.

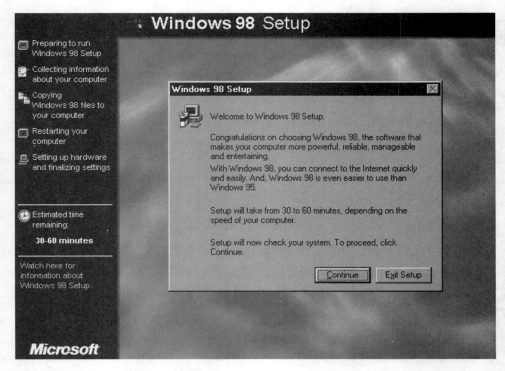

FIGURE A.1:   You're on your way!

When doing a clean install, you'll be asked at this point to choose a directory for installation—the default is C:\WINDOWS, but you can choose another location or a different name for the directory.

Setup will then perform a more thorough check of your system, including looking for installed components of Windows and making sure you have enough hard drive space to complete the installation.

Saving System Files

The next dialog box asks if you want the install program to save your Windows 95 system files. These files make it possible to quickly uninstall Windows 98 should you run into trouble. So it's a good idea to select Yes.

You can then skip down to the section on choosing an Internet channel set. Select your country and choose Next. You won't see the Setup Options dialog box because Windows 98 will set up the same options and components as what you had in Windows 95. Remember that after installation you can use the Add/Remove Programs function in the Control Panel to easily add or remove any components.

NOTE If you're doing a clean install, you won't be offered the save system files option because you're not overwriting anything.

Setup Options

The next choice you have to make, for a clean install only, is about how much of the OS you want to install. You can select:

Typical The major components (as defined by the setup program) are installed. This is the default setup. This is also the option we recommend selecting.

Portable Includes options appropriate for laptops. You can choose the components you want to install or let the system install the major components (as in the Typical install).

Compact Selects a minimum configuration—for situations where space is tight.

Custom Lets you make selections at every step. Don't be put off by the designation of this choice as for "experts." Even a reasonably competent beginner can handle this installation.

Selecting Components

If you selected Custom install, you choose the components you want. For a Typical, Compact, or Portable installation, you can choose the components you want or let Windows 98 choose what to install based on the type of installation selected.

The main categories of components are listed in the window. Click Details to see the total items that make up the category. Check the ones you want installed. A click of the mouse will also remove check marks in front of items you don't want.

Identifying Your Computer

This dialog box asks you to give your computer a name which will identify it on your local area network. You are also asked to enter the name of your workgroup and a description of your computer. This is the information you gathered from the Identification tab of the Network dialog box before you eliminated Windows 95.

Choosing an Internet Channel Set

Channels are designed to offer easy access to selected parts of the Internet. Windows 98 Setup comes with default channel sets based on country and language. Choose the set that you want installed.

Making a Startup Disk

The setup program asks if you want to create a startup disk so you can boot your computer in case of trouble. The answer is definitely, positively, YES!

The Startup disk contains several programs that will enable you to boot your system and edit important files in case something gets horribly mangled. It also contains the invaluable UNINSTAL.EXE, which enables you to get rid of all of Windows 98 and start over in case things are severe enough to require reinstallation.

NOTE   Like the seat belts in your car or the smoke detector in your home, you'll only need a startup disk if things go very badly, indeed. If you do need it, however, nothing else will do.

After the startup disk is made, there's a long pause while Setup copies files. Go get a cup of tea.

NOTE   If you must, you can cancel making the startup disk by selecting Next and then choosing Cancel. This isn't advised, however.

The Finishing Touches

After all the copying, the Setup Wizard needs to restart your computer and finish up. Your system might not be able to restart by itself. Wait five minutes or so and if nothing appears to be happening, then hit the Reset button. This won't harm your installation and is not a sign of installation failure.

After the restart, Windows 98 still has a few chores. It will detect and set up plug-and-play devices and possibly other hardware whose settings couldn't be taken over from Windows 95. This may involve restarting again.

If you did a clean install, Setup will ask you to set your time zone. Use the right and left arrow keys on the keyboard to move east and west. This is important for network connections and so that daylight savings time is properly scheduled. Then Setup will run through a series of other tasks, including setting up the Control Panel and putting your programs on the Start menu. The last one, updating system settings, may take quite a while. Finally, there will be another restart, and you will see the Welcome to Windows screen, which offers online registration and an introduction to Windows 98 features.

Installing Additional Hardware

If a piece of your hardware wasn't detected during the install, use the Add New Hardware function in the Control Panel to tell Windows 98 about it. You may have to restart yet again after installing your hardware.

Deleting Unnecessary Files

After Windows 98 is installed and you feel safe and secure with the new system, you can free up the hard drive space occupied when you chose to Save System Files early in the installation. Go to Add/Remove Programs in the Control Panel. On the Install/Uninstall page, choose the Delete Windows 98 Uninstall Information option, and click OK.

Appendix B

INSTALLING FOR WINDOWS 3.1 USERS

The recommended-by-Microsoft approach is to install Windows 98 right over the top of your existing Windows 3.*x*. Advantages to this approach include:

- You'll keep all your programs and their settings.
- If you have problems, you can use the uninstall program to automatically remove Windows 98 and get your original DOS and Windows 3.*x* back intact.

Hardware Requirements

Microsoft has upped the hardware ante with Windows 98 just as they did with Windows 95. This time, you must have:

- A 486DX/66 or better microprocessor
- 16MB RAM
- CD-ROM drive (3.5" disks may be available)
- 175MB available free hard drive space

Some 50MB of that space is used to save your Windows 3.1 system files so you can uninstall Windows 98. You can reclaim that space once you feel safe and secure with Windows 98.

The installation will fail on a lesser processor, a machine with less than 16MB of RAM, or if you have insufficient hard drive space.

Starting the Installation

Place the Windows 98 CD in the CD-ROM drive and start Windows 3.*x*. Open File Manager and double-click the icon for your CD-ROM drive (see Figure B.1). In the right pane, double-click SETUP.EXE to start the installation.

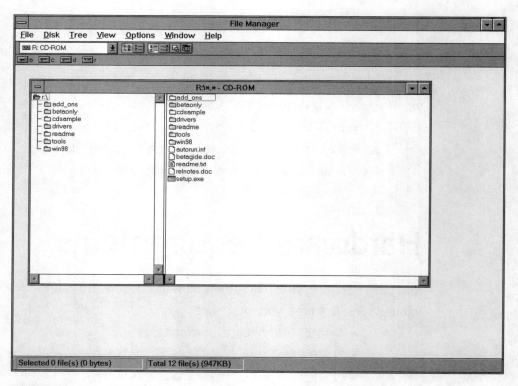

FIGURE B.1:   Use File Manager to view the files on the Windows 98 CD-ROM.

Welcome Screen

The first screen "welcomes" you to Windows 98 (as if it were a hotel) and gives an estimate of the time it will take to install. On most machines this will be 30-60 minutes. Click the Continue button.

Next, a setup window will open announcing that the Setup Wizard is starting. Look at the list of installation steps on the left side of your screen. The step being performed will be highlighted.

License Agreement

A window will open like the one in Figure B.2, showing the license agreement. Click the button next to I Accept the Agreement and then click the Next button. (If you don't accept the agreement, the installation stops right here.)

FIGURE B.2: The license agreement

Select the Directory

In the next dialog box, you're asked to specify the directory for the installation of Windows 98. The default is C:\WINDOWS. Unless you have a good reason to install elsewhere, accept the default.

If you select Other Directory, you'll be prompted for the directory name and location.

Checking Your System

The next procedure looks at your system to first determine what Windows components are installed and then to see if you have enough hard drive space to install Windows 98 (see Figure B.3).

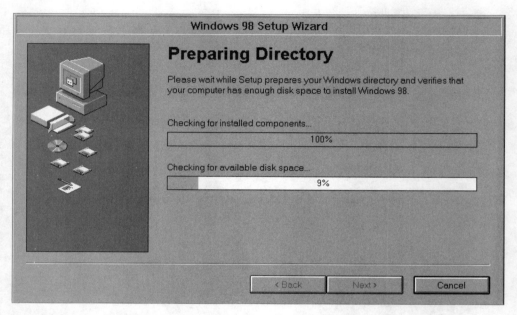

FIGURE B.3:   Setup checks for installed components and for available hard drive space.

Save System Files

The Save System Files dialog box gives you a chance at an additional bit of security. If you select Yes, the Setup Wizard will save enough of your existing Windows 3.x files so that (should worse come to worst) you can uninstall Windows 98.

This is highly unlikely to be necessary, but "Better safe than sorry" is our motto. So, we strongly recommend selecting Yes.

NOTE   This step will require additional hard drive space but once you're up and running with Windows 98, you can delete the old system files and free up the space.

After you click Yes, another dialog box (see Figure B.4) will show the progress of the system files being located and then saved.

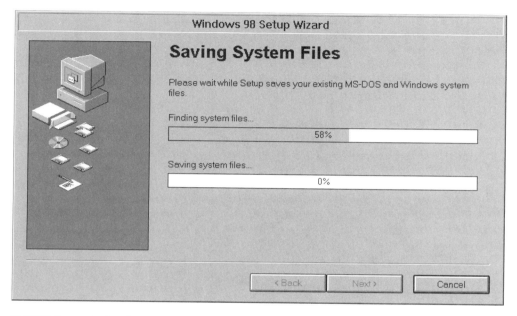

FIGURE B.4: Saving the Windows 3.x system files

If you have more than one hard drive, you'll be prompted for the preferred location for the system files. You can pick any drive where you have enough open space.

Setup Options

The Setup Wizard presents you with four possible setup options (see Figure B.5). The four options are:

Typical   For the majority of people, this is the best option. It requires the least input from you and anything you later decide you want to install is easily available.

Custom   This is also a perfectly good option, especially if you're an experienced Windows user and a bit of a control freak. You have to provide more information and make more choices as you go, so installation is a little slower, but in exchange you get the opportunity to customize as you go.

Portable   This is useful for laptop computers, but it is not necessary. The regular installation can detect PC Cards and built-in pointers without being told that a portable computer is involved.

Compact   This option is recommended only when hard drive space is limited and cannot be enlarged. You'll get the basic functionality, but most applets and many system tools will not be installed.

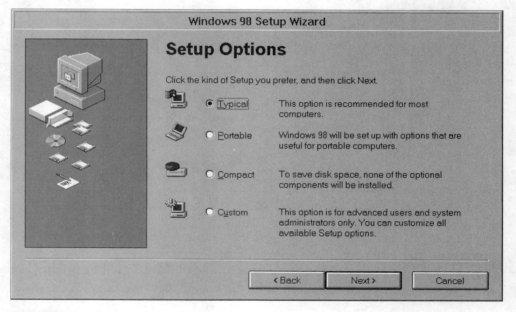

FIGURE B.5:   Choosing a setup option

After you choose the option you want, click Next.

NOTE   **The rest of the steps for installation in this appendix are based on selecting the Typical option for installation. If you select another option, these steps may not apply to you.**

Windows Components

The next dialog box for the Typical installation asks if you want to view the components and decide which to install. If you select Yes, you'll see the window shown in Figure B.6. (If you say No, you're telling the installation program that you don't want to see the components.)

NOTE **The Custom install choice takes you directly to the Select Components window.**

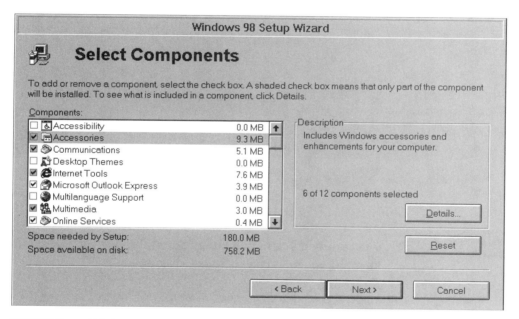

FIGURE B.6: Windows components

To decide what to install, view each option in turn. For example, in Figure B.6 Accessories is highlighted, and a description for it appears to the right. Directly under the description you'll see how many of the components have already been selected (by the Setup Wizard) to be installed. For Accessories, it's six of the 12 available.

Click the Details button for a list of the 12 Accessories (see Figure B.7). As you highlight each item, a description appears to the right. Items with check marks next to them will be installed. Remove the check marks next to items you *don't* want installed.

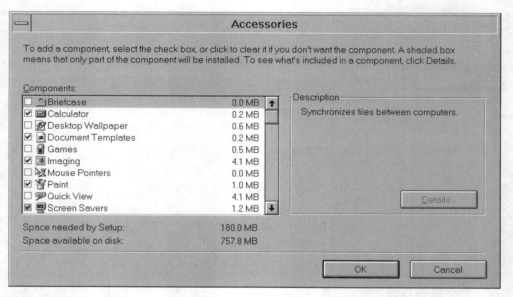

FIGURE B.7: Selecting the Accessories to install

NOTE   **Don't worry if you're not sure about everything you want to install. Anything you miss can be installed later.**

When you've made your choices, click the Next button.

Identification

The next dialog box, Identification, asks for the name of your computer, the workgroup name, and a description of the computer. If you're on a network, provide the correct information. If you're not connected, leave the default information and click Next.

Computer Settings

In the Computer Settings dialog box, you'll see a list of the keyboard and language settings that will be installed. If any are incorrect, highlight the setting and click the Change button.

Internet Channels

The channels that Windows 98 starts with as the default listing are tailored to specific countries. In the Internet Channels window choose the country whose channel set you'd like to see.

Emergency Startup Disk

The next step is to create an emergency startup disk. In case of a complete freeze, you can use this disk to start your computer. You'll need a single, high-density floppy disk. It doesn't have to be new, but anything already on the disk will be deleted in the process of making the emergency startup disk. To create the disk:

1. Click Next.
2. Put the floppy disk in the drive when the Setup program requests it.
3. When the process of creating the disk is completed, you'll be notified to remove the floppy disk and then click OK.

Start Copying Files

The process of copying files is the longest stage of the installation. It'll go quickly if you have a high-speed CD-ROM drive, slowly if you don't. But expect a half-hour or so before you have to do anything more.

Identifying Hardware

After all the copying, the Setup Wizard needs to restart your computer and finish up. Your system might not be able to restart by itself. Wait five minutes or so and if nothing appears to be happening, hit the Reset button. This won't harm your installation and is not a sign of installation failure.

Windows 98 then builds a driver database and attempts to identify all the hardware attached to the computer. That includes the video card, monitor, sound card, modem, and printer. In general, plug-and-play technology does a very good job of figuring everything out. If it doesn't, you can later manually install a modem, printer, or other device.

TIP   **You'll be asked at some point for a Windows password. If you're not on a network, don't provide one. Just press Enter. You can always add a password later but once you provide one, you won't be able to get rid of that password window at boot up again. To stop being asked for a password, after installation, right-click the Network Neighborhood icon on the desktop and select Properties. On the Configuration page, under Primary Network Logon, select Windows Logon. Click OK. When you reboot, the password window will not appear.**

Welcome to Windows 98

After a restart or two, Windows 98 will begin and you'll see the Welcome to Windows 98 dialog box (see Figure B.8). Click a subject to register the product or for a lesson on how Windows 98 works. Or, click the X in the upper-right corner to close out of this box and start using Windows 98.

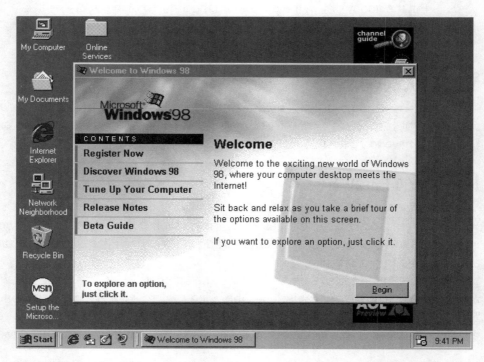

FIGURE B.8:   The Welcome to Windows 98 screen offers a tour of some of the Windows 98 features.

Glossary

16-bit, 32-bit   Refers to how certain programs address memory and other technical details. In general, 16-bit programs refer to those written for DOS or versions of Windows earlier than Windows 95. Windows 98 allows the use of 32-bit programs which can do true multitasking (as opposed to task switching). If designed correctly, 32-bit programs can be faster than 16-bit programs but they are not inherently so.

Active Desktop view   A Windows 98 desktop view where the Desktop looks and functions like a Web page. In Active Desktop view you can link active documents, show World Wide Web sites, and use Channels.

Active window   The window that keyboard or mouse movements act on. Many windows can be open, but only one is active at a time. You can spot the active window by its title bar, which is a different color than the title bars of other windows.

Application   An application is a collection of files that may include several programs. WordPerfect is an application that consists of any number of files constituting a single package. Applications are also grouped by type such as word processing applications, database applications, and so forth.

ASCII   Pronounced "As-key." Stands for the **A**merican **S**tandard **C**ode for **I**nformation **I**nterchange. It was developed back in the '60s as a standard numerical code for characters used on all computers. Today, ASCII usually means normal text as opposed to code unreadable by regular folk.

Associate   To connect files having a particular extension to a specific program. When you single-click (also stated simply as "click") a file with the extension, the associated program is opened and the file you clicked is opened. In Windows 98, associated files are usually called registered files. *See also* Register.

Attribute   A bit of code in a file that determines an aspect of the file's status. The four file attributes are read-only, hidden, archive, and system. A file can have none or any number of these attributes. You can modify a file's attributes, but you should only do so if you have a good reason.

Background   The screen area behind the active window. Can also refer to a process that is going on somewhere other than in the active window.

Baud   The speed at which data is transmitted over a communications line or cable. This is not *really* the same as BPS (bits per second) but the terms are used interchangeably.

Bit   Represents a single switch inside a computer set to 0 or 1. There are millions of them in every computer. Short for **b**inary dig**it**, 8 bits make up a byte, the basic unit of data storage.

Bitmaps   Picture or image files that are made up of pixels. Pictures made in Paint are automatically saved as bitmaps (with a .BMP extension).

Boot   A simple name for the complicated process your computer goes through when starting up.

Bootable disk   A disk containing the *system* files needed to start the computer. When your system starts up, it looks for a disk first in drive A, if none is there it goes to drive C. When a disk is found, the computer examines the disk to see if it contains the system files. When a disk with system files is found, the computer uses that disk's information to start the system running. If a disk with system files is in drive A, information on that disk will be used to tell the computer about itself. Computers can normally be booted only from drive A or drive C. The emergency disk that Windows 98 creates during installation is a bootable disk.

BPS   Bits per second. A unit of measurement for the communication speed of modems and fax modems.

Browser   A program such as Internet Explorer that is used to explore the World Wide Web.

Byte   The basic unit of data storage. A byte is made up of 8 bits. For all intents and purposes, a byte equals a single character.

Channel   A Windows 98 feature that allows you to automatically copy content from a particular Internet site.

Classic Style view   This desktop style is very similar to the desktop view from Windows 95. It requires a single-click (often stated as simply "click") to select desktop items and a double-click to launch them.

Configuration   A set of values in a program or for a device such as a printer. The values will be things such as how menu options work or a particular size of paper for a printer to use.

DDE   Stands for **D**ynamic **D**ata **E**xchange. An older standard for making information updated in one program available in another program. It's been replaced by OLE.

Default   The configuration settings that a device or program will have without any intervention from you. Usually you can change the default settings, but care should be taken.

Defragment   The removal of extra space on a disk. Sometimes used to store the same program in more than one place.

Dialog box   A window that opens to ask you impertinent questions or request input. Windows 98 programs are knee-deep in dialog boxes.

DLL   Short for **D**ynamic **L**ink **L**ibrary. A file with information needed by one or more programs. Don't delete files with this extension willy-nilly because your programs will be dysfunctional without the DLL files they need.

Double-click   Two rapid clicks on the left mouse button. In the Classic Desktop Windows 98 interface, this is the necessary mouse move to launch a program or open a folder. Many of the programs you use with Windows 98 will require double-click maneuvers as well.

Driver   A program made up of instructions to operate things such as a printer, modem, or mouse that are added to your computer. Windows 98 includes most of the drivers you're likely to need, but there are rare times when you need to acquire a newer driver (and instructions on installing it) from the manufacturer of the device.

Explorer bars   A browsing tool used to access search engines and favorite Web sites. You can access the following Explorer bars in any window: Search, Favorites, History, and Channels.

File   A collection of information stored on a computer with a unique name.

Folder   A means of organizing files. Each installed program will make its own folder and perhaps several subfolders. The user can likewise make folders to organize programs and files. Folders are analogous to directories in Windows 3.1 and DOS.

Home page   The primary or main page on a Web site, usually containing links to other Web sites or pages.

HTML   Stands for **H**yper**t**ext **M**arkup **L**anguage. It's the language that is used to create Web pages.

Initialize   To prepare for use. With disks, this means to format the disk so it can be read. Programmers use this term to mean getting everything in the program to a known, beginning state.

Internet   A worldwide collection of computers and networks that are all connected either directly or indirectly to one another.

Kilobyte   One thousand bytes (actually 1,024). Abbreviated as K or KB.

Landscape   A setting for displaying or printing where the characters are viewed or printed with the longer side as the width and the shorter side as the length. The opposite setting is Portrait.

Megabyte   One million bytes (actually 1,048,576). Abbreviated as M or MB.

Modem   A contraction of **mo**dulator-**dem**odulator. A device that hooks up to phone lines so your computer can communicate with other computers, either individually or through an online service.

Multitasking   Using more than one application at a time. Most of the time in Windows 3.1, you were *task switching,* moving back and forth between applications, not actually using more than one at the same time. Windows 98 makes true multi-tasking possible, but to get the full effect you need to be running 32-bit programs.

OLE   Pronounced "O-lay." Short for **O**bject **L**inking and **E**mbedding. An automatic way for Windows programs to share data.

Online   To be in a state of readiness. A printer is said to be online when it's ready to print. These days, online is mostly used to mean being connected to another computer via modem. The connection can be to a commercial service, an Internet Service Provider, and so forth.

Online Service Provider   A private company such as America Online or CompuServe, that provides a connection to the Internet, plus connections to proprietary services such as chat groups and recommended sites.

Optimize   Computer jargon for "improve the performance of."

Parallel   A port on your computer usually used to connect a cable to a printer. Can also be used to connect other devices, such as an external drive or network adapter, to your computer. Information transmitted through a parallel port travels through multiple side-by-side paths inside the cable.

Peripheral   A device attached to the outside of your computer. This includes the monitor, keyboard, mouse, and printer.

Plug and Play   A recent standard for hardware. Hardware that adopts this standard can be installed on a Windows 98 computer with very little intervention by the user. The hardware will be detected and configured by Windows 98 to run properly. Manufacturers of disk drives, modems, network cards, and other devices have been rapidly adopting Plug and Play.

Port   A connecting point on your computer for plugging in external devices. At a minimum, most computers have two serial ports and one parallel (printer) port. Computers also have a specialized port for the keyboard; some have a special mouse port, too.

Portrait   The way text is typically displayed or printed, with the shorter side as the width and the longer side as the length. The opposite setting is Landscape.

Protocol   A set of rules that determine the flow of data and how it's used. The modems at either end of a communication line have to be using the same protocol to talk to each other. Likewise, computers on a network need to be speaking the same protocol in order to connect.

RAM   Short for **R**andom **A**ccess **M**emory. In a nutshell, memory is where things happen in your computer. The processor (CPU) does the work, but it can hold only so much information. Programs and files are retrieved from the hard disk and stored in RAM so that operations can proceed rapidly.

Register   Is used to tell Windows 98 what program to use to open files of a certain type (that is, files with a particular extension). If a file type is registered, double-clicking it in Classic Desktop view or clicking it in Active Desktop or Web Style view will start the necessary application and open the file. For example, a file with the .DOC extension will automatically be opened in Word. A .TXT extension will cause a file to be opened in Notepad. *See also* Associate.

Serial   A particular type of port that transmits information one bit at a time. Mostly used by a modem or a mouse, and occasionally by a scanner.

Shortcut   A tool that acts as a pointer to a file, folder, application, or device. Shortcuts are very small files that you can place almost anywhere. When you double-click a shortcut in Classic Desktop view or click it in Active Desktop or Web Style view, the object it points to will be opened. You can have shortcuts to objects in various places without having to physically move or copy files.

Single-click   A single click on the left mouse button. Also expressed simply as "click." In the Active Desktop view or Web Style view, this is the necessary mouse move to launch a program or open a folder.

Start button   The button in the lower left corner of the Windows 98 desktop. Used to start programs, open documents, and customize desktop settings.

Subscribe   To choose Web pages that are automatically delivered to your computer. In Windows 98, you can read information from a list you subscribe to either on line or off line.

Swap file   Space on the hard disk that Windows 98 uses to increase the amount of memory available to Windows programs. The swap file in Windows 98 is dynamic, so it automatically grows larger or smaller based on current activity on the computer.

System resources   A finite portion of memory that is set aside for Windows to keep track of all of its pieces. In Windows 3.1, running out of resources was not uncommon even if you had a lot of memory, because the amount available for system resources could not get larger or smaller. Windows 95 was better, but memory management still created problems. Windows 98 has more space for system resources and manages those resources much more intelligently, so you can have many more programs open at once.

Taskbar   A tool located initially at the bottom of your screen that contains the Start Menu button, clock, program icons, and other icons.

URL   Stands for **U**niform **R**esource **L**ocator. The address for a page on the World Wide Web. For example, `www.onlieepicure.com`.

Virtual memory   Simulated RAM that is created by taking advantage of free space on the hard drive, also called a swap file. If you start more programs or processes than your RAM has room for, the programs actively doing something will be placed in RAM while the less active or inactive ones will be moved to the swap file space on the hard drive. Windows 98 will automatically swap programs back and forth as needed. The swap file is dynamic in Windows 98, which means it will also automatically grow and shrink as necessary.

Web Style view   This desktop view style acts like a Web page but doesn't have the Web page functionality of the Active Desktop view. To highlight a file or program in this view, simply move the mouse pointer over it. To open a file or folder, single-click it.

Wizard   A Windows 98 feature that helps you complete tasks such as connecting to the Internet or tuning up your computer. You will find such Windows 98 wizards as Windows Tune-Up, Add Printer, and Add Hardware, among others.

World Wide Web   The portion of the Internet that allows you to view graphics and video, hear sound, and read text.

Index

Note to the Reader: Main level entries are in **bold**. **Boldfaced** page numbers indicate primary discussions of a topic. *Italicized* page numbers indicate illustrations.

G

H

J

K

L

O

P

U

V

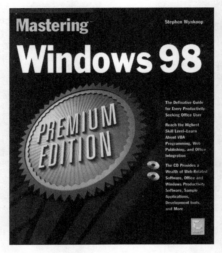

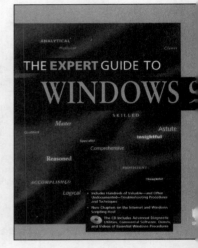

MAKE THE TRANSITION TO
WINDOWS® 98
QUICKLY, PAINLESSLY, AND SUCCESSFULLY

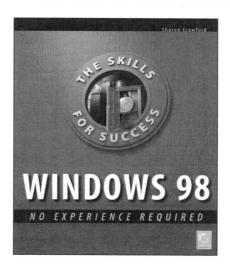

...is easy-to-use guide gives Windows ...5 and 3.1 users all the information ...y need to upgrade to Windows 98. ... gives users the tips and tricks they ...ed to get the most out of Windows ...—easy networking, troubleshooting, ...rdware upgrading, Internet tips, and invaluable connectivity advice.

ISBN: 0-7821-2190-X
...32pp; 7½" x 9"; Softcover; $19.99

This no-nonsense guide teaches the essential skills necessary for using Windows 98 effectively at home or at the office. Each chapter presents scores of real-world examples that let readers learn the practical skills they need to succeed in today's workplace.

ISBN: 0-7821-2128-4
576pp; 7½" x 9"; Softcover; $24.99

Learn about the Windows 98 features you need—ignore the ones you don't. This straightforward, easy-to-read guide is designed for users familiar with computers, but new to Windows 98. The book also includes a comprehensive index and a useful glossary of the latest Windows terminology.

ISBN: 0-7821-1953-0
384pp; 7½" x 9"; Softcover; $19.99

SYBEX®
www.sybex.com

START USING NEW
WINDOWS® 98
FEATURES IMMEDIATELY

This convenient, almanac-sized book has over 1,000 pages of Windows 98 and essential PC information. It includes coverage on the Windows 98 operating system and command reference, PC upgrading and maintenance advice, guides to Microsoft and Netscape browsers, an Internet/Hardware/Software resource directory and a PC/Internet dictionary.

ISBN: 0-7821-2219-1
1,008pp; 5⅞" x 8¼"; Softcover; $19.99

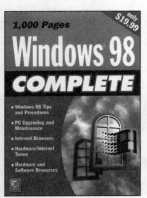

This easy-to-use guide gives Windows 95 and 3.1 users all the information they need to upgrade to Windows 98. It gives users the tips and tricks they need to get the most out of Windows 98—easy networking, troubleshooting, hardware upgrading, Internet tips, and invaluable connectivity advice.

ISBN: 0-7821-2190-X
432pp; 7½" x 9"; Softcover; $19.99

Easy to use and alphabetically organized, this guide is your key to every command, feature, menu, toolbar, and function of Windows 98. This book also provides fast answers about Internet Explorer, WebView, and all of the Internet features and functions of Windows 98.

ISBN: 0-7821-2191-8
304pp; 4¾" x 8"; Softcover; $14.99

SYBE
www.sybex.e